WHEN WOMEN CALL THE SHOTS

Other books by
LINDA SEGER

Making a Good Script Great

Creating Unforgettable Characters

The Art of Adaptation:
Turning Fact and Fiction into Film

From Script to Screen:
The Collaborative Art of Filmmaking (coauthor)

LINDA SEGER

WHEN WOMEN CALL THE SHOTS

The Developing Power and Influence of Women in Television and Film

AN AUTHORS GUILD BACKINPRINT.COM EDITION

When Women Call the Shots
The Developing Power And Influence Of Women In Television And Film

AN AUTHORS GUILD BACKINPRINT.COM EDITION
Published by iUniverse, Inc.

For information address:
iUniverse, Inc.
2021 Pine Lake Road, Suite 100
Lincoln, NE 68512
www.iuniverse.com

Originally published by Henry Holt

ISBN: 0-595-26838-2

Printed in the United States of America

To Carolyn Wendy Barzelay,
whose thirty-year friendship
has been one of my
life's greatest blessings

CONTENTS

PART THREE · WOMEN AS STORYTELLERS

PART FOUR · CREATING WOMEN CHARACTERS

PART FIVE · SEX, LOVE, AND ROMANCE

PART SIX · A SOCIAL AND GLOBAL PERSPECTIVE

ACKNOWLEDGMENTS

Many thanks . . .

TO MY EDITOR, Cynthia Vartan, whose care, professionalism, and collaboration has made all five books a joy to write. To my agent, Martha Casselman, whose cheerfulness and support are a pleasurable part of the process, and to my consultant Dr. Leonard Felder, for the title and for his advice and encouragement.

To my assistant, Marsha Parkhill, who faxed, phoned, transcribed, and organized for two years. Her competence, ability, and steadfastness are evident on every page.

And to my other assistants, who filled in at important moments: Nancy Rhee at the beginning; Dunya Bean and Pamela Shandel in the middle; and Ellen Irwin, Kathleen Becket, and Cara Haynes Latham at the end. Thank you to all these women, who got me through and cheered me on.

To film historian Anthony Slide, for guidance, information, and all his constructive help in chapter 1. His generous and open spirit were a great gift.

To my researchers and helpers: Lynn Brown Rosenberg and Mary A. Roberts, from the Homestead Museum; Joshua Jeffrey Todd, Elaine Sinclair, Sarah Rich, and Teri Diller, at the Academy of Motion Picture Arts and Sciences.

To my readers, who gave me invaluable feedback: Judith Claire,

Sharon Cobb, Devorah Cutler, Sara Duvall, Sunny Lee, Cathleen Loeser, Anne Milder, Ralph Phillips, and Lindsay Smith.

To Donna Crowley and Dara Marks, for reading parts of the manuscript, for friendship and advice.

To Todd Coleman, for his feedback on chapter 5; to Loreen Arbus and Carol O'Leary, for their comments on chapter 2; to my mother, Agnes Seger, for reading parts of the manuscript and giving comments.

To Dulcie Smart, for translating Leni Riefenstahl's letter from German into English.

To novelist Gayle Stone, who helped me refine the title and the proposal.

To Jesse Douma and the folks at the Writer's Computer Store, who got me through my many computer problems, and to Meg Johnson from Vidiots for her help and suggestions.

To Kino International, the U.S. distributor of *The Wonderful Horrible Life of Leni Riefenstahl,* for sending me Ray Mueller's film.

To the many people who helped me arrange interviews, including Sharon Cobb, Jack Ong, Babu Subramaniam, and Jhony Bakshi for leading me to the filmmakers in Bombay, India; Marion Dorring in Europe; Carolina Riviera in Mexico City; Andrea Shaw, Gail Singer. and Myra Fried in Canada; Hilary Linstead, Viccy Harper, and Cathy Robinson in Australia; Philippa Boyens in New Zealand; and to the hundreds of assistants who took my phone calls, responded to my faxes, and paved the way.

Thank you to several women historians whom I have only met through their books but who have done important groundbreaking work in this area. Their work has been of immeasurable help in my own research. They include Ally Acker (*Reel Women*), Jeanine Basinger (*A Woman's View: How Hollywood Spoke to Women, 1930–1960*), Lizzie Francke (*Script Girls*), and Marsha McCreadie (*The Women Who Write the Movies*); and to senior staff writer Rachel Abramowitz and Holly Sorensen from the "Women in Hollywood" issue of *Premiere* magazine, Fall 1993.

And always to my husband, Peter Hazen Le Var, who helps keep me calm.

PREFACE

IN THE MID-1980s, the University of Richmond, Virginia, held several television conferences on the role of women in the media. Among our group of seventy-five were Emmy Award–winning producers, directors, and writers of some of the most popular television shows. The subject came up: "Are women different than men? Do they bring something unique to this industry?" Most of the women were horrified by the thought, and gave a resounding "No." To them, different meant "unequal to," "not as good as," and an excuse not to give them equal opportunity.

In the spring of 1994, I sat down for lunch with seven women from the television and film industry. Included were one of the most successful women television directors, two producers whose films were rated among the one hundred most watched films of all time, and executives at successful production companies. Again the question was asked, "Do women bring something different to the industry?" This time, the answer was "Yes, of course. And that difference is our gift and our strength."

When I first began writing this book, several women joked, "If it's about our influence, it's going to be a short book." In my research, I talked to more than two hundred women and about forty men. I visited China, Australia, New Zealand, Canada, Mexico, Spain, Germany, France, Denmark, and Sweden, and also talked to women and men from Great Britain, India, Bangladesh, the Philippines, Egypt, Japan, Belgium, Switzerland, Norway, the Netherlands, Iceland, Eastern Europe, and Africa.

I found a remarkable consistency in their responses to my questions. Although some women were uncomfortable with seeing their replies as gender-related, it became clear after a number of interviews that there was a pattern. Women all over the world were asking for more diversity and balance in the films we see, teamwork and partnership with men, and more authentic female characters. To check my results, I studied the current literature to see if what I discovered was consistent. The pattern was evident. The opinions of those I talked to are, in general, representative of women in the industry.

Women want to be equal partners with men—not more than or less than, but equal to—and they have many ideas about what needs to change in this industry. Women feel that their stronger presence will not just benefit them, but will benefit the film and television industry, leading to increased effectiveness, greater profitability in an industry where money is usually the bottom line, and expanded and more satisfied audiences. Women can provide a hope and a vision to an industry in need of change.

There is no doubt that some change in the industry is inevitable. The industry is becoming more international, more multicultural, and more technologically advanced. New approaches to storytelling are occurring through the development of interactive media and the work of minority and women filmmakers. Actresses demand better roles, audiences respond favorably to more interesting women characters, and talented women ask for a stronger voice in an industry whose audience is more than 52 percent women.

By 1994, women's numbers began to be sufficient to begin to see a difference. Thirty-five percent of executives at the major studios were women. Twenty percent of all production deals at studios were with women. Some of the most successful movies and television shows were created, produced, directed, or written by women. These numbers are increasing all the time. Today Women in Film is an international organization with more than five thousand members. Other groups are active in giving women a voice: CineWomen, Women in Radio and Television, Women in Entertainment, the Hollywood Women's Press Club, the Hollywood Women's Political Caucus, Women Behind the Lens. Women are out there asking questions, making suggestions, demanding, confronting, advising, and talking, not only to each other about what they'd like to bring about, but to many men as well who feel that change is needed. I hope that readers will find these ideas as exciting, inspiring, and invigorating as I did.

PART ONE

THE WOMEN PIONEERS

SOME IMPORTANT BREAKTHROUGHS FOR WOMEN

1896: Alice Guy Blaché directs *La Fée aux choux* (The Cabbage Fairy), the first fiction film.

1915: Director Julia Crawford Ivers is the first female general manager of a Hollywood studio, Bosworth, Inc.

1915: Viola Lawrence, considered the first female film editor, begins her editing career. In 1929, she edits *Bulldog Drummond,* Goldwyn's first sound picture.

1916: Lois Weber becomes the highest paid director at Universal Studios and the highest-paid woman director of the silent era.

1917: Marion Wong starts her Chinese-American production company, Mandarin Films.

1919: Mary Pickford cofounds United Artists with Charlie Chaplin, Douglas Fairbanks, Sr., and D. W. Griffith.

1928: Janet Gaynor wins the first Academy Award for best actress for three films, *7th Heaven, Street Angel,* and *Sunrise.*

1936: Dorothy Arzner is the first female member of the Directors Guild of America.

1938: Costumer Edith Head becomes the first woman to head a studio design department. She is nominated for thirty-four Academy Awards, winning eight of them, more than any other artist, male or female.

1940: Film editor Anne Bauchens is the first woman to receive an Academy Award for film editing, for Cecil B. de Mille's *Northwest Mounted Police.*

1942: Mary McCall, Jr., becomes the Writers Guild's first woman president.

1945: Virginia Van Upp becomes executive producer at Columbia Studios.

1973: Cinematographer Brianne Murphy becomes the first woman accepted into the American Society of Cinematographers.

1

THE EARLY YEARS

This thing we call "failure" is not
the falling down, but the staying down.[1]
—Mary Pickford

THE MOVIES. We're entranced with them. Those splendid characters in those wonderful stories. More than a hundred thousand fiction films have been made to enchant audiences around the world. How did it all begin? It began with a woman.

At first, the moving picture camera was seen as a scientific invention, a new technology that would document in moving pictures what the still camera did with photographs. It recorded real-life moments and news footage.

In 1894 several men were working on the invention: Thomas Edison in the United States, Auguste and Louis Lumière and Leon Gaumont in Paris, William Friese-Greene in Great Britain, and Max Skladanowsky in Germany. In the early exhibitions, people were fascinated by watching the most ordinary movements—people walking down a street or workers leaving a factory. Anything that moved was a good subject for the camera.

Some of the early moving pictures were humorous—a man boxing with a kangaroo, a woman twirling in her full dress. And some of them had a character but no story, such as an early film of a gardener who waters himself instead of the garden. But no one yet considered fictional stories suitable subjects.

In 1895 Leon Gaumont opened a photographic studio and patented a motion picture camera. Some months earlier, Gaumont had hired the young Alice Guy, who had the foresight to learn to work a new invention—the typewriter. Like many women who would follow after her in the film industry, Guy broke into the business as a secretary. At her interview, she was told, "I fear, Mademoiselle, that you may be too young." "But Sir," Guy pleaded, "I'll get over that." With this charming rejoinder, she got the job.[2]

In December of that year, Gaumont was invited to view the first public exhibition of a film from the Lumière brothers. He invited Guy to join him to see this new invention. She did, and she saw an exciting possibility for the camera that had not yet been tapped.

"She had the idea of making a story film in 1895," says Guy's granddaughter, Madame Regine Blaché-Bolton. "It took time to fix it. to dream, to talk to Gaumont about it."

"Might I try to write one or two little scenes and have a few friends perform in them?" Alice Guy asked Gaumont. He agreed, on one condition—that she still fulfill her secretarial duties.[3]

Guy's first film, made between March and August 1896, was a short fairy tale about children who grow in a cabbage patch. *La Fée aux choux* (The Cabbage Fairy). "It was a fairy story with a beginning. middle, and end, costumes, actors playing characters, a backdrop, a set," explains Regine Blaché-Bolton. "It was about a minute and a half long."

Gaumont was so impressed with her work that he set up a film studio for her to continue to produce fiction films. He even rented a house for her behind the studio. Guy became the first producer-director-writer and production head of a studio. For the next ten years, Guy produced, directed, and wrote almost four hundred films for Gaumont. She never stopped experimenting with the possibilities of film. Look at any contemporary film and you'll see techniques that began with Guy. She was one of the first, if not the first, to move the camera to follow the action of the story rather than keeping the camera stationary. She used close-ups, double exposures, fade-outs, and reversed the film to show a house demolished *and* rebuilt. She pioneered location filming, shooting many of her films on the streets of Paris. She was the first to use sound and color in films, experimenting with techniques developed by Gaumont as early as 1900.

Special effects? Guy created them for her film *The Life of Christ,* including one that showed Jesus rising from the tomb. Car chases? Collisions? Explosions? Guy did those in the early 1900s. She made movie spectacles seventeen years before Cecil B. de Mille began his first Biblical epics.

Guy did romances, adventures, comedies, and science fiction. In 1905 she did one of the first film adaptations—of Victor Hugo's novel *La Esmeralda.*

Guy's approach to female characters set a tone for others to follow. At a time when male filmmakers were objectifying the woman, Guy focused on strong female protagonists who took charge of their lives and their destinies. In 1912 she directed *In the Year 2000,* a film about a time when women rule the world.[4]

In 1907, after making almost four hundred films in Paris for Gaumont Studios, Gaumont sent Guy with her husband, Herbert Blaché, to the United States, where he was to represent Gaumont's interests. After a three-year domestic hiatus, Guy was able to allow her ambition and talent to blossom in America. For the next ten years she wrote, directed, and produced another three hundred films under the banner of the Solax Company, the studio she created in 1910 in Fort Lee, New Jersey. It was the best-equipped studio in the world, designed at a cost of $100,000, using the latest techniques in laboratories, carpentry shops, darkrooms, projection rooms, sound stages, editing rooms, and offices. That studio became a model for the modern film studios that were to follow. Only one other woman in film history would own and completely control a film studio.

That woman was Lois Weber, the first American-born woman director. She began as an actress working for Herbert Blaché with

Gaumont's American subsidiary. By 1911 she was writing, directing, and acting in films. By 1915 she was as famous as D. W. Griffith or Cecil B. de Mille. A year later Lois Weber was reputed to be the most important and highest-paid director at Universal Studios, making $5,000 a week. Universal financed her own production unit, which they also did years later for Steven Spielberg on the Universal lot. And, like Spielberg in the 1980s, Weber was allowed to put her own creative stamp on this environment.

In 1917 she formed her own production company, Lois Weber Productions, and by 1920 she had a five-picture contract with Paramount Studios. She brought an important new point of view to moviemaking, tackling controversial social issues such as birth control, divorce, abortion, and promiscuity. Weber set the stage for the many social films that followed, and established film as socially relevant, provocative, and influential.

In 1914 Julia Crawford Ivers, the first woman general manager of a studio, wooed Weber from Universal to Bosworth Studios. Although Weber would return to Universal the next year, she was at Bosworth long enough to hire writer Frances Marion.

Frances Marion, one of the most important screenwriters in the history of film, created scripts for such stars as Lillian Gish, Greta Garbo, Marie Dressler, and Norma Talmadge. It was Marion who helped form the image of the first great Hollywood star, Mary Pickford, by writing many of Pickford's most successful films. Between 1915 and 1953, Marion wrote about 130 produced screenplays. She pioneered the prison film as a new genre and was the only screenwriter, male or female, to win an Academy Award two times within three years, for *The Big House* (1930) and *The Champ* (1932).

While Frances Marion's career blossomed, Lois Weber's films declined in popularity. Perhaps it was the social climate of the times, or a certain heavy-handedness with her social themes that no longer interested audiences. Her last films, in 1927 and one talkie in 1934, had limited releases and were attacked by critics. Weber directed more than one hundred films before her death in 1939, although fewer than twenty have been preserved.

IS THERE ANYTHING THEY COULDN'T DO?

From the early 1900s to the early 1920s, there were hundreds of successful and prolific women in film. Anything seemed possible. The film industry was open to anyone with talent and determination and a dream. And it was open to women primarily because women already in the industry either directly supported other women or influenced them as role models. Under these conditions, women excelled.

According to film historian Anthony Slide, "During the silent era, women can be said to have dominated the industry. There were over thirty women directors prior to 1920, more than at any other period of film history. Women writers were considered the best of this era, and in 1918 alone, some forty-four women were employed in the film industry as scenario writers. Many of these women were considered the top screenwriters of this period, and the women directors were considered equal to, if not better than, their male colleagues.[5]

"During this period, there were many women fulfilling more than one role," continues Slide. "Many of the most famous actresses had their own production companies. Not only major stars such as Mary Pickford, Gloria Swanson, and Norma Talmadge, but also lesser-known actresses such as Ethel Grandin, Marion Leonard, Gene Gauntier, Margery Wilson, Colleen Moore, and Corinne Griffith. A number of actresses, including Lillian Gish, Cleo Madison, and comedienne Mabel Normand, also directed."

Some of the women became executives. In 1919 Mary Pickford—along with Charlie Chaplin, Douglas Fairbanks, Sr., and D. W. Griffith—cofounded United Artists, the first company established to distribute and exhibit the films of independent producers. Just as Alice Guy Blaché's Solax Studio became a model for other early studios, the distribution setup at United Artists was a forerunner of the distribution companies of the 1970s, 1980s, and 1990s—acquiring the best independent product to release under its name.

Some women excelled in what became known as the "female professions," such as script continuity, makeup, and costumes (even though throughout the years there have been many males in these jobs). Edith Head began work in 1923 and became the only woman to oversee the design department of a major studio. She worked at Paramount from 1938 to 1967, and then at Universal until her retirement in 1982. She was nominated for thirty-four Academy Awards and won eight of them—more than any other male or female—for such well-known films as *All About Eve, A Place in the Sun, Roman Holiday*, *Sabrina,* and *The Sting.*

RUGGED INDIVIDUALISM

Early filmmaking was not just confined to Hollywood and New York. "There was probably no state without a film company during the 1910s," notes Slide. "Anyone could dabble in filmmaking who had access to a camera. Even in small towns, the camera was used to record local events, as well as to shoot fiction stories."

Among the women pioneers in independent filmmaking was actress-producer-director Nell Shipman. "Shipman was never very happy working for someone else," says journalist William Arnold, "and was quite willing to trade traditional stardom for creative control over her film projects.[6]

"The company's first effort, *Back to God's Country*, was filmed in 1919 in the Lesser Slave Lake area in Alberta, Canada," says Arnold. "Her leading man died of pneumonia." But the film was a success, although "part of its success may have had to do with the fact that the star happily appeared in a much-publicized nude scene."[7]

Having fallen in love with the wilderness, Shipman moved her production company to Priest Lake, Idaho, where she continued to do extensive location shooting, under hazardous and difficult conditions. It was a perfect setting for Shipman to tell her adventure stories and explore environmental and feminist themes. She had a special love of animals, using them in her films and basing many of her scripts on novels that featured them.

Nell Shipman was not the first person to use wild animals in her films—Alice Guy Blaché used them in 1913, and director Kathryn Williams used them in 1914—but she made them the focus. She also went one step further by pioneering animal safety on the set. Although now the film industry has strict codes for the treatment of animals, in the early days the film industry had no misgivings about abusing or even killing animals to get the shot. Shipman's work foreshadowed the work of the Society for the Prevention of Cruelty to Animals, which began to protect animals on the set in the 1930s.

By the mid-1920s, Shipman's career was over, as were the careers of almost every woman director and producer and many women writers. After pioneering some of the best work in cinema, women suddenly disappeared—from film work and from film history.

How could this happen? Women had proven themselves to be as skillful, as talented, as capable as men. Once glorified by the industry, why were women suddenly unable to continue their creative work, to be hired, to compete?

CHANGES

Between 1910 and 1920, the center of the film industry had moved from the East Coast to the seasonless West, where there was plenty of cheap labor, land, and good weather. A number of production companies in New York and New Jersey were unable to make the change. Alice Guy Blaché's Solax Studios was taken over by her husband, Herbert, who renamed it Blaché Features, drove it into bankruptcy, and then ran off to Hollywood with his mistress. With two small children and a bankrupt studio, Alice Guy Blaché's career was ended. She didn't have the money to relocate or to continue. As a woman now in her fifties, she was not wanted. She tried to freelance but was unable to get work in either the United States or Paris. Even credit for the first fiction film was taken away from her and given to Georges Méliès. Many of her other films were credited to male assistants.[8]

Nell Shipman experienced the same fate. As the head of an independent company without studio distribution of her films, she was unable to compete. Her company went bankrupt, leaving her, at the end of her life, penniless.

The movie industry was changing. No longer could anyone take a camera, shoot a good film, and sell it. All the means of production were being consolidated into one large system that would change the way films were created and distributed—the studio system.

2

THE RISE OF THE STUDIO SYSTEM

THE BEGINNING OF the studio system can be traced to the formation of MGM in 1924. The studios were run by men, and men hired men. They ran their studios to make money—a lot of it—and to create an efficient business that had control over every aspect of moviemaking, from production to distribution to exhibition. Although women had made successful films, their contributions were not recognized and they were bypassed in the development of the studio system. By the 1930s, the studios were firmly in place, and the independent film, to a great extent developed by women, could no longer compete.

"In the beginning, there was this pioneer attitude—you didn't know what you were doing, and everything was experimental and exciting," says Meta Wilde, one of the early script supervisors. "Then the studio system came, and suddenly you had much more of a hierarchy and everything was much more compartmentalized." The more corporate the business became, the fewer females there were.

"By the 1930s, the only women on the set were the wardrobe women," says Wilde. "The wardrobe department had to dress the women who were the stars. There were men's wardrobe people and women's wardrobe people. And they had women down on the set to see that stars had the right costume on, or the gloves, or the hat, or whatever was necessary. They had hairdressers for women and hairdressers for men."

THEN THERE WERE TWO: ARZNER AND LUPINO

Women directors were no longer wanted. In Hollywood, the only woman directing for a studio during the period 1927 to 1943 was Dorothy Arzner.

"In the beginning, Dorothy Arzner was considered the leading film cutter in the business, and later was considered one of Hollywood's top ten directors," says director Francine Parker, who knew Arzner, studied her films, and produced a retrospective of her work at the Directors Guild in 1979. "As an editor, her close-ups to create the bullfighting scene in Valentino's *Blood and Sand* were stunning—no one had ever intercut a scene like that." To create the scene, Arzner intercut shots of Valentino and shots of the bull, giving the impression that Valentino was actually fighting the bull, even though they were never in the same ring. Although this technique is used often in Hollywood today, it was revolutionary for the 1920s.

She also made her mark through her approach to female characters. "Her use of peripheral characters was extraordinary," continues Parker, "as was her insight into how women talk and relate to each other and how they view the world. Her artistry encompassed outlandish wit, dazzling characterizations, warmth, humanness, meticulous imagery, technical virtuosity, as well as a spectacular command of the language and mechanics of the motion picture. And, in its day, top box-office draw."[9]

Parker also acknowledges Arzner's influence on other film artists. "She helped save the career of the brilliant cinematographer Charlie Lang, who was going to be fired on one of her shoots. She said, 'Let's give him another chance.' Francis Ford Coppola was her student and called her one of the major influences in his life."

Dorothy Arzner gave a number of women their first starring roles, including Esther Ralston in *Fashions for Women* (1927), Katharine Hepburn in *Christopher Strong* (1933), Rosalind Russell in *Craig's Wife* (1936), and Lucille Ball in *Dance Girl Dance* (1940). She gave the starring role in Paramount's first talkie to Clara Bow in *The Wild Party* (1929) and helped develop Bow's screen persona as the girl who had "it"—sex appeal. On the set of *The Wild Party,* Arzner invented the boom microphone by fastening a microphone to a fishing pole, to give the stars greater flexibility.

Arzner was the first woman member of the Directors Guild of America. Six years after she directed her last film, another woman director came on the scene—Ida Lupino.

Lupino acted in more than fifty films beginning in the late 1930s but turned to directing in 1949 with *Not Wanted,* although she received no directing credit. It was made for $110,000 and grossed $1 million. She formed a production company with her first husband, Collier Young, and went on to direct six more feature films and, later, more than eighty-eight shows for television. She was known for films that stayed within or below budget, for her willingness to tackle complex social issues, for her ability to direct both action and love stories, and for her good taste.

Director Parker describes Lupino as daring. "She shot entirely on location for her feature films, which was a daring innovation and which set the stage for future feature-film production. She was daring to sacrifice security to realize a vision rather than playing it safe for comfort, daring to be inventive in concept and different in techniques, daring to do A movies on Z budgets long before it was fashionable, risking unknown faces, gambling on untried subjects, daring to shoot big while shooting fast, daring to direct at a time terrifyingly tough for women, daring to be daring."[10]

Lupino was the only woman who had directed a major feature film until Elaine May directed *A New Leaf* in 1971.

AN ACCEPTABLE WOMAN'S JOB

Although early women directors were few, in one aspect of the profession women were active and continued to be influential throughout the history of film—the role of film editor. Viola Lawrence, considered to be the first female film editor, began editing as early as 1915 and edited *Bulldog Drummond* in 1929—Goldwyn's first sound film. Rose Smith coedited D. W. Griffith's *Intolerance* (1916). although some accounts say she also may have worked on *Birth of a Nation* in 1915. Anne Bauchens may have begun at about the same time as Lawrence and Smith, although her first published film credit is in 1918.

Other women began in these early years and had long, sucessful careers as editors. Margaret Booth began working as a negative cutter in silent films in 1920 and became supervising editor of all MGM pictures in Europe and America in 1937. For the next thirty-two years she oversaw the editing on as many as forty-two pictures per year. She herself edited some of MGM's best-known films. including *The Mutiny on the Bounty* and *The Way We Were.*

Barbara McLean edited thirty of Darryl Zanuck's films and was nominated for seven Academy Awards between 1935 and 1950 for such films as *Les Miserables*, *Lloyds of London*, *Alexander's Ragtime Band*, *The Rains Came*, *Song of Bernadette*, and *Wilson.* She won the Academy Award for editing *All About Eve.*

Adrienne Fazan edited many of the great musicals, including *Singin' in the Rain*, *An American in Paris*, *Kismet*, and *Gigi.*

Many of the great male directors used female editors. Alfred Hitchcock's editor was his wife, Alma Reville. Anne Bauchens edited for Cecil B. de Mille. Martin Scorsese's editor, Thelma Schoonmaker. cut several critically acclaimed pictures, including *Raging Bull.* Woody Allen's editor on all his films since *Annie Hall* has been Susan E. Morse. Verna Fields worked as editor on some of the memorable films of George Lucas (the final edit of *American Graffiti*) and Steven

Spielberg (*Jaws*). Carol Littleton edited *E.T.* and most of Lawrence Kasdan's films, including *Body Heat* and *The Big Chill. Bonnie and Clyde* (directed by Arthur Penn) and *Dog Day Afternoon* (directed by Sidney Lumet) were edited by Dede Allen.

Margaret Booth says of her profession, "Editors get credit, but I don't know if it's enough. They receive much more now than they used to. We would receive credit on the screen but not really credit for all we did—which was working night and day with thousands of feet of film."[11]

In spite of their success as editors, women have never been a majority in the profession. They are, according to Carol Littleton, a "healthy third of the Editors Guild. In spite of our few numbers, many of the top-notch editors of American films are women."

Littleton has a theory about why women make such good editors. "In life, as in editing, we may wield little power, but we exert great influence. We may not participate as players, but we observe. When your only participation is being a spectator, and if you are a passionate spectator, you become an extraorinarily keen observer. Historically, men do and women watch. As a result, women have an intuitive sense of what is true in human behavior. As film editors, we influence the material by heightening or focusing the emotional life of the film. We can change the tone of the film and the emotional weight of the story. Editing is about making choices based upon observation. The editor includes the best possible moments to tell a story."

THE SUBTLE INFLUENCE

The lack of opportunity in most jobs did not prevent women from continuing to have influence in the film industry, but their influence was largely behind the scenes. Throughout film history, women have had an impact on many of the most important decisions and have stood behind many of the most important men in Hollywood.

A list of the men in Hollywood who have had the most influence on the film industry might include directors Howard Hawks, Cecil B. de Mille, John Ford, Orson Welles, and Alfred Hitchcock; studio heads Irving Thalberg (MGM), Jack Warner (Warner Bros.), and B. P. Schulberg (Paramount); and actors Rudolph Valentino, Douglas Fairbanks, Sr., Tyrone Power, Charlie Chaplin, and Clark Gable. The success of these men depended on the behind-the-scenes work and support of women.

Actress-director Mabel Normand, for example, helped launch Charlie Chaplin's career. Normand, a leading actress for Mack Sennett when he started Keystone Pictures in 1912, was a daring and inventive actress, director, comedienne, and stuntwoman. Her humor was a model for such later stars as Lucille Ball, Carol Burnett, and Debbie Reynolds, as well as Charlie Chaplin.

Norman helped get Chaplin his first job, prepared him for the camera, and was his director at least five times (several times uncredited), though he didn't much like being directed by anyone and decided he'd do better himself.[12]

"Perhaps [Chaplin's] greatest debt is owed to Mabel Normand," says Raymond Lee in *Movie Memories*. "A study of her films, made before Chaplin came to this country, shows entire routines, gestures, reactions, expressions, that were later a part of Chaplin's characterizations."[13]

Such important studio heads as Irving Thalberg and B. P. Schulberg needed and valued the "woman's touch" that women writers brought, to help define the many women stars of the 1930s and 1940s. Even Jack Warner, who disliked women writers, felt he had to employ some to write for his major women stars.[14]

It wasn't just women stars who were being created by women writers. Writer Anita Loos helped define Douglas Fairbanks's image by adding humor to his actions, "making him superior in words as well as deeds."[15] The screenplays of Bess Meredyth helped shape the careers of John Barrymore (*Don Juan*, 1926) and Ramon Novarro (*Ben-Hur*, 1926) and created Tyrone Power's swashbuckling image in

The Mark of Zorro (1940). Writer and executive June Mathis is credited with launching Rudolph Valentino's career and his romantic image; in 1921 and 1922 she insisted he appear in two films she wrote, *The Four Horsemen of the Apocalypse* and *Blood and Sand.* Clark Gable's career was dependent upon his drama coach and first wife, Josephine Dillon, who sanded down his rough edges, polished his diction, and prepared him for the talkies.[16]

Many of the great male directors also surrounded themselves with talented women. Howard Hawks, known for his strong women characters, hired Leigh Brackett to write the scripts to many of his films. In *The Big Sleep,* which Brackett cowrote with William Faulkner, Humphrey Bogart took for granted that Brackett had penned the lines he found too genteel—only to discover that those lines had been written by Faulkner and that Brackett was responsible for the tough-guy lines. She went on to be instrumental in creating John Wayne's he-man characters in such films as *Rio Bravo* and *Rio Lobo.*[17] Hawks gave Brackett what he considered the supreme compliment: "She wrote like a man—she writes good."[18]

For most of Cecil B. de Mille's career, his screenplays were written by Jeanie MacPherson and his films were edited by Anne Bauchens. These included such epics as *The Ten Commandments, The King of Kings,* and *The Buccaneer.*

Many of Alfred Hitchcock's best-known films, including *Rebecca, Suspicion,* and *Jamaica Inn,* were written by Joan Harrison, who first worked as his script editor and then helped establish his style of suspense. In Hitchcock's early years in England, he worked closely with Alma Reville, who later became his wife and coscripted and edited some of his films. His producer was another woman, Peggy Robinson.

Virginia Van Upp began her career as a child actress for Lois Weber, wrote more than twenty films, and later produced and doctored the script of Orson Welles's critically acclaimed film *The Lady from Shanghai.* Van Upp was an exception—not only was she a writer, but she was one of the few producers who continued to work in the industry in the 1930s and 1940s, eventually becoming second in command to studio head Harry Cohn at Columbia in 1944.

When the studios ran into financial trouble, it was usually the glamour, talent, and screen presence of the women stars that saved them. According to film historian Jeanine Basinger, Mae West is credited with "single-handedly saving Paramount Pictures from financial ruin. Shirley Temple was given the same credit at 20th Century–Fox during the 1930s, as was Deanna Durbin at Universal."[19]

IT DIDN'T HAPPEN JUST IN HOLLYWOOD

In the early 1900s, women were active in film throughout the world—in France, Australia, New Zealand, China, India. Like their sisters in the United States, they left their mark by making some of the most influential films. And, like them, they rose and fell in the industry they helped create.

France's Germaine Dulac is known as the first feminist filmmaker. Her early films were conventional, but by 1917 she had begun to experiment with methods of making the film more subjective. She emphasized atmosphere over story and used dissolves, slow motion, and superimpositions to show unconscious processes on the screen. Working with French theoretician Louis Delluc in 1917, she formulated the basic concepts of French avant-garde film. She then joined several other filmmakers and intellectuals to create the first *ciné-clubs*, to promote the art of film.[20]

In Germany in the 1930s, another woman filmmaker emerged who is considered by many to be the most controversial and one of the most important filmmakers, male or female, in the history of film. Leni Riefenstahl started her filmmaking career as an actress in a uniquely German genre, the mountaineering film, but after six years she moved into directing. Now in her nineties and living near Munich, she discusses her early work in an interview by letter. "At the same time as I was producing and directing *Das Bläue Licht* [The Blue Light, the first film she directed], there was another woman director, Leontine Sagan, who was also making a feature film, called *Mädchen in Uniform* [Girls in Uniform]."

Das Bläue Licht brought Riefenstahl to the attention of Adolf Hitler. In 1934 she shot *Triumph des Willens* (Triumph of the Will) about the Nuremberg Rally, considered to be the most effective propaganda film ever made. For the 1936 Berlin Olympics, she directed *Olympia,* arguably one of the ten best films of all time.

In these films, she created, experimented with, and revolutionized film technique. Riefenstahl says, "Especially through my first documentary film, *Triumph des Willens,* I revolutionized film reportage by use of the moving picture. Up until this time film reportage was static, not moving, therefore not filmic. I got my camera-people to use roller skates to get moving shots, and to make not only tilts and pans but as many traveling shots as possible—my favorite saying was 'movement and more movement.' Through this, life came into the pictures. That was new—and much more. The dynamism of our sport filming in my Olympic film came about not only through movement but also by shooting with different speeds. Then the use of lots of handheld cameras, the effect of longer telefocal lenses, which I got specially made at that time, the production of Agfa R film-stock with which twilight and night shots could be made in sunlight during the day through special filters."

Riefenstahl created other techniques used in later films, including digging pits for the cameramen so that the athletes could be filmed against the sky (a technique used to great effect by John Ford in *Stagecoach*). She put a camera in a balloon to float above the athletes, although she adds, "None of the shots were of use."

For *Olympia,* Riefenstahl used large film crews. "One day, at the opening of the Olympic Games in Berlin, I had sixty camera-people, some of whom I had trained myself. But on many of the other days of the Olympics I had thirty camera-people working. On *Triumph des Willens* I had eighteen cameramen."

For *Triumph des Willens,* Riefenstahl used traveling shots and intercut scenes. She looked for patterns and contrasts, finding ways to link the images as in a musical composition, making the film tell its story without a commentator. She says, "I shot the subject matter as good as I could and shaped it into a film."

The film went on to win a gold medal in Paris, a gold medal in Venice, and a National Film Prize in Germany. The film was so successful, so intense, so persuasive, that it was charged with being greatly responsible for the rise of the Nazi Party. Riefenstahl's triumph was her downfall. After the war she was ostracized worldwide as a director and never made another film. She says, "I've never been proud of it, neither now, nor then. So not only am I not proud, I'm deeply unhappy I made it."[21]

In another part of the world, and under very different circumstances, Matilde Landeta, known as the grandmother of Latin American film, was having the same type of problems as her female counterparts in the United States. Landeta was not the first woman director in Mexico (the first woman to write, act, direct, and produce was Mimi Derba, in 1919), but she may be the most important. Landeta, working in the late 1930s and 1940s, was known for subject matter that was rarely, if ever, expressed through male filmmakers.

Landeta made films about remarkable women. In one, *La negra angustias,* she dealt with a woman's rebellion against an unjust society, men's violation of the human rights of women, and rebellion against machismo in Mexico. In *Lola Casanova* she told the story of a woman who helped the Serra Indians. Her last film, *Trotacalles/Streetwalker* (1951), was about the exploitation of two Latinas.

Landeta says, "I fell in love instantly with film. I knew it was my kind of world—a world I had imagined but didn't know existed. I wanted to direct. I started as script girl for sixty to seventy films, then I did fourteen films as an assistant director."[22]

It isn't unusual for filmmakers to encounter obstacles, but Landeta's were uniquely related to her gender. In the late 1930s she tried to move from script girl to assistant director, the natural development process in order to learn the art of directing. She encountered great difficulty getting a promotion but finally did become an assistant director.

"Film directing isn't easy," she says. "It's hard work. But they managed to make it harder. They threw every possible obstacle at me. Negatives would get lost. I'd have no equipment. I'd need something and it wouldn't be available. After I finished my first film, they refused to show it for over a year. When it finally opened, it was in a local cinema without any publicity."

Although Landeta made 110 short films, she was allowed to make only three feature films. Her loss was also the world's loss, according to film critic Gustavo Garcia. "Mexican cinema was not ready to accept such a dynamic, progressive, and intelligent figure. So Mexican cinema, which had in a way created her, ended up destroying her, and with her they destroyed as well for several decades any kind of woman's cinema in Mexico."[23]

The woman's film in Mexico had a brief flowering under Landeta. In the United States, the woman's film was the mainstay of U.S. cinema for almost twenty years.

3

WOMEN WRITERS, WOMEN STARS

DURING THE 1930s, eighty-five million people went to the movies each week.[24] Many of these moviegoers were women, attending matinees to watch their favorite female stars. A number of these star vehicles were based on the novels of women writers: Daphne Du Maurier (*My Cousin Rachel* and *Rebecca*), Margaret Mitchell (*Gone With the Wind*), Fanny Hurst (*Back Street*), Rachel Crothers (*Susan and God*), Vera Caspary (*Laura*), Patricia Highsmith (*Strangers on a Train*), Carson McCullers (*Reflections in a Golden Eye*), Kathleen Winsor (*Forever Amber*), Olive Higgins Prouty (*Stella Dallas*), and the many films made from Agatha Christie's novels.

Many screenplays with great female roles were written or rewritten by women, or by male and female partners. In fact, from 1930 to 1950, 21 percent of all scripts nominated for an Academy Award were written or cowritten by women, even though women made up a much smaller percentage of Hollywood writers.

MGM, under Irving Thalberg, had the best record for employing women writers throughout the 1930s and 1940s, and it showed in the success of their films. Anthony Slide says, "Women writers were clearly in a minority at MGM, but the caliber of these women stands out. They were writing some of the most memorable and most important films of this period." These included *Pat and Mike* and *Adam's Rib* by Ruth Gordon, *Queen Christina* and *Anna Karenina* by Salka Viertel, *The Women* by Anita Loos, *Christopher Strong* and *Camille* by Zoe Akins, *A Star Is Born* by Dorothy Parker, *The Thin Man, Seven Brides for Seven Brothers, Rose Marie,* and *Father of the Bride* by Frances Goodrich, and *Singin' in the Rain, Auntie Mame,* and *Bells Are Ringing* by Betty Comden.

Women writers created good roles for up-and-coming actresses who looked as if they could make it big—if only they had the right script. Frances Marion helped launch Greta Garbo into talkies with *Anna Christie.* Writers Helene Deutsch and Sally Benson wrote *National Velvet,* which gave Elizabeth Taylor her first starring role. Writer Isobel Lennart wrote *Love Me or Leave Me,* the film that proved Doris Day could do more than lighthearted comedies. Producer-writer-executive Virginia Van Upp helped create one of the great screen legends, Rita Hayworth, by writing the sultry lead role of *Gilda.*

The women didn't always receive credit for their work. Not all accounts credit Catherine Turney with the screenplay for *Mildred Pierce,* although the Writers Guild later restored her credit. In several accounts, Vina Delmar is not given credit for *The Awful Truth,* although according to Marsha McCreadie in *Women Who Write the Movies,* "There were plenty of contemporaneous newspaper articles which credited Delmar with the script; oddly enough, Leslie Halliwell's *The Filmgoer's Companion* . . . lists Leo McCarey as the writer as well as the director."[25] McCreadie admits, "It is the same problem of uncredited writers—woman and men alike—throughout film history, though it may be more acute with women writers."[26]

But the opportunity was there. "They needed us," says Catherine Turney, who wrote a number of these women's pictures of the 1930s and 1940s. "With the advent of sound, the studios were desperately looking for people who could write dialogue. So the studios turned to playwrights—women or men, it didn't matter, as long as they could write. I had a play in New York, and on the strength of all these play reviews, MGM said they wanted me to come over."

During the 1940s, there was another reason why women were hired. "Most of our work was during the war, when a lot of men were away," says Turney. She and Lenore Coffee were the only women writers at Warner Bros. in 1942. "The war had a lot to do with the change in attitude toward the women. Women objected to being treated as if they were frail flowers who couldn't function on their own. The studios, theater, entertainment business, they're chic. If they see a trend, they jump on it quickly. That's where the box office is. Since women were taking an active part in the war, the studios were tailoring vehicles for women, to show them to be strong and able to function without the man. The star was the epitome, and everything was built around the star—finding a vehicle for her or him."

In turn, many of these stars wanted more control over their scripts. Some actresses, such as Bette Davis, became producers. Others, like Jane Wyman, persisted until they got what they wanted. "I was under contract to Warner Bros. from 1935 until I went into television in 1954," Wyman says. "I worked for Jack Warner for all those years and never had a fight with him. Ever. I would ask him for certain parts and he would say no, and I would say, 'Well, I'll get you yet,' and I would go back again and he would give it to me." Those great roles won her an Academy Award for *Johnny Belinda* in 1948 as well as four Academy Award nominations.

Women agents too were finding and nurturing some of the great talents of the screen. Kay Brown Barrett not only launched the American careers of Ingrid Bergman and Laurence Olivier but was instrumental in bringing *Gone With the Wind* to the screen. She immediately saw the novel's potential as a film but had trouble convincing anyone until David O. Selznick finally agreed to buy the screen rights.

THE WOMAN'S FILM

Although there were woman's films throughout the silent era, the heyday of the woman's film was during the Golden Era of the studio *system, in the 1930s and 1940s and continuing on somewhat into the* 1950s and 1960s. Film historian Jeanine Basinger defines the woman's film as "one that places at the center of its universe a female who is trying to deal with the emotional, social, and psychological problems that are specifically connected to the fact that she is a woman."

The woman's film usually showed a strong woman at its center, her life more independent and empowered than the life of the ordinary female moviegoer. "Working within the confines of the studio system, women screenwriters hesitated to criticize traditional gender roles," says Laura Kaiser in an article on women screenwriters. "Yet many of their scripts clearly comment on women's desire for power."[27]

This dichotomy between reality and film served many functions, including a political one. By showing independent working women, the films gave women permission to work outside the home, particularly during the Second World War. For wives whose lives were oppressed, it gave images of freedom. For wives lonesome for husbands, it showed them the ultimate female fantasies of love restored, or that if the first husband died (as was the case in many films of this period), there would be an even better man to take his place. Although love always prevailed at the end, the strongest message of the film was not always the giving up of the job for the man, which came at the end, but one of the gutsy, emotionally involving independent woman doing exciting deeds.

Basinger sees the function of the woman's film as subversive because it presented a role model that women didn't fulfill, allowing the woman to vicariously take part in action and adventure and then moving back to the traditional by telling the women in the audience that they've made the right choice in not living those lives. Basinger contrasts the independence of the characters with the social milieu of the 1930s and 1940s and what women had to resort to in order to get what they wanted. "Subversion is not unknown in a woman's daily life. If a woman does not have power in her daily life, she has to find some way to accomplish her goals, some method for getting her way.

The wife who teased money out of her husband, who flirted with her husband's boss, who appeared to go by the men's rules while secretly manipulating, was a woman who had mastered subversion. Such women were very common in this period, and such behavior was typical in the woman's world."

The adventure that was part of the woman's film was necessary because dramatic conventions demanded that the woman character move out of her traditional world. "In order to tell a story about a woman, something has to happen to her," explains Basinger. "Nothing happens to her if she's obedient, dutiful, stays at home like a good girl, has her children. You've got to get her out of that context in order to have an interesting story. She can't just do nothing. She has to break with tradition."

The star's persona also created a subversive message for women—that it's all right to have strong wants and desires, and that women's lives and concerns mattered. "In the 1930s and 1940s, there were an enormous number of strong women stars who had to be nurtured by the studio system," continues Basinger. "That meant a lot of stories of different kinds. There were mature women, with mature women's problems."

Then there's the audience. "What does an audience want to see?" asks Basinger. "There was a huge audience of women coming to the movies then. They went to see clothes and glamour. They went to see romance. They went to see all the things they didn't have, and one of the main things they didn't have was power, or a career, or freedom. The movies gave them those things, which was very fulfilling for them, and then the films brought it back around at the end by saying, 'But those things aren't nice, they aren't good for you, they'll ruin your life. Women shouldn't want those things.' The subversive message partly is in the story because you need conflict for drama, but it's also there because of an honest observance of female behavior. The woman screenwriter was leading an exciting, independent life and she knew how to write about that. She knew how to speak to her sister in the audience about these issues."

These movies, rich in subtext, were subversive because they weren't absolutely clear in their message. Basinger watched hundreds of woman's films to form her theories, and she noticed over and over again one important fact: "I saw how ambivalent they really are. According to who you are, you can take the message of these films in many different ways."

With the end of the woman's film in the early 1950s, women's influence seemed to disappear. The men had come back from war and began to take back the writing jobs that women had so ably done for the previous fifty years. The image of women was changing—they had left the workplace and moved back into the home in large numbers, changing the image from strong, independent woman to homemaker with the loving support of a man. True, an occasional script was written by a woman. Ida Lupino still directed, in television, until the 1960s, but there weren't women decision makers, women in the mainstream of Hollywood films. Not until the 1980s would women appear in any significant numbers as executives, and not until the 1990s would there be a significant emergence of women as directors, writers, and producers.

4

THE END OF AN ERA

BY THE EARLY 1950s, the studio system was changing. Government regulations said that studios could no longer have control over every aspect of filmmaking. Theaters were sold, and studios began to focus on distribution of films. Their profits diminished. Paramount profits dropped from $20 million to $6 million a year.[28] The number of people attending the cinema dropped from ninety million a week in the 1940s to sixteen million a week in the mid-1950s. Television was changing the entertainment business, and with it came changing opportunities for women in film.

"The studio system almost all of a sudden went out of existence," explains Catherine Turney. "It's so ironic because, in the beginning, when television first came in, the studios could easily have controlled television, but they were so anxious to get rid of it that they lost perspective and the networks took it over."

Turney reflects on the problem: "Each time something new happened in this business, things started out so promisingly for women, and then the squeeze came. The only thing I can think of is that the men, when they began to see where things were going, would behave more aggressively. In the beginning, quite a few of the screenwriters looked down upon television. It was the poor relation. When they did work in television, they were shunted off into obscure little offices down at the end of the street. My agent wouldn't even send me to the television networks for any jobs. He said, 'You can go there if you want. I'm not sending you there.' He saw television as a B-picture unit and he didn't want to be caught dead in such a place. That was the attitude about television."

But television had arrived. Although there were no women in executive positions in television, a number of actresses nevertheless dominated the new medium and produced and starred in their own shows. In comedy, the most famous name was Lucille Ball. Ball was employed by Dorothy Arzner at RKO Studios in the early 1940s, and then, with her husband Desi Arnaz, she bought out RKO and renamed it Desilu Productions. Actress Ann Sothern had two production companies, AnSo Productions to produce *The Ann Sothern Show* and Vincent Productions (named after her favorite patron saint) to produce *Private Secretary*. Others were stars in their own series: Gale Storm in *My Little Margie*, Eve Arden in *Our Miss Brooks*, Donna Reed in *The Donna Reed Show*, Dale Evans (with Roy Rogers) in *The Roy Rogers & Dale Evans Show*.

Some of the biggest names in variety programming were women—Martha Raye, Rosemary Clooney, Dinah Shore, Giselle MacKenzie, Imogene Coca, Gracie Allen, and Jane Froman. Loretta Young, Jane Wyman, and other Academy Award–winning actresses began drama anthology series, playing different characters each week and producing their own shows. "I produced as well as starred in my show," says Wyman. "It was necessary to get involved in producing because we had more training than a lot of people who were coming into television at that time. I couldn't find anybody to produce it because I couldn't find anybody that would do it my way. But I didn't take a producing credit because it splits you, and it splits your audience. Loretta Young also acted in and produced her show without credit, but we all had control. Of course, at that time we worked for the sponsors. We had to please them. The networks had nothing to do with it. The sponsors stayed on the set. They would make decisions on the selection of the script. They changed the name of the show from *Fireside Theatre* to *The Jane Wyman Theater.* But I could develop the material. Television changed the whole symmetrics of entertainment. Anything goes, whatever is successful will go, whether it's a woman, man, animal, ape, whatever. It was open season. You could do anything you wanted to."

Even such famous film actresses as Barbara Stanwyck, Bette Davis, Grace Kelly, Ida Lupino, Betty Grable, June Allyson, Arlene Dahl, Betty Hutton, Frances Langford, and Polly Bergen appeared in television in the 1950s and 1960s, usually with their own shows, sometimes making guest appearances.

Although the actresses made their mark in the early years of television, women writers and producers found that, once again, they weren't wanted. Comedy writer Irma Kalish had had a successful career writing short stories and magazine articles, but when she tried to write for television, no one was interested. "The producers did not believe that women could write comedy because they didn't think we could be funny. My husband, Austin Kalish, had to go into partnership with other men because it was the only way he could support us. I wasn't salable. He was. Finally, when his most recent partnership dissolved in the middle of a script assignment, I was able to get a job by writing with him. It was the only way I could get my foot in the door. Even after that, one producer believed that the only reason my name was on the script was because I had typed it."

Jane Wyman and Loretta Young hired women writers, and a few others did too, but these were the exceptions. "Not until *My Three Sons* was I able to get back into a writing job. That was in 1959," says Kalish. "And I was never able to produce a show until the late 1970s."

In its early years, television repeated the problems that women encountered in Hollywood from the late 1920s until the 1970s. So when women weren't accepted as producers, directors, or writers, they continued in the more typical female professions—script continuity, makeup, and costumes.

"The people going into television were also pioneers," says script supervisor Pat Miller, who began working in the industry in the late 1940s. "I alternated between feature films and television because jobs in television became more frequent. At the time I was script supervisor on *The Ann Sothern Show;* the networks owned the shows and the woman star held the most power. Ann Sothern was the producer of the series and its star. She controlled every detail concerning the production."

Eventually there were some changes for women, because television needed them. "As more and more shows were going on the air, they needed good writers," says Kalish. "If a woman was a good writer, that was it. And, sometimes women were hired because the lead actresses in shows believed only women could write for another woman."

THE RISE OF THE INDEPENDENT FILM—AGAIN

With the decline of the studio system and the development of television, a new opportunity opened—the independent film. Since women had pioneered the independent film, one might think they could make their comeback through the same medium. But it didn't work that way. The independent film still needed investors, producers, and theaters, and few were going to take a chance on a woman, who usually had little experience and few connections. The old stereotype still held that said women weren't as strong, as authoritative, or as capable as men. Many men believed that women could not be trusted with a lot of money. Others felt an all-male crew wouldn't listen to a female director. The break women needed came with the help of men. For some, it came from producer Roger Corman.

"Roger Corman began making independent films in the late 1950s and was among the first to break away from the Hollywood system," Pat Miller remembers. "Corman was able to produce inexpensive films, independently, with very talented people who opted to forgo cash compensation to get a toehold in the industry. Some later prestigious personalities in the industry were Roger Corman protégées." Corman gave opportunities to women who had little chance in the studio system: producers like Gale Anne Hurd, who went on to coproduce *The Terminator* and *The Abyss* with James Cameron; Barbara Klein and Gwen Fields, who produced *Reflections in the Dark;* directors Katt Shea Ruben and Debra Brock Calso, as well as Penelope Spheeris, who directed *Wayne's World,* which grossed $122 million in 1992—the biggest moneymaker ever directed by a woman.[29]

Why was Corman willing to give opportunities to women when others would not? "I believe in hiring the best talent," says Corman, "and since women are 50 percent of the population, I expect them to be 50 percent of the talent. Perhaps I give a bit of an edge to women because they haven't had as much opportunity."

Corman's work was followed by the work of several women who themselves helped change the landscape for independent film distribution. In 1979, Sandra Schulberg founded the Independent Feature Project (IFP) and its market, the International Feature Film Market (IFFM), to foster production financing, distribution, and exhibition of independent American films. In 1980, Shulberg, along with Maxi Cohen, filmmaker and founding board member of IFP, and several other producers, cofounded First Run Features, the first film distribution company committed solely to distributing American independent films in this country and proving there is a market. Cohen explains that "there was virtually no theatrical film exhibition of independent films in the late 1970s. First Run Features distributed—and still does—the first films of Lizzie Borden, Spike Lee, and Victor Nunez. After First Run came other independent film distributors, such as Cinecom and Alive."

OTHER BREAKTHROUGHS

Slowly women began breaking in, one at a time. A role that opened up for one woman was that of cinematography. Women had operated cameras in the early years, but by the 1920s they had disappeared from any positions with cameras, lights, and sound. They still wanted these jobs. "The Cinematographers Union goes back to the 1930s," says cinematographer Brianne Murphy. "There were no women in the union, except perhaps for animation photographers. In order to work and not be exploited by producers, a group of us who weren't in the IA [the Cinematographers Union] formed our own union, called the American Film Craftsmen. Then the male cinematographers in our group started getting into the IA. This was in the mid-1960s. When I did get in several years later [1973], I was warned, 'You probably won't work. Who's going to hire a woman cinematographer?' But I took the chance, and fortunately NBC called the union shortly afterward and said, 'We're doing a special on breast cancer and our subjects would like to have a woman crew or at least a woman cameraperson. Would you please see what you can do.' They said, 'Of course, we've got *a* woman.' They sent me over there and I shot that documentary on breast cancer. NBC was happy with my work and asked me to go on staff. I said I wouldn't because I was afraid they would have me do the flower shows and PTA meetings. I said I wanted to do riots, the hard news. So I worked on a daily basis for them, which was actually more lucrative, mainly doing news and documentary."

Women in a nontraditional profession had trouble being taken seriously. "At first, time after time someone on the crew thought it was a mistake I was there," explains Murphy. "When I went to Universal for my first television job, on *Colombo,* a guard at the gate told me to go to makeup. I told him I wasn't an actor, that I was coming to shoot *Columbo,* but he didn't believe me. I finally had to go to makeup in order to ask them where the camera department was."

The executive offices also opened up for women—one at a time—beginning with attorneys. When Barbara Boyle entered the profession in 1960, she, like Murphy, had trouble getting in the right door. "My last year in law school I was told there was an opening for an attorney at a movie studio. The studio was located at La Brea and Sunset, at what is now A&M Studios but in those days was the old Charlie Chaplin Studio. I drove to the gate, the guard looked me over. 'Oh, yes, honey, they are expecting you.' The gate opened. I drove to Building B, found a small reception area, and sat down. There were four gorgeous, color-coordinated women sitting there. There were only three law schools in California at that time: Stanford, Bolt, and UCLA. 'My God, I thought I knew all the women law students in California.' Lo and behold, another absolutely gorgeous woman came out of the office. What affirmative action. I was impressed; they wanted to hire a woman.

"My turn came. Inside the office, behind a large desk, smoking a large cigar, was Lou Rusoff. The only items missing were gold chains, just not in vogue then. Lou looked at me and said, 'Take off your jeans.' I went into a long diatribe about women, images, and what Hollywood generated about both. Finally he said, 'Do you ever think you're wrong?' I said, 'About what?' He said, 'I'm casting for a beach party movie. You're supposed to have a bathing suit on underneath. Who are you supposed to see?' I said, 'Sam Arkoff—for a job as an attorney.' He said, 'How did you get to me?' I said, 'Probably because of the stereotypes Hollywood creates.' So he called Sam and said, 'Listen, I have never heard anyone talk so much. I have a feeling she's bright if you can get a word in edgewise. Let me talk to her for a few minutes and then I'll send her over.' After a half an hour with Lou, then head of production for American International Pictures, I went to see Sam, who gave me the job on the spot."

In order to compete, women have had to put up with the usual comments about being a woman, or subversive comments to make them feel uncomfortable. Women have learned to negotiate with humor, to ignore some remarks, give a smart rejoinder to others.

"By the second meeting, none of those remarks were made," says Boyle, who recognized her need to work harder and longer to be accepted. "I did my homework. I never walked into anything unprepared. I knew everything about everybody in the room that I possibly could. All the things a good young lawyer should do, I did it in spades. By the second meeting, it was 'Let's get down to the negotiations.' "

Like many women who would follow her, Murphy usually ignored the comments and just went about her work. "Lighting a set takes communication with electricians and the gaffer and the grips and the camera operator. I'd give them an f-stop, or tell the electricians and the gaffer in foot candles what I wanted. It's a whole different language you're not going to know if you're somebody's daughter who just fell onto the set. Then they realized maybe I did know what I was doing. On *Columbo,* which was the first thing I'd done on a major lot, the producers came down to the set after they had seen the first day's dailies. One of them said, 'They're up there in the tower looking at your film for the third time.' I said, 'Is something wrong?' He said, 'No, they just can't believe that a woman did it.' "

A NEW ERA

By the 1970s, women were returning to work, gaining independence, educating and preparing themselves for professional life. Family structures were changing, the economic situation was changing, and women began demanding opportunities. If women were equal to men, then they should have equal opportunities. Organizations sprang up to support these changes. The National Organization for Women was founded in 1967. *Ms.* magazine began publication in 1972. In the film industry, a group of women decided it was time to organize for change.

Prior to 1973, the only women's group in film was the Motion Picture Mothers, which began in the early 1930s and whose members raised money, volunteered, and met for lunch. Women in Film had another agenda—to improve roles for women and help them move into decision-making positions within the corporate structure.

"The women's movement was just beginning to bubble over," says author Sue Cameron, one of the original founders of Women in Film. "In 1973, because we were upset that there were no women anywhere, I went to the Writers Guild and gathered some statistics and found out how many women wrote episodes for television over a whole season. If there were forty episodes of a show, thirty-nine were written by men and one was written by women. I printed the statistics in my daily column in *The Hollywood Reporter.* Tons of phone calls from irate women started coming in, so I went to the owner and publisher, Tichi Wilkerson Kassel. We realized there was no place to go, that we needed to help each other, and we had to meet, and we had to organize. Enough was enough."

So Wilkerson Kassel said, "Let's start an organization." Wilkerson Kassel recognized that it was lonely at the top and decided to do something about it. "I felt there must be other women in positions of power who needed to talk to other women about their problems. I asked several women—Sue Cameron, Marcie Borie, Zelda Bogart—to help me ferret them out. We began brainstorming, searching for the best strategy to promote talented women to key positions in the industry."

Although women across America were marching and protesting for change, Wilkerson Kassel recommended another method. "I felt it was essential to avoid a radical stance; that the best way to achieve more than a token status in the industry was to work within it. We had to be smart and diligent, to network, to prove that women have the talent, drive, and technical know-how to become an indispensable part of the establishment."

Wilkerson Kassel called Sue Cameron and said, "Call your friends and invite them for lunch." The first person Cameron called was Nancy Malone. Others joined them in Wilkerson Kassel's office over lunch, to talk about the formation of this new organization.

The beginning of Women in Film started the erosion of the exclusive male hierarchy, began to raise consciousness about women's desires and ability, and encouraged the founding of groups that would find other ways to support women.

Nancy Malone helped found one of them. "When I was at Fox, I went to Dennis Stanfield, who was then president of the studio. 'I'd like to do something for the women here at the lot,' I said. 'Why don't we put together something called 20th Century–Fox Women's Council?' And without batting an eye he wrote out a check for $5,000 to start it up."

After Women in Film came such groups as CineWomen, Women in Radio and Television, Women in Entertainment, the Stuntwoman's Association, Women in Show Business, Women in Communication, and Women Behind the Lens. Creating opportunities for women was the first agenda of most of these groups. But the long-range plans included more than just fitting in to the boys' network. As women's sense of power and identity developed, many wanted to be part of the creation of a film industry that left room for women to be women. They didn't want to become one of the guys so much as a part of a diverse team that calls upon all their talents and that sees the possibility of a true partnership among men and women. As women broke into the business, they wanted to influence changes in the power structure, believing that there are more effective, efficient, and diverse ways to conduct the business of film. To do that would take women in decision-making roles—as executives, producers, directors, and writers.

5

CASE STUDY

Loretta Young

LORETTA YOUNG was a pioneer in both film and television, beginning her work in silent films, winning an Academy Award for *The Farmer's Daughter* in 1947, and then moving to television in the 1950s, when there were virtually no role models for women except for the ubiquitous mother roles. Loretta Young gave us many. But she also gave us herself.

I was one of the girls who grew up watching Loretta Young's weekly series. She had an enormous impact on my life. It was not the glamour of Loretta coming through the door in beautiful flowing gowns that most influenced me. It was her graciousness and wisdom that served as a guiding light.

Loretta says: "I was four years old when I made my first picture. I'm eighty-one now. My uncle was a production manager. One day his picture needed some extra fairies to fly around the garden in a picture called *The Primrose Ring* with Mae Murray. So he just went right across the street to his own backyard and picked out the kids. I was one of them. The rest of the kids didn't like it too much, but I really thought I was flying.

"I also did three other silent films. My first lead was in a silent picture, called *Laugh, Clown, Laugh,* with Lon Chaney. I was fourteen years old.

"In the beginning, it was a big family. Everybody was terribly excited about the business. Nobody knew what they were doing, but they just ploughed ahead and did it anyway. There were many women stars, no women directors (heavens no!), I'm sure there were women writers, but it was a long time before I realized the script was written. I thought the directors made it up. Oh, no, they didn't give me any script. You went on the set in the silent days and the director said, 'Now, you go over here and you see this man. You're in love with him. So you get very excited when you see him.' They told you what to do.

"In the early days, Lillian Gish produced her own pictures at Metro and they were brilliant. She was wonderful and when she stopped producing her pictures, they stopped making money. D. W. Griffith taught her everything he knew and he was apparently a very good director.

"At that time, men did these jobs just because women were thought of as more delicate and their home life was more delicate and very seldom did a woman go out—maybe a secretary. Even then, when they left working, they got married and went home and had children. That probably is reflected in the fact that there were no women directors. The first woman director I heard of was Dorothy Arzner in the 1930s and 1940s. I was a big hot-shot star by that time, I thought. I knew there was a woman director and I hoped I never had to work for her. My attitude was I paid more attention to men then I did to women.

"I lived in kind of a dreamworld. I was never conscious of any facts, whether it be money or houses or what I got. It was geared to all the pretense and all the beauty and all the niceness. I didn't know you had to act to be a movie star, I thought you just were one. Men intrigued me because I didn't know anything in the world about them. I knew all about women and I liked them. Frank Capra was the first man to open me up about acting. We were rehearsing *Platinum Blonde* and he said, 'What do you think about that, Loretta?' I said, 'Mr. Capra, it doesn't make any difference what I think. You tell me what you want me to do and I'll try to do it.' Capra said, 'No, that's not the game at all. I say something, you listen, and you answer. What you think is vital.'

"When I was choosing roles, I made conscious decisions about what kinds of stories I wanted to be in. I am a rip-roaring practicing Roman Catholic. I was looking for good women to play. I decided a long time ago that I wanted to be an influence for good, for productive decisions and actions. I would play a bad woman if the story was clear that this is what you're not supposed to do. But if it condoned adultery, stealing, murder—the breaking of any of the Ten Commandments—I wouldn't do it.

"In motion pictures I was a great admirer of Bette Davis and of her work. Bette preferred to be the villainess. She preferred it because there were more opportunities to act. The good girls were often plastic, simply pretty and nothing else. Since Bette was a superb actress and had no other qualms about dos and don'ts in her life, everything went into her work. Not so with me. First come my convictions.

"The producers would never even think of me in that part when Bette Davis was around, because she would do it so much better than I would. They knew that. I knew that. I think part of living a fairly happy life is knowing your limitations.

"One time I was loaned to Metro to do a picture and I read the script about a mistress. She doesn't marry the man, and to me that's adultery. They said, 'You can't let that influence your work.' I said, 'Of course, my work influences me and everybody who sees it. It's going to be for good or bad. I know that.' I went to my studio and finally they said, 'Only Mr. Mayer can get you out of it.' So I went to Mr. Mayer, who I knew had two daughters, and I said, 'I don't want to play the part. Would you want your daughters to do it?' He said no. So Carole Lombard got the part and she was very good.

"I was more interested in influencing the audience. That's one of the reasons I wanted to go into television, because I wanted to get, if possible, one good idea into the mainstream of life once a week.

"I was the first Academy Award winner to go into television. I started the show about 1952. [*A Letter to Loretta* began in 1953; *The Loretta Young Show* began in 1954.] I had my Academy Award. I'd made my money. I had some real estate. If I didn't make money, that wasn't the main point. The main point was the timing was right for me to leave motion pictures. Both Mr. Mayer and David Selznick came to see me and said, 'If you do this, you will never get another motion picture script because television is our enemy.' I said, 'It shouldn't be, Mr. Mayer, because it's here and you can't stop it. You should embrace it.'

"We were one of the first people in town to have a television. My husband was an advertising man and he knew television was here to stay. But there wasn't any money in doing television in those early years, and they wanted me to wait for three or four years. Finally I said, 'If I wait until there's money in it, I'll be too old to do the kind of thing I want to do.' I was forty when I went into it.

"I had already turned down three or four series. I said, 'No, I don't want to play the same person all the time. I'll bore myself and everyone to death. I want to play an anthology—a different person every week.' They said, 'But that means thirty-six parts.' I said, 'Fine, fine, thirty-six parts. I'll do them all, maybe not well, but I'll do them.'

"NBC had no control over anything on my show except policy. They gave me a certain amount of money each week and I gave them the finished product. I had complete control, for nine years.

"And the show was designed in three parts, because somebody said to me one time, 'If you want a child to understand something, you have to tell it to them three times and usually in three different ways. So I came through the door. I hooked the audience with glamour if I could. Then I presented the thought, such as 'Pretty is as pretty does.' Then I would show them a story about pretty is as pretty does. And the third part was to read a known truth about the subject, usually from the Bible or Confucius.

"Because I'm a woman, it was a woman's show. I was hoping to influence the young women of twelve, thirteen, or fourteen. So I usually tried to make stories about a woman who has to learn something.

Very seldom would I blame anything on a man. Most of the time, it was what the woman had to learn.

"I had a lot of women writers on the show. And I produced the show, although that was never on the credits because I decided, 'Enough's enough. It's enough to say *Loretta Young Show.*'

"I had many people coming up to me to tell me how that show influenced them. One woman said, 'I just have to tell you I have reared my four children on those quotes after that show.'

"We got an awful lot of mail, but I said I only wanted to see the critical mail. A lot of the critical mail came almost like a stamped-out letter. Groups, atheistic groups, could get 125,000 letters on anybody's desk they wanted to within twenty-four hours. So one day, after six years, Procter and Gamble came to me and said, 'You've got to stop making pictures about priests and nuns because we've gotten so much mail.' I said, 'I warned you about this. I told you you were going to get an awful lot of bad mail about me because there are an awful lot of bad people and they're as anxious to spread their ideas around as I am mine. Only I've got the show this time. So don't let it frighten you.' Then when they said, 'You're going to have to stop this,' I said, 'No, I'm sorry because they're some of my most successful shows. Besides, I'm leaving tomorrow to make a show in France called *The Road,* which is about a miracle at Lourdes. If they don't like my other shows, they're going to hate this one and it's going to be an hour because I'm going to ask for an extra special half-hour next year. You can cancel my show if you want but you're not to tell me what I can make and what I can't make!'

"I left the next day for Paris. My agent called me and said Procter and Gamble canceled the show. I said, 'Well, I told them they could.' So after I cried myself to sleep, I borrowed money to make the picture, figuring I'd sell it to ABC or CBS as a movie. Now, that year I was the most important female on television. But Procter and Gamble canceled the show, and then Toni and Listerine picked it up.

"Throughout the show, there were often men who tried to overpower me. I finally got to the point where I wouldn't argue or reason, but just say no. One day I said to my husband, 'When it's called the *Tom Lewis Show,* I'll do it your way. But it's called the *Loretta Young Show.'*

"As the show continued, I tried to get men's stories to pull in the men, too. These were about good guys, not jerks. I did one show about a priest friend of mine who had been in prison in China for four years, in solitary confinement. They were about the heroism of a man.

"We also did shows on racism, on abortion, one on pornography. You have to touch on all those subjects because that's what society is made of. To influence society, good or bad, you have to touch the subjects that are good or bad.

"I also played many different kinds of characters—a judge, a teacher, a nun, a doctor, a blind lawyer, a model. I wanted to play successful people in those jobs. I wanted to say, 'Whatever position you're in, you can do it in a positive way instead of a negative way or an indifferent way.'

"During those years, women were becoming influential in television. There was Lucille Ball, Dinah Shore, Donna Reed, Barbara Stanwyck, Jane Wyman, Jane Froman, June Allyson, and of course Ida Lupino. My story editor was a woman—Ruth Roberts.

"Sometimes people question the influence of television. But of course television is influential. If it didn't have any influence, why then do they advertise so much?"

PART TWO

WOMEN IN POWER AND MANAGEMENT

SOME IMPORTANT BREAKTHROUGHS FOR WOMEN

1960: Barbara Boyle becomes corporate counsel for American International Pictures.

1974: Marcia Nasatir becomes the first woman vice president at United Artists; Rosilyn Heller and Nessa Hymans become vice presidents at Columbia.

1977: Kay Koplovitz is founder, president, and CEO of the Madison Square Garden Network, which is renamed USA Network in 1980.

1980: Sherry Lansing becomes the first woman to head a studio, as president of production at 20th Century–Fox. In 1992 she becomes chairman of the Motion Picture Group of Paramount Pictures.

1981: Paula Weinstein becomes president of production at United Artists.

1981: Suzanne de Passe becomes president at Motown Productions; she is the first African-American woman to head a major entertainment company.

1984: Helene Hahn becomes the first woman to head the business and legal affairs department at a major motion picture studio, Disney.

1984: Barbara Corday becomes the first woman president of Columbia Pictures Television and the first woman president of a TV division of a major studio.

1986: Ann Daniel becomes president of Winkler-Rich Productions.

1987: Dawn Steel becomes president of Columbia Pictures.

1989: Geraldine Laybourne becomes president of Nickelodeon. In 1995 she becomes president of Disney/ABC Cable Networks.

1992: Stacey Snider becomes president of production for Tri-Star Pictures.

1993: Lucie Salhany becomes the first woman to head a television network, Fox Broadcasting. In 1995 she becomes chair of the new United Paramount Network.

1993: Stacey Sher becomes president of Jersey Films.

1994: Lisa Henson becomes president of worldwide production at Columbia Pictures.

1994: Laura Ziskin becomes president of Fox 2000 Pictures.

1994: Amy Pascal becomes president of production at Turner Pictures.

1996: Nikki Rocco becomes president of distribution at Universal Studios.

6

REENVISIONING BUSINESS

Success can make you go one of two ways.
It can make you a prima donna,
or it can smooth the edges,
take away the insecurities,
let the nice things come out.[1]
—*Barbara Walters*

IF POWER IS DEFINED as the authority to green-light a movie, then there are few women in power. In spite of a growing list of women in high positions, in 1995 in the United States there is only one woman who can decide what feature films you'll see—Sherry Lansing at Paramount Pictures. At the three major networks of ABC, CBS, and NBC, three white men decide what you see on television. More progress has been made at the two new networks of Fox and Paramount, where Margaret Loesch heads the Fox Children's Network and Lucie Salhany heads the new United Paramount Network. Women have made the most inroads in cable television. There are four woman presidents who make the final decision on programming: Kay Koplovitz at USA Network, Geraldine Laybourne at Disney/ABC Cable Networks, Sheri Singer at Lifetime Television, and Betty Cohen at Turner Cartoon Network. In other nations around the world, particularly Canada, Australia, and New Zealand, women do slightly better.

If power is defined by the hierarchy of the corporate ladder, no woman sits at the very top. Although the women mentioned are making programming decisions, over them are male CEOs and owners of the networks and studios and boards, which are made up predominantly, or totally, by men. Behind the boards are multinational corporations—all governed by men. As one male executive says, "Our company has a lot of women executives in Hollywood, but the board that governs us in New York is almost all men." As another says, "It's still an old-boys' network."

Many women are in middle management. Why so few at the very top? "People are in the movie business because you can make a lot of money, you can have an exciting life, and you can make a difference to a lot of people," says Marcia Nasatir, who was one of the first women to crack the glass ceiling. In 1974 she was hired by United Artists as the first vice president of a studio since Virginia Van Upp was executive director of Columbia Studios in the 1940s. To her, the answer is simple: "Why would men want to give up those jobs?"

Executive Barbara Corday, the first woman president of Columbia Pictures Television in the 1980s, believes there's another reason. "I don't think men feel comfortable with women around. I think the high, high level men just do not know how to deal with women in the room." In spite of her own high position, Corday knows the ultimate decisions are still being made by the men at the top. "It's like all the daddies went into a room and decided how things were going to be run, and maybe they'll tell us and maybe they won't. They give us a job and we think we've got a pretty good job, but in the end a lot of things get decided somewhere else."

Women look through the glass ceiling and want to sit at the top. They want equality, the opportunity to decide policies, choose films, have a say in many of these decisions. As some of them moved into positions of power, they began to define areas in the industry that needed changing. Some women in middle management, and some men, also reached the same conclusions about the problems: Film, all over the world, is dominated by sex and violence and antifemale images. Millions and millions of dollars are spent on high-budget male movies, many of which fail, and little is spent on women's stories or more realistic human stories, which can be done for less money and have a better chance of being profitable. Time is wasted in the executive offices on political maneuverings. Money is wasted to satisfy egos rather than the bottom line of the product.

Women, as the outsiders, have looked at the problem and said, We think we have some answers, some new perceptions, a fresh point of view. Could we just discuss them?

OPENING THE DOORS

The solution to any of these problems begins with access, and the problem of access is not just a problem for women. The film industry is one of the most difficult industries to enter and to stay in. People in many corporate positions are hired and fired about every two years. Many top executives lose their jobs, form new alliances, and sometimes, with large severance checks, unexpectedly move to small towns deciding that this life is no life for raising children, spending time with a spouse, and staying healthy.

But thousands aspire to make an impact on the media. This is considered the most exciting, the most glamorous, perhaps the most influential industry in the world. More than two billion people watch the Academy Awards every year. The film industry is the second largest industry in the world, just after aeronautics. Films make more than $25 billion a year.[2] More than 85 percent of all homes worldwide now have television. Film and television are a way of life, whether in a remote mountain village in China, on a small South Seas island, or in a city of millions. The opportunity for influence is enormous. People come to this business with stars in their eyes, but they also come with great stories to tell and a desire to make better pictures. Considering that it's difficult for anyone—man or woman—to enter, and considering that there are plenty of women as well prepared and as accomplished as men, why are women still so far from equity?

The problem of gaining power in order to make an impact is complex, because it manifests itself at every level of the business. If the film schools do not have equal numbers of men and women, the pool of prepared filmmakers to feed the industry is not equal. Since many of the top executives have had a mentor, the natural tendency of men is usually to mentor males. If there are few women in power, there are few women to mentor other women. Those new to power have to balance taking the risk of helping others with playing it safe in order to keep their position. If power is gained because you play raquetball and tennis with your boss and have locker-room conversations, then women are already out of the playing field. If preparation for the top executive positions includes the all-male rafting trip (and at some studios it does), then women can never jockey for an equal position.

Men sometimes make different judgments about what constitutes qualifications for a job. Is it the ability to play politics? To be competitive? Or is it an intuitive ability to sense a commercial script? The nurturing ability to form a good team? The insight to select and develop talent?

WOMEN IN BUSINESS—THE FIRST WAVE

In the 1970s and 1980s, as they moved into the corporate structure, women were aware that they were playing by men's rules. Some were good players but got criticized for being too much "like a man." The stories circulating around Hollywood in the 1980s about tough and abusive female bosses were many. Some felt the abusive woman boss acted that way partly because of insecurity, partly because she was not comfortable with the accoutrements that go with the job—the toughness, the aggressiveness, the competitiveness. They didn't seem to wear as well on women as men. (Although some would say they don't wear well on either gender.) Women were taking jobs in a system they didn't design, imitating a gender they didn't belong to, trying to accomplish objectives they never defined.

Sometimes the woman's assertive behavior was misinterpreted. When Barbra Streisand received the Women in Film Crystal Award in 1992, she described the problem of the perception of female versus male authorities: "A man is commanding—a woman is demanding. A man is forceful—a woman is pushy. A man is uncompromising—a woman is a ball breaker. He strategizes—she manipulates. He's committed—she's obsessed. If a man wants to get it right, he's looked up to and respected. If a woman wants to get it right, she's difficult and impossible. . . . Men and women are measured by a different yardstick."

Although many of the first wave of women have come in for their share of criticism, much of it unfair, the way could only be opened by women who could get along with male power. The greatest changes began in 1980, when Sherry Lansing became the first woman president of a studio at 20th Century–Fox. Changes continued throughout the decade, as Paula Weinstein became president of production at United Artists; Dawn Steel became president of Columbia Pictures; Barbara Corday became president of Columbia Pictures Television and the first woman executive vice president in charge of prime time at a network; Margaret Loesch became president of Marble Productions; and Ann Daniel became president of Winkler-Rich Productions.

As more women entered the industry, they began to find ways to balance their own personal style with the demands of the business. "I don't feel I ever had to change my style of doing business," says Betty Cohen, president of the Worldwide Turner Cartoon Network, "but I've had to understand that dealing with men at the top is surprisingly more about style than about substance. I've learned to walk more lightly, be less strident and less demanding. I've learned to keep a sense of humor about things. To not act like your ego is deeply on the line over anything seems to be working better than to be constantly drawing lines in the sand and being overly aggressive."

Dawn Steel, known as one of the toughest women in the business in the 1980s, changed her personal style, and she attributes this change to having a daughter. "There's nothing like having a child around to clean up your mouth. And I sure had to clean up mine. It was like, 'Oh my God, she understood what I said?' That's the end of that. So, just in terms of my truck-driver mouth, she cured that for me. And when you have a daughter, she becomes your mirror. I saw myself in her so much that it allowed me to become softer, more nurturing, more interested in the creative, artistic side of my work. Being a mogul was no longer attractive to me. I was once called 'the most powerful woman in Hollywood' and I thought, That's not what I aspire to be. I aspire to be the most creative woman, or the person who made the best movie. All those things are now more important to me than power."

Today most women report feeling much more supported by other women than in previous years, and they find that most women bosses have mellowed. Having more women in the industry has helped them further put their stamp on the business. Many began questioning whether power and money, which seem to define success in this business, are really what it's all about.

POWER: IS IT WHAT WE WANT?

The film industry is an industry based on power. It takes power to get a movie made, power to have creative control over the film, power to get a top executive to take one's phone calls. Power is expressed when one person has the money to invest (or can get others to invest) in films, or has access to the big box-office stars, or has produced the latest hit film. The image of power is integrally linked with the concepts of hierarchy and competition and ego. As women move into this world, they'd like to change the definition. The history of the abuses of power have brought women to rethinking what power is all about in an industry that yields both subtle and overt power over millions of people and billions of dollars.

"Power is about getting the job done and having the opportunity and the ability to do that," says Sheri Singer of Lifetime Television.

"Power is about empowerment, power *with* rather than power *over*," says New Zealand actress and writer Dulcie Smart. "Making people open up, rather than close up. Helping people, not hurting them."

For producer Sara Duvall, power is a win-win situation that relies on reading the emotions of the situation. "Real power is learning to negotiate from strength. As women, part of our negotiating skills come from the fact that we are in touch emotionally. We use our emotions to connect and to strategize. If you negotiate with a man and can identify what he's really afraid of and what it is that he really wants without fear, and if we can find a way for him to have what he wants and still have what we want, then we're there. It's a workable, constructive, effective negotiation."

Television producer Marian Rees sees power as a "prickly word" and prefers the term *authority.* "Authority is far more definitive. You have the authority to say yes, being in a position to make a difference through your own position and leadership. A collaborative model of power spreads information around. People have authority in their various areas. They are empowered. There might be a producer who has the authority as the custodian of the project. But there's also the personal authority of the director, writer, actors, and all the many people working on the film. It's about shared power."

Women want the power that can help them accomplish their goals. "Yes, I want it," says Amy Pascal, president of Turner Pictures. "To be in a position of power is to be very clear about how you feel about things. It's not clouded by what everybody else is doing." This view of power means knowing what you want and communicating it. "The greatest thing we can do as professionals is to make that voice inside ourselves stronger and stronger."

Tecca Crosby is executive coordinator of the Ontario Film Development Corporation (part of the Ottawa Film Board), which gives money to develop and finance/produce Canadian film and television projects. She heads up a production department of two women and two men and sits on a senior management team of six women and one man. She describes real power as "a deep, hidden power that can be a very quiet thing. It's not a cape you put on, it doesn't have to be beating your chest and flexing your muscles to prove it. I think women have always known that they have power. That's the idea of the matriarchy—you do influence people, you raise the children, the survival of the species is in you."

Power is nurturing. It is also building up, looking in the same direction, sharing the same vision. Alexandra Raffé is head of the Ontario Film Development Corporation. "Power in our organization is being trusted sufficiently by our board of directors and by our government that they will not interfere with the policies and the goals that we set and the directions that we take," she says. "It's getting away from intimidation and bully tactics so we can get done what we need to do. Power comes from autonomy and trust."

"There are many different kinds of power," says Barbara Corday. "There are people who have power because of personality. There are people who have power because of their talent. There are people who have power because of their jobs. Certainly in this town, anyone who can say yes has a certain amount of power. My thing about power is not so much who has it but what they do with it and how they use it with other people."

For Corday, as with many women, the key to power is the ability to use it well. "I have always said to anyone who works for me, 'You already have the power, so you have to be extra nice to people. You have to really be on your toes about treating people well, because if they don't want to come to us, you have no job.' I have seen network people abuse their power. With a wave of their hand, they dismiss people. 'Oh, I've heard of her, she's not very good.' Or, 'That guy, isn't he over fifty?' That means that person has no career at that network for as long as that executive has the job."

"Power, for men or women, can be a very evil thing," says actress Jane Wyman. "It takes away any humility anybody has. If you're powerful, you think you've got it all made. But when that's taken away from you, that fall down that ladder is so long and so hard and nobody is going to catch you. The word *power* in my vocabulary has been eliminated. Instead I use the words *choice* and *opportunity*. Opportunity, if it presents itself, is up to you to go after it—man, woman, beast, or child. If it's there and it's something you feel you really can do, then it's up to you to be imaginative enough to pursue it."

THE COMPETITIVE MODEL

The traditional definition of *power* depends on competition where someone is on top, others below, someone winning, others losing. Traditionally the world of business has been defined by the male metaphor of sports and competition. The film industry is no different.

"If there's one thing that predominates in the way I hear men talk in the business," says John Matoian, the man who green-lights prime-time programs for Fox Television, "it's the use of sports metaphors. I suppose the dominance of males in the sports world has spilled over to the dominance of males in our bureaucratic world. It has historically been a pretty male-dominated business. It's all about playing the game, keeping your eye on the ball, going to bat for the script, and winning—winning at any cost. It's what men learned in competitive athletics."

Competition is not all bad. It develops strength and determination and has the potential to develop teamwork. It can motivate one to succeed. It can build a healthy ego. On the surface, a spirit of competition seems to be essential to any business, and certainly to the film business. On any given weekend, one film will always do better than the others. On any given night, one TV program will have higher ratings than another. Competition is always part of a business that depends on immense profits. And some women thrive on competition, as do men. After all, doesn't everyone like to be the best, to be on top?

Not necessarily, say many women who see the destructive aspects of competition dominating many businesses. The competitive model has destroyed people more than it's built them up. Many women question this model of winning at any cost, of trying to be better than the other guy.

"I think it goes back to the way we were raised," says Lucie Salhany, president and CEO of the United Paramount Network. "It's somewhat counterintuitive and the opposite of the conventional wisdom on the subject, but I believe that because women haven't participated that much in team sports, they tend to be better team players. Men do team sports but they are all really looking for individual recognition in them, and it's a rare man who learns from sports to subordinate his ego for the good of the team. Women tend not to be threatened by having good people around them. Perhaps it's because women were discouraged from believing in themselves enough to think they could accomplish things all by themselves, so they tend to want help from the very best people they can find. At every step of growth or achievement, they look around and say, whether to men or women, 'Come with me, let's all join in and collaborate on making it succeed.' "

Although the first wave of women had to play by the competitive rules of the game, the second wave, who are riding on the breakthroughs made by the Sherry Lansings and Dawn Steels of the film world, are questioning competition as a metaphor for business, because they see the dangers of a win-lose approach. They see that competition *between* companies also can lead to competition *within* companies, which becomes ineffective and ultimately leads to wasted energy, inefficiency, and an inferior product.

Many men find this different approach refreshing and more productive to the business. Richard Rashke, who has written television movies, sees competition as getting in the way of art and productivity. "Women have had a lifetime of dealing with people in a more noncompetitive way. It's easy to explore story ideas with them. With men, it's difficult to get past the competition to a feeling level. Men have not taken the time to get out of their heads and down to their feelings and live with their feelings and be comfortable with their feelings, so they get nervous as soon as you start talking about things on the feeling level. We don't expose our vulnerability as easily. If I'm developing a story with a woman and feel awkward and nervous about the inevitable sex scene, I feel confident that I can ask her to help me. I can say, 'I'm really scared about this scene,' and know that will be accepted. I won't be diminished in her eyes. But I couldn't do that with a man. First of all, there wouldn't be an opening, and if there were an opening, I'd be put into the position of 'mine's bigger than yours.' It would be like, 'What's the matter, Richard, don't you know about this?' It's there. It's not always spoken, but it's there."

As part of their desire to make the business more effective, more humane, women are creating different rules and metaphors by which its played. To this end, they're asking different questions—about teamwork versus competition; about how time is managed in corporations; about the emphasis on doing nothing but work, to the detriment of a personal life; about how choices are made as to which product to produce, and for whom are they producing it. Women are proposing new and effective solutions that are changing the atmosphere of the business on all levels—from the corporation to the set, from the independent producer's office to the small businesses that feed the industry.

7

THE COLLABORATIVE VERSUS COMPETITIVE MODEL

WHAT IS THE ALTERNATIVE to the competitive model? The model which seems the most conducive to women, and may be the most conducive to the film industry, is the collaborative model. It's not a new model. We can find it in sports when teamwork is really working well, in early agrarian societies, and as part of the consensus model for the woman's movement. It's used by some of the most successful men and women in any business. In the film industry, it is the model emphasized again and again by women executives, producers, directors, and writers.

Many women find this model to be a more effective way to work because it removes the internal competition that can be found in so many other companies. Producer Janet Yang uses it because she recognizes that a competitive attitude can work directly against the goal of producing great films.

"So much of this business is built on hype and goals," says Yang, a partner with Oliver Stone in Ixtlan Productions. "It's like children: 'My father is bigger than yours.' It's about who got the most nominations, whose movie cost the most. It's that kind of game people play. I like to think there are more important considerations, such as the quality and content of the movie. But this is not the kind of thing that's easily written about in headlines."

One of the elements in competition can be the building up of individual ego to the detriment of a positive working environment. "With some men I have to be very careful, because you can bruise their ego so easily," says British writer Sue Teddern, who has often been the only woman on a writing team. "Sometimes I find myself pussyfooting with them. When women are working toward the same goal, it's far easier to be open and up front than if you have to worry about bruised male egos."

Sometimes working with the competitive ego can be wearing. Teddern adds, "If you're in a difficult meeting where you're dealing with ego, it's vital to appear assertive and confident. In difficult circumstances, I'll get through the meeting as best I can without losing my temper or without getting upset. But it's tiring. Sometimes I think men are better at this, or more used to it. I don't know. But it's not behavior I like."

To Kay Koplovitz, president of USA Network, competition can waste time and be counterproductive. "In many corporations there is an inordinate amount of time spent in corporate politics. Some people like to manage by fear and intimidation and pitting people head to head against one another. They encourage that sort of political gamesmanship within a company. They encourage the jockeying for position. I very definitely don't want to have an environment where people are always looking over their shoulder and spending 40 percent of their time speculating about internal politics and not putting their best efforts into the achievement of the company."

The collaborative model can be more efficient, since it removes the need for politicking, but it still needs to be used well or it too can be ineffective. At Canada's Studio D, which produces women's documentaries, Anita Taylor researched this model and discovered that trying to reach consensus can create delays confronting problems because no one wants to hurt anyone's feelings. It can also create discomfort when there's conflict, because conflict seems inconsistent with the warm, nurturing atmosphere that is supposed to be part of collaboration. But Taylor discovered that even though sometimes the reality and the vision don't match, "feminist visions and processes can survive . . . feminist goals and outcomes can be achieved."[3]

When it works well, collaboration can still include aggressively pursuing one's goal. But the cutthroat aspect of competition where someone's success comes because of someone else's failure is removed. The collaborative model has a different emphasis.

"I emphasize collaboration and delegation," says Sherry Lansing. For her, this model not only works well on the job but makes it possible for her to have a more balanced life. "I've tried to find time for my personal life. I've managed to do this by delegating and by starting early in the day and by not having any distractions during the day."

It emphasizes efficiency. "Women seem to be better at juggling more balls at once, so to me, I think of efficiency as balancing a career, a marriage, and four kids," says Sheri Singer, vice president of movies and drama series at Lifetime Television. "The juggling is easier if there is a team supporting the boss."

Canadian development executive Michaelle McClean recognizes the collaborative model as including the ability to hear and support the good ideas of others. "It may be common for people who are put into a position of power after being disempowered to have much more respect for everybody around them. I always feel responsible to everybody. If I have to criticize somebody, I tend to think a lot before I say something, and choose my words carefully. I hate to generalize, but I think perhaps men don't always do that. They either don't say anything, or when they say it, it's presented in a way that the person walks out feeling absolutely demolished."

It means caring about the team. Turner executive Amy Pascal says, "I'm more worried than a man may be about how people feel. I think women have had to be incredibly perceptive about what's going on in a room, because our livelihood has depended on how other people feel. I listen emotionally. A woman knows how to breathe what people need."

It promotes strategic and creative thinking. Geraldine Laybourne, president of Disney/ABC Cable Networks, emphasizes "nurturing the creative process. A lot of the other senior managers are more financially oriented or acquisition-based as opposed to creatively oriented. But creative thinking includes intuition, which is sorely undercredited in management."

Intuition can lead to effective, profit-making decisions. Television producer Susan Baerwald believes that "many women are instinctual and therefore are often more willing to take risks. As executives, if we're given freedom to make decisions, and if we make the right choices based on our intuition so our new direction attracts a large audience, then change can happen. But it won't happen until we have the freedom to say yes to something different and it succeeds."

Collaboration recognizes that compromise can be part of good teamwork. "I think we're trained in the art of compromise, which makes us good managers," adds Amy Pascal. "We're good at taking a little bit from here and making people feel okay with not getting everything they wanted but getting some of it. And nurturing is important. It's the different strategy of nurturing people by loving them, not by making them afraid."

A number of men attest to the effectiveness of this model. Herb Scannell, who was vice president of Nickelodeon and worked for Geraldine Laybourne before her move to Disney/ABC Cable, found that this model taught him new approaches. "Gerry is representative of the kind of women who are emerging into positions of authority and power. She brings a different kind of management style that is good for the people who work for her and good for the business in general. In a corporate world, your boss is the decision maker and authority. But Gerry involves us in decision making. She cares about what the people who work for her think. She wants to see things discussed and argued along the way. And she wants the people who work for her to come out of the process with a point of view and to come together in a consensus of opinion. The emphasis on process for her is an important thing."

The model emphasizes a humane approach to treating other people. "Gerry expects us to treat each other in a certain way," continues Scannell. "One time a woman left the company to work for a competitor. When somebody leaves the company, you basically make it uncomfortable for them. You want them to get out. Gerry said, 'Maybe this is the way you guys do it, but it's not going to be the way I am going to do it. We don't need to be so irrational or impulsive about this.' "

WOMEN AND THE COLLABORATIVE ADVANTAGE

The collaborative model seems to rely on qualities that have traditionally been called "feminine." These qualities that have often been undervalued, or have been relegated to the home but not to business, are considered by many women to be their most important strengths.

"My greatest power as an executive is that I'm a woman," says Amy Pascal. "If I pretend otherwise, then I'm denying everything that comes naturally to me and trying to do something I can't possibly get away with. The only thing I can do is embrace the femaleness and the good things about being a woman and apply that to everything."

For many women, that means to be yourself. Lucie Salhany emphasizes finding one's own personal style. "In some ways you can bring your own management style to a corporation; in fact, you must. Each employee, at every level, brings something of him- or herself to the corporation. I think for women it's even more important that you have to be yourself. If you can't be natural in your job, then you can't be effective, you can't even survive. Women must constantly battle those issues—the express and the unspoken unconscious male dominance, the inability to break into some circles, the differences that I feel exist between men and women. Since you have to use every bit of energy and expertise you have just to do the job and do the job well, you can't waste energy in trying to change who you basically are. If you do, you simply won't survive."

Affirming one's natural qualities and applying them to business takes many adjustments. Canadian filmmaker Myra Fried said she often has had "mushy boundaries. This is the year I turn into an armadillo—get boundaries and learn to just say no."

Some women, trying to emphasize teamwork and accessibility, find that if they're not careful, they can become ineffective. Canadian producer Brenda Greenberg's desire for an open-door policy got out of hand. She had to make new decisions about how to apply it. "The project can eventually suffer, because I can get to the point that I'm so debilitated by trying to be accessible that I can't function anymore. I have to learn the ability to say, 'I'm a little busy right now. I know I said I have an open door but it's gotta close right now.' "

Some women struggle with their desire to be effective and their desire to be well liked. Greenberg finds that this can be a problem. "If I've had to be tough on somebody, I suffer so much for it afterward. I go home and angst about it. I think maybe I could have said it a different way. And then someone on my crew might say to me, 'I think you were pretty nice about it.' "

"But," points out Canadian producer Andrea Shaw, "being well liked, for many women, may be one way we keep our jobs."

It is presumed that everyone wants to be well liked. But women seem particularly driven by it. Perhaps it's our enculturation—we were taught to be nice. That was one way we learned to be ladylike, and one way we could get a man. Some women are taking that quality from our culture, deciding that it's a good quality, worth keeping. Part of that quality is the ability to work as a team and to create a group with good team spirit. "We have a tremendous capacity for participation, for the collaborative spirit," says executive-turned-director Devorah Cutler. "As women, we have tended to think that we either have to dominate like men or be submissive as our cultural patterns have dictated. We have to find what's unique about ourselves and contribute that. Some of that uniqueness may come from our sensitivity to others, from our ability to listen to people's needs. These qualities have been devalued by society, but our legacy is to reweave the myth—to take these qualities off the shelf and recognize their value. We become good leaders by listening and delivering that shared, collaborative vision. In doing so we create true power, an inclusive power, power with grace."

THE COLLABORATIVE SET

Unlike many businesses, the entertainment industry is not made up of just the corporation. What is most unusual about this industry is the various business structures necessary for the production of a film. Women are also rethinking these models and impacting film production where the film is created—on the set.

The metaphors of the badly run set have been based on competition and hierarchy. It's been described as a dictatorship, run with an iron hand by the director or producer, a dysfunctional or nonfunctioning family, a war zone, a caste system, with the emperor at the top and the coolies doing his bidding.

Women have had enough bad experiences on sets to know what they don't want. What's a miserable set? "The worst sets are like a barnyard," says Canadian producer Andrea Shaw. "Cocks crowing, bulls pawing the dirt, pigs snorting. It's all about marking territory and creating behind-the-scenes drama as a way of dominating. People get hurt for no good reason. Energy that could go into the creative work has to be spent in mediating and giving pats on the back. On those sets I learned how *not* to produce."

This is not to deny that there are aspects of the set that are intrinsically hierarchical. "That hierarchy never goes away," says cinematographer Brianne Murphy. "There's the producer above everybody, and then there's the director, and right under the director is the director of photography. The director of photography is in charge of the entire technical crew, and nothing disturbs that hierarchy. It has to stay that way. There's a chain of command that has to be adhered to."

But within this model, the hierarchy can be benevolent, and collaboration is essential. "I tell my crew immediately that I can't do the job without them, that I need their cooperation," continues Murphy. "I tell them I expect them to be in earshot of me and that I won't scream so they'd better be quiet so they can hear what I want, which works very, very well. I thank them. I praise them for anything exceptional they do. I try to get to know them enough so if they have special talents, I ask them for advice that goes beyond their job as grip or electrician."

But collaboration includes everyone, she adds. "If you're friendly with a caterer, someone not in your station, some think that you're going to lower your status, but you don't because those people are the ones who give you your status. If I'm busy doing something, they might ask, 'Can I get you coffee?' "

In a badly managed set, the atmosphere can pit one group against another. "It can become extremely stressful. Every single day they're after you." Murphy believes some of the stress and inefficiency is unnecessary. "You can hear me mutter on the stage that Winston Churchill fought a war in fewer hours than it takes us to make a movie. As a result, among the stress I become very calm. People can't figure out why I'm so quiet on the set, but I'm fully aware how hectic things are. It doesn't help to get hectic along with it, or someone will say, 'She's acting just like a woman.' So I go the other way. Quiet and calm."

This same approach was shared by Ida Lupino, the only woman studio director from 1949 to 1966. In an interview by letter written not long before her death in 1995, Lupino explained her process. "Keeping a feminine approach is vital—I hate bossy females. Instead of saying, 'Do this,' I tend to make everybody a part of it. I'd say to a cameraman, 'I've got a wild idea. What do you think of it?' Often I pretended to know less than I did. That way I got more cooperation. I tried never to blow up. A woman can't afford to do that. They're just waiting for it. As long as you keep your temper, the crew would go along with you. With the exception of one or two pills I've met along the line, most of the crews I've worked with have been wonderful."

The collaborative set not only works differently, it can be defined by different metaphors. By rethinking what the set needs to be, the work becomes more comfortable and productive. "A set is like a kitchen," says Lee Grant, director of such award-winning movies as *Nobody's Child, Tell Me a Riddle,* and *No Place Like Home.* "If my production company had a name, we'd call it Kitchen Table Productions because I don't believe anybody does any good work unless they're totally relaxed. Comfortable. The kitchen is the most comfortable room in the house, where you can show up in your pajamas and just hang out."

Marian Rees uses another image. "I think of the script as the circle around which our films are built, not as a pyramid. I never think of myself as at the top as much as a person in the circle around which we gather. The story of the film becomes the campfire." Rees adds other metaphors she finds useful. "All you can do is be a good helmsman and steer the course for others so that it's a steady environment. I speak to my crew as the custodian of the idea."

Canadian director-producer Gail Harvey observes that this kind of set takes some getting used to. "Sometimes it's hard for the crew to get the hang of it at first. I talk to everybody. I listen to everybody. It's a very collaborative effort. A couple of the crew members were used to working with real autocratic male directors. I remember the location manager came up to me after the screening. He said, 'We didn't really get what you were doing at first. We were surprised that people were asking us our opinion on things.' But he admitted that toward the end of the shoot, we were all on the same wavelength."

The collaborative model allows creativity. Actor-director Jodie Foster sees this as essential. "You have to be sensitive and interested and fascinated and allow people to fly. Otherwise you break their spirit and then they won't go for anything. So it's like good management. A good parent wants to protect her children and make sure they're on the right path, but still kind of allow them to fly out."[4]

For some, collaboration seems like a sign of weakness, as if the director lacks vision. But some of the best films, whether directed by women or men, have used this collaborative model. Some women would say that the collaborative set is the only way to create a great film. "To get your best work," says director Devorah Cutler, "there has to be trust, and you have to let everyone know they're very important. They are valued. Then, the potential is there for magic on the set, a loving atmosphere. And that atmosphere, although seemingly invisible, is tangible and is recorded, one way or another, on film."

FACING THE DIFFICULT DECISIONS

The urgency and stress of making a film demands fast decisions that can affect people's lives, both positively and negatively. One of the hardest decisions that any producer or director faces on a set is the need to fire people. This seems to go directly against the collaborative model. Some women attest that this is a particular problem for them, perhaps even more so than with men. Yet even these situations can be handled well with the skills of compassion, trust, intuition, and teamwork.

"This is a business where you need to do things quickly," says Denise Di Novi, who has produced such hits as *Batman, Batman Returns, Edward Scissorhands,* and *Little Women.* "You shoot for only eight to twelve weeks, so you don't have time for someone to improve or prove themselves. When you're on the set, everything moves quickly. It's a rare movie where you're not forced to fire somebody. It's a terrible thing. When I first started my job, I found it so hard that I would not confront them with the facts. I would try to get out of it as easily and quickly as possible. Now I feel if you're going to fire somebody, you really owe it to them to explain why and also try to explain what they did wrong so they can try to avoid it the next time.

And take the time to find out why it happened from their personal standpoint. It's always agony for me. Unless the person has done something dishonest or unethical, I usually have a great degree of sympathy for them."

Her maternal instincts come to the forefront in dealing with the problem. "Usually the problem occurs," continues Di Novi, "because the person is going through personal problems or something. If they're a younger person, I feel very maternal. What if this ever happened to my son? If they're my age, I think, What are they going to tell their kids? I put myself in their position."

"When I first started producing, I hated to fire anyone," says producer Susan Landau, who coproduced *Cool Running* with Dawn Steel. "Now I've learned—fire early and don't wait. I'm getting better at that. Years ago, there were four of us women who sat around long tables, day after day, trying to decide whether to fire someone. We thought about firing him, talked about firing him—and I don't remember if we ever fired him. Conflict is the hardest thing. I'm getting better, the more competent I feel. But when I do fire, I try to make the person feel better. Usually I first try to straighten it out and see if any adjustment can be made."

The work of one person has a ripple effect upon the work of everyone else on the set. Director Gillian Armstrong recognized that the ability to fire a leading actress was essential for the good of everyone, including the success of the film. "On *My Brilliant Career* we had cast someone, and after looking at the screen test we knew she wasn't right. If Margaret Fink hadn't been such a strong producer, I wouldn't have been able to fire [the actress]. So I learned that I had to be tough. Of course, then we found Judy Davis and I realized what a disaster it [not firing the other actress] would have been for everyone."

Producer Penney Finkelman Cox (*'Til There Was You; Honey, I Shrunk the Kids; Broadcast News*) recognizes that the decision to fire demands a recognition of this interrelationship. "On the one hand, we need to recognize that we've made an evaluation of their talent, made a commitment to them that has had an effect on their lives. But we also need to have a sense of the people around that person and how each department interrelates. If you fire a prop master, the set decorator will be affected. If you fire the cinematographer, that's going to affect the grip and electrical crew. It's not just an isolated situation. Everything has a ripple effect. Once the dynamics have been altered, you begin to realize that a lot of people have been affected by that person's bad work habits or attitude."

8

WORK, FAMILY, AND BALANCE

ONCE WOMEN got in the door, they began to question other aspects of the business. The film business, like many others, demands long hours. Many male executives say with great pride that they work sixteen-hour days, take scripts home on weekends, never take a vacation, and only socialize with people in the business.

Women, particularly women with children, do not have that alternative. As a result, their entrance into the business brings with it questions that men need not ask: How can I be a mother and have a career? Are the two mutually exclusive?

Writer Naomi Foner, who created the scripts for *Running on Empty* and *Losing Isaiah,* found that new questions emerged for her when she had her first child. "I was surprised by the strength of my commitment to parenting, to being a mother, because I always thought of myself as being this independent, very political woman. It was a huge issue for me because the woman's movement was giving me too simple an answer. The answer at that time seemed to denigrate the parenting part. I wasn't comfortable with that. I found myself in deep struggle, which has been a struggle all through. It was not that kind of struggle for my husband. When he went off to work, he knew they were with me and they were safe. When I went off to work, I took them along."

The situation can seem impossible to balance. Dawn Steel says, "I felt guilty when I left my house, I felt guilty when I left my office, and I could never get it balanced. You can have it all, but not all at once. There's an umbilical cord that's attached between a mother and a child. It's a profound relationship."

The problem also carries with it the potential for creative solutions that can benefit both men and women. Women, and some men, who are successful producers use their influence to find ways to care for children. One of the people who has done the most to raise the consciousness about child care in the industry is Gary David Goldberg, producer of the television series *Family Ties*. Because of his efforts, a child care center was set up at Paramount Studios in 1986, the first on-site facility at any studio. Rhea Perlman and Danny DeVito were also instrumental in this effort. As a result of Goldberg's influence, most studios now have child care facilities. But that doesn't always solve the problem when filming on location. The women producers—the women with money—are arranging the set to help the production secretaries and staff who are unable to hire nannies. "It's not a big deal to have child care on the set, but you have to do it yourself," says Steel. "You have to organize the parents on the shoot."

Producer Denise Di Novi set up a playroom, to be shared with the children of other departments, and she found it provided other benefits. "Everybody said that it gives a nice vibration, a good feeling. Many women would work eighteen hours a day on a film and never see their children. My heart goes out to them because they don't have as much flexibility as I do. As the producer and the boss, I can bring my kids in anytime. They may feel they're not allowed to do that, so I try to make it clear to people that as long as they take certain measures so their child is occupied, they're welcome to come. To have kids visiting the set is always nice."

With women and children and parenting needs entering the business, many men's attitudes also change. "Most of the men, if they see you are balancing it well, are really respectful," says producer Wendy Finerman (*Forrest Gump*). "Of course, when I'm at work, I'm giving my all." But working it out also means training everyone you work with. "I have worked out my life in a way that most people who work with me—movie stars, staff—know that from the time I leave the office until I go home and put my kids to bed, I am not to be disturbed. But from 8:30 P.M. on, anybody can call me at home."

The maternal instinct can be a benefit in Hollywood, as it softens and relaxes work attitudes. Mothers and certainly some fathers understand the need to balance family and work. But it's not just about raising great kids or having a well-rounded life; it's also about being effective. "I've always attacked the job of producing as a very maternal job," says Di Novi. "I think the good men producers are maternal [or paternal] as well. It's almost to me by definition a maternal job. You have to be organizational. You have to know what everybody's feeling and thinking. You have to take care of everybody's needs and facilitate for everyone, which is sort of the stereotype of the self-sacrificing mother. After having a child, it heightens those instincts. It also heightens your empathy level."

PUTTING WORK INTO PERSPECTIVE

Mothers need to balance family and work. But many women, whether mothers or not, see balance as essential to being healthy and effective. Although it's not unusual to hear from workers in any field that they want less work and more play in their lives, there's a difference in the film industry—much of the work is exciting, joyful, and just plain fun.

"Working can be a very emotional and seductive experience," says Trina McQueen, president of the Discovery Channel in Canada. "There is a huge element of almost emotional attachment to the work you do, and it can give you such pleasure and such a rush that it's easy to become addicted to it. In some ways, it's the same kind of joy you get from being on a team."

But in spite of the emotional satisfaction, in this business the hours get longer. There are more scripts to read, more meetings to go to, more screenings to attend. When women first entered the job market, they adopted the male system of long hours, no time for family, work, work, work. Now women are saying no.

Barbara Corday says, "Every woman I know is seeking balance, because women want other things in their lives. Too many men are willing to give up their lives for work, for all different reasons. In their thirties, it's because they think they have to. In their forties, it's because at home the kids are crying, out of their control, and work is quieter. In their fifties, they're afraid they're going to get fired. They're always nervous about what's going to happen to them, because men's identities are so tied up in their work. But ours are not. I think most of us believe that if you can't do it in ten hours, you're not going to do it in fifteen either. There's no desk that is clean at the end of the day. I don't care how many hours you work. You have to cut off at some point. You have to say, 'They don't get blood. They get my best possible effort and as many hours a day as is reasonable to work, but they don't get blood.' We've added breakfast meetings. We've added dinner meetings. We've extended the day on both ends to such a degree that I believe we work longer hours than any other business I've seen."

Most women are clear about this issue—they don't want work to be their entire life. For some women it's an absolute necessity. While holding the position of industry executive, Margaret Loesch developed breast cancer. "For my life's sake, I have to exercise. It doesn't matter if I feel guilty, I've got to go to that gym three days a week because I don't want my breast cancer to come back," she says. "As women, we're in a state of flux. Women try so hard to be good at everything. Some men seem very complacent being okay, and they feel it's okay to be okay. We don't."

What does she advise? "We need to come back to center at some point. We need to learn to take care of ourselves more. I don't think it's natural what we're trying to do. We're burning every candle we can at every end possible. Very intensely. But I don't know how much joy we're getting out of it. We need to smell the roses. Ultimately it comes back around to how fulfilled we are; the calmer and more serene we feel, the better we do our jobs."

Canadian executive Marilyn Belec says the problem is on all levels: "I have gained fifteen pounds since I've come to Halifax. Stress, health. Sore necks go with the territory. I have not filed my nails. Hair is growing on my legs. My house is filthy. My husband and I spend far too much money eating out. We finish work at seven or eight at night. We're both so tired we can't go home and cook, so we eat out. Most of my salary goes to restaurants. I'm fed up with it."

But if our lives are nothing but work, we no longer have the life experiences that feed our business. How can we make movies about life if we don't live life?

To get this balance, women are deciding that it's time to live a little. And what are they doing? A variety of pursuits: dancing, horseback riding, getting away to a cabin in the woods. It's essential, for many, to have something in their lives that has no relationship to their work.

"I had always vowed I was not going to be someone who worked fifty weeks a year to take a two-week vacation," says Helene Hahn, formerly of Disney Studios and now in charge of business, legal affairs, and administration at Dreamworks, the company founded by Steven Spielberg, Jeffery Katzenberg, and David Geffen. "Several years ago, I became passionate about skiing. I bought a second home and started going every other week. Usually I would go on Thursday evening or Friday. I really found that in some ways it made me more effective. Knowing I wasn't going to be in the office on Friday, I pushed myself. Sometimes I worked longer hours during the week or just pushed myself to be more efficient and get everything done. I had a system where I would have all my mail Federal Expressed to me on Fridays, so any paperwork I had to do I could do on Saturday or on the plane coming back. I had a cellular phone so I could check in and see if any questions had to be answered. Many of them I could answer from the chair lift or at four P.M. Friday afternoon. I found being in the office four days and being out of it three days refreshed me and gave me the ability to do my job better."

Producer-executive Loreen Arbus turned to dance to give her balance. "The Argentine tango is body and soul. I don't have to conform to any standard other than an artistic vision. In the entertainment industry, compromise is too great a part of our lives, because the process gets in the way of the vision and distorts the objective. This is not true with dance."

For some women this balance comes about not just through their personal decisions about how to organize their lives, but through the natural balance that happens when male and female energies are combined. They see the collaborative model as the best model to forge productive working relationships with men.

9

THE COLLABORATIVE MALE

WOMEN WANT TO WORK with the collaborative male. In fact, some of the most successful partnerships in film and television are male-female partnerships. Some of these partners are also married. Diane English and Joel Shukovsky created *Murphy Brown* and *Love and War.* Linda Bloodworth-Thomason and Harry Thomason have done the same with *Designing Women* and *Woman of the House.* Paul Junger Witt and Susan Harris cocreated *Golden Girls* and *Empty Nest.*

In feature films, successful married partnerships include Lili and Richard Zanuck, producers of *Driving Miss Daisy, Cocoon,* and *Clean Slate;* Kathleen Kennedy and Frank Marshall, who produced *E.T., Alive,* and *Congo;* and Tony Bill and Helen Bartlett, who produced *Untamed Heart, A Home of Our Own,* and *Beyond the Call.*

Some are life partners but are not married; Nancy Meyers and Charles Shyer, who wrote and produced *Private Benjamin,* now write, produce, and direct all their films, including *Irreconcilable Differences, Baby Boom, Father of the Bride,* and *Father of the Bride, Part II.*

Others have worked together for many years. Marcy Carsey and Tom Werner are the creators of *The Cosby Show* and *Roseanne.* Ishmael Merchant, James Ivory, and Ruth Prawer Jhabvala have collaborated on many films, including *Room with a View* and *Howard's End.* Kevin Bright, Marta Kauffman, and David Crane are creators and producers of *Friends.* Oliver Stone's partner at Ixtlan Productions is Janet Yang.

There are many successful writing partnerships, usually married, sometimes not: Lee and Janet Scott Batchler (feature films), Jonathan Estrin and Shelley List (series, Movies of the Week [MOWs], miniseries), Debra Frank and Jack Weinstein (television series), Harry and Renee Longstreet (MOWs), Steve Wasserman and Jessica Klein (hour-long series), Martin Sage and Sybil Adelman (sitcoms), and so on.

These partnerships are not set up along gender lines. The woman is not necessarily the negotiator and the man the "tough cop." The man doesn't necessarily do business while the woman does the artistic work. They break down more through the diversity that each brings to the job and the ease in their own working relationships.

"My relationship with Marcy is extremely healthy," says Tom Werner. "There is little competitiveness. That doesn't mean I couldn't have been in partnership with a man and had the same lack of competitiveness, but I think it's extremely rare. I was at an extremely male-oriented network, and I think that most workplace relationships are more about competition and ego than about doing the job well. My relationship with Marcy has always been about doing good work, having fun, caring for each other, and positive reinforcement. At the network it was more about 'you didn't do this' or 'we have to increase our sales this month by X percent,' which seemed more of a male idea.

"Marcy has a quality of clarity. She taught me to think clearly. One learns a lot of bad habits growing up in our society. One learns that success is based on income or being number one. Marcy's values are such that success is based on character. It's so clearly the right approach that it's nice to be in an environment where that approach is both recognized and rewarded.

"Although we're not married, we do care deeply for each other. We feel that the care we have for each other somehow works its way into the product, and I do think we run a company that's extremely sensitive and healthy."

"She's the yang to my yin," says producer-writer-director Oliver Stone when talking of the president of his company, Janet Yang. "Janet has an extraordinary amount of patience and sensitivity to certain issues to which I may not be totally enlightened, so she gives me a dimension and another perspective. She brings an Eastern quality, a nice wisdom and a sense that there's time and that patience is required."

Says Harry Thomason of his wife and partner, "Linda is much more interested in ideas; I'm more interested in details."

"Janet is more visual, I write more of the dialogue," says Lee Batchler, who wrote *Batman Forever* with his wife and partner. "I have an edge on people who are driven by emotion. When it comes to political characters, manipulative characters, I'm more naive than Jan. She understands the inner workings of people who strategize their way through life. Also, working with Jan balances me. If it were up to me, I probably would be a bit of a hermit and go away for nine weeks to write, then come back and rejoin the world. That's not an option in our household, especially now with our little boy, and it's good that it's not an option."

"I think we bring very specific points of view to our work, and it becomes more well rounded," says Charles Shyer of his relationship. "Nancy has the ability to cut right to the heart of the scene. She creates humanistic, more sensitive characters. Of course, when you live together and you work together, there's a positive and a negative to it. You have to be willing to expose yourself to the other person and be completely vulnerable, because when you're working, if you posture and act cool, the work is going to be removed and reserved."

THE COMPLIMENTS ARE MUTUAL

Some of these partnerships work because of the understanding and insight each has for the other.

"Oliver Stone is a very complex man," says partner Janet Yang. "There's a part of him that wants to do good and be good, and there's another part that can't resist the temptation to be a little devlish. He likes to stir things up, to agitate, to push, explore. He doesn't settle. He's not serene. I know how to give him his distance and space. But he's very direct. With many people, you don't know what they are thinking. With Oliver, you always know. So, I can speak my mind. He demands precise, forceful communication. He's tough because that's what works. He looks for results. That I can buy. It's about doing the work, being effective. Working with Oliver, I can be myself. He's a male's male but he's been more actively encouraging of me than anybody else."

"Lee is more a single-task person and I'm a multitasker, to use computer terminology," says Janet Scott Batchler. "He does one thing at a time. Does it well. Finishes it and moves on. He's very direct in his thought processes and in his actions. And he deals with people in that same focused way, meaning exactly what he says, with no hidden agenda. I'm the one who can juggle a hundred balls at once, and can realize that other people may be doing the same thing, professionally or emotionally. Our partnership works because we provide different strengths to each other. And we trust what each other brings to the relationship."

"Tom's more patient than I am," says Marcy Carsey. "I'm tougher. He's more thoughtful and he carries that into personal relationships too. Sometimes he can put himself into somebody else's shoes a little more readily and a little more fully than I am willing to. Sometimes, on a person-by-person basis, he might have a greater understanding of a particular actor and I might have a better understanding of a particular writer. It really is equally divided—whoever is least mad at that person creating a problem. Whoever can really take this issue on without wanting to shake the person is the one of us who deals with that person."

Carsey continues: "The best thing about the partnership is that there is somebody with whom you've worked together for years and whose opinions and mind you respect tremendously that you have to be smart for, day in and day out. If I can't convince him of something, an idea or project or show or an actor, then we don't do it. In the meantime, you've jumped through hoops trying to present a case as well as you can to your partner. But if he says no or I say no, then it's no. We really both hold each other in high regard."

"Harry is a man who has evolved over time," says Linda Bloodworth-Thomason about her husband. "He was raised by a very feminist mother who taught him to love women. And that makes a big difference in our partnership."

Polly Platt had been a long-term partner with producer-director Jim Brooks. For ten years they produced such film as *Broadcast News*, *Terms of Endearment*, and *The War of the Roses*. She understands how important a good partner can be, because "there's always trouble when you make movies. There's trouble with the studio, there's trouble with money, there's trouble with making decisions, there's people you want who don't want you, people you want to write the script who aren't interested or you can't get them; there's always trouble. The longer you make movies, the more you know that everything that you don't think about going wrong is what's going to go wrong this time. You say, 'This is going to be a problem because we need snow,' and of course what's really a problem is that you have a bitch of an actor. You never can really figure out what's going to happen! There's always something unexpected. It helps to be balanced out by a man. It helps to have a male partner."

Charles Shyer is also delighted by true collaboration. "When we get rolling together—like when Nancy'll write something and it makes me laugh and we get some ideas and we start pumping off each other—it's very romantic, very sexy, it's a real high, it's like one of the great feelings in life. When you're really cooking, when you're working together and you happen to be also in love with the person you're working with, it's pretty incredible."

WHAT'S IT GOING TO TAKE?

Many of these male partners want the balance and perspective that women bring. Oliver Stone recognizes the importance of having women in powerful positions, "because they reflect life. If it were all men, perspectives would be skewed. It's a need for balance, in order to be truthful to the world."

John Matoian sees the need for women because the predominant viewership of television is women. "It's very critical that we have the female voice. I need to have women tell me whether this is a story women will respond to, because the kinds of stories that women are attracted to are different than the ones men are attracted to. Anytime anyone in a group can give me a perspective about something I'm not party to, it's a big help."

Executive Trina McQueen hopes for a society that values diverse contributions: "The human condition is such that the more people, the more ideas that are considered and included, the better society is. The more different kinds of thinking and attitudes and values that you can bring to bear on a problem, the more valuable the solution will be. We can't say that men have built a society that has no value. Men drafted the Magna Carta and invented the Ferris wheel. We've had Shakespeare and Leonardo and Ben & Jerry. Our system has benefited from male creativity and enterprise. But we'll be even better when society values people for their talents and acts and thoughts, and not for other reasons. That's the central reason to me for the women's movement. It will make things better for women. But it will also make things better for the world."

To achieve diversity, the industry needs more women, lots of them.

"We need sheer numbers of women bumping on those walls to break them down," says Harry Thomason. "Ultimately, it will equalize itself."

HIRING WOMEN

Hiring in the film industry has often depended on who you know and who has access to insider information. Most jobs are never advertised. Many women encounter the problem of not being able to gain access to the people hiring, and even when prepared are not being considered.

"You all start out the same," says one executive who clarified the process but asks not be named. "Men and women usually start as secretaries or in the mail room. Or maybe you've been to film school, produced your first short film. You know how to do the job. But a year goes by and you're still at the same level, and then another year. You begin to see that the men's careers are moving; they're moving up, or getting better jobs at another company. Or they're doing their second and third film, and even though your first film won awards, you can't get anywhere. With every success, they're getting more contacts, more opportunities, more experience. At some point it's difficult to make up for all that lost ground, because this business is about momentum. It's not about one break, but about having someone help you follow through from one job to the next. The thing is, you're going to be hired for the next job based on the job you did before. With each job, you make contacts which lead to other contacts. It's all about that web."

Even when one job leads to another, the moves for many women may be lateral or backward rather than up. Or, the next job may not be there—just because no one noticed her good work.

Not noticing may be the main form of discrimination in the entertainment industry. Many men do not notice that the most qualified person for the job may be a woman, or that there are only two women in their twenty-person department, that their film has only five women on the crew, that they have no woman producers, and that they've never hired a woman writer or director. Women easily become invisible, in spite of their achievements, because no one asked them to the job, to the film, to the class. As a result, all the ways that they can achieve visibility are closed to them. Some qualified women are invisible because the moderator of the professional panel never asked the female experts, or because the professional award-ceremony coordinators forgot about the qualified female presenters. The dais at professional luncheons often has only one or two women out of thirty august celebrities.

Producer Polly Platt is puzzled by the peculiarity of discrimination against women and how it works in this industry. "There is some kind of network that keeps the men who are biggies from falling down and losing their jobs. Not that they don't fail. They do. But there seems to be a safety net for men. It fascinates me the way they simply fail upward."

Recognizing the problem, some women, and some men, as a matter of course make it a policy to hire women, to try to make up for past discrimination. Executive Barbara Boyle always prefers to hire women, given two equally qualified people. "We haven't had the opportunities and the choices. Of course, men haven't had the opportunities and the choices either. We have both been the product of five thousand years of imposed roles. I make an effort to have my immediate staff half and half. I never wanted an all-girl team or an all-girl production. I like the sexual energy that occurs between men and women, because I like differences and I believe that women have a completely different way of looking at things than men. It's more interesting to have fifty-fifty."

Kay Koplovitz of the USA Network looks for diversity. "Diversity is important to us. I found an odd thing a few years ago when I took time to analyze how the spread of executives and employees are throughout the company. I found certain departments were enclaves of certain minorities. I want to have a mixture of women, blacks, Asians, and Hispanics integrated throughout the company. It's something that you have to work aggressively on all the time. You can't really release your effort on it because people revert to what they feel most comfortable with."

Statistics show that women are apt to hire women. "At USA Network, our management staff is now about 53 percent women," says Koplovitz.

At Dreamworks, Helene Hahn says, "Women are well represented. We have more than 50 percent executive women. In animation I would say it's also at least equal."

Sherry Lansing points out that her company, Paramount/Viacom, has one of the best records for hiring women, with four women as top corporate heads. "We're user-friendly and gender-blind and color-blind. I like to think I simply hire the best person. But I don't hire a woman over a man if she's not equally qualified. That would be a mistake."

Looking at departments headed by women at the studios, Paramount Pictures has one of the best overall averages, with 46 percent women as managers or above, as compared to 30 percent women at most of the other studios. Margaret Loesch at Fox Children's Television has seven women and three men in her department. Amy Pascal, president of Turner Pictures, has a staff of five men and three women.

Joan Penefeather, former member of the National Film Board of Canada, talked about hiring at a Toronto Women in Film conference. "When we talk about power and control, we're not talking about just who's sitting at the top of the hierarchical structure. We're talking about putting women through this whole spectrum of various functions. What's important is that all levels advance. Everyone has an opportunity to reach where they want to go. If that's not happening, find out why and change it, but change it perhaps in a way that doesn't involve just putting someone in charge, because that doesn't necessarily solve the problem."

Hiring women just in the corporate offices will not change the industry. A quick look at the credits of most film and television shows finds women are still not well represented on the crews, many times serving only in what are known as the "female professions" of makeup, costumes, and sometimes as a second assistant director.

Hiring needs to come from a true recognition of talent. But until there is greater equity, the first woman hired in any job is in a difficult position—she can feel that she's representing all women, that her success or failure will determine the possibilities for all women. "When I made *My Brilliant Career* in 1979," says Australian director Gillian Armstrong, "it wasn't just me being judged about whether or not I could direct, but I was actually carrying all women in Australia on my shoulders. If that film had failed, they would have said, 'Women can't do it.' I was the first woman director in fifty years, and journalists would make a big fuss about me, saying how small I looked amongst the crew, or saying that we're having problems in the cutting room. Being female meant that I probably wasn't competent to know how to cut a film together and that I would probably faint or collapse from the grueling shoot or that the male first assistant director or cinematographer was secretly directing the movie. With women, not only does their first film have to be very promising, but their second film also has to do very well."

Many women are hopeful, provided the gains made in the 1990s can continue. Entertainment attorney Mary Barnes assumes a "trickle up theory, which will result in a lot more women producers and executives about ten years from now. In theory, these women should be able to rise through the ranks to the top so that eventually we'll be running the company. I think that will have a real impact on the attitudes toward women in the business and the actual product."

Other women see a problem. Although there are those who think that repealing affirmative action laws will not affect women's employment, many women are afraid of the consequences. Entertainment attorney Janet Stott explains, "As affirmative action laws are peeled back and there will be little government enforcement or requirements, you will not find most male executives actively looking for women. There are certain perceptions in the corporation about why they hire women—because they don't want to be vulnerable to lawsuits. Maybe because they feel guilty. Once there's not a legal reason, I don't think they will care so much about providing opportunities for us." There aren't yet enough women in the business to counteract the effect of men not caring, not noticing, or just deciding there's enough and it's not necessary to do more. And without enough women, those who are in power may take fewer risks in hiring women. All their energies may go to just keeping their jobs.

HOW MANY WOMEN ARE ENOUGH?

What do women think is fair in this industry? What are they looking for? Affirmative action? Quotas? A fifty-fifty split?

Executive Trina McQueen has an opinion of percentages that is echoed by many women: "In my belief, most men will let women in the door up to 20 percent, and then comes a real resistance. That's where you get a lot of the backlash and a lot of the horror stories, as men actually see that these women can threaten their jobs. I think it eases off somehow at 35 percent. At around 35 percent, women have a freedom to develop a great many models. I don't think we can underestimate that there is that streak in women who want to behave exactly like men, only tougher and only more brutal and forceful and aggressive in their behavior. I think that model failed when there were only a few women, because men just got their backs up and resisted it. But when there is a critical mass of women, and when the mind-set has changed so that a woman boss becomes acceptable, women who are by nature aggressive, brutal, and forceful in their natures can get ahead. Another model is a more inclusive, consensual model. It's a kind of management theory that women fit into very well—the empowerment that comes from the lack of hierarchy. When we reach a critical mass, there will be many different models adopted by women. We contain multitudes of ways of behavior, multitudes of ways of thinking, and multitudes of ways of working."

Janet Yang agrees. "As one person, you're one lone voice. At two, you're not yet a threat. When women first entered the business, they were very much on their own. Other women were threats to them. They did not work together. They had to be real ball busters and get out there and be tough as nails. What I have found, almost uniformly at this point in time, is an abundance of support from other women. There's immediate networking. There's enough there that we don't feel one person is taking someone else's job away and enough so that we can really help each other. And there's still enough to go around."

If 35 to 50 percent women is the ideal according to most women, is there a point where the balance is favored too much toward women, just as it has for so long favored men unfairly? Although some women have worked with all-women crews and all-women offices and found these experiences to be comfortable and empowering, women don't want reverse discrimination. At Ixtlan Productions, Yang is aware when it goes too much the other way. "Even in this company, although Oliver Stone is my partner, there have been times when almost all of the employees were female. We would look around at all the women. To me, it didn't seem we were missing anything at the time. But it did seem that—just in case—we better get some men in there. I have two key executives; one's male and one's female. I think it's healthier and more balanced to have a mix."

Roger Mayer, who did a great deal to bring women into positions of power at MGM and later at Turner, is also aware when there often seems to be a particularly unequal mix. "The ideal is that we would hire based upon the quality of work and the fact that the person's qualified for the job. The thing you have to watch out for is if the percentage is very different from department to department or from division to division. Then you may have a supervisor who doesn't want to hire women, men, or minorities. I would never say you have to have a company with 50 percent men and 50 percent women because the population is about fifty-fifty. I don't believe in that. But I do believe in that as a goal. And it is a good policing tool. But I don't see why one department can't be thirty-seventy, the next one sixty-forty and the next one fifty-fifty. If I saw a department with only 15 percent women, I would do something about it because I would know there is a problem. I think a third as a goal is a fair enough figure. And that can go either way—35 percent women or 35 percent men. We now have departments that don't seem to be willing to hire anyone but women. If I ran it, I would walk by and say, 'Aren't you ever going to hire a man?' "

Some countries, such as Canada, set certain affirmative action standards, which gives that country one of the best records for women in the film industry. Out of six new Canadian television cable networks that began operations on January 1, 1995, three of them had women at their head. "The government is apt to be less sexist in its pronouncements," says Trina McQueen. "They do set policy. For example, our Canadian Regulatory Agency [the CRTC] requires every television station to have equity in hiring or they lose their license. It also has policies on stereotyping."

This is not true in Hollywood, which is adamantly against any kind of censorship or government regulations about what they have to do. Yet in the film industry, as in industries in general, women in the boardrooms are essential for there to be equality. Lucie Salhany clarifies this necessity. "As women become represented in the real positions of corporate ownership and control, the decisions that are now made in boardrooms and golf courses and locker rooms will also be made in beauty parlors and on shopping trips and in women's locker rooms. But that day is a long way off. And I don't just mean a token seat on a board. I mean that when the positions of ownership or significant stock stakes of major corporations are held by women in their own right, and not simply as widows or daughters, then business will begin to change."

What to do about it? Of the more than two hundred women I interviewed, one word kept being repeated: *diversity*. Labor Secretary Robert Reich emphasized this same point and applied it to business. "Diversity is good for business. Women and minorities don't have to change, companies do."

Finding balance, creating new structures, for some women has not been possible within the corporate structure. Sherry Lansing recognizes that some women do not want these corporate jobs—by choice. "I may be the only woman here now, but I won't be the only woman in this position forever. But many women find when they get to a certain level of executive height in the movie business, the hours are extraordinarily difficult. The pressures are extraordinarily difficult and it's not as satisfying as they would like. They wish to spend more time having a balanced life. They choose to be producers or directors or to have more control of their destiny as compared to being corporate executives. I think the opportunities for women are unlimited. Women are more and more making choices not to pursue those opportunities but to pursue others, which is a very valid choice."

Some women are making these choices because of what they see happening to men.

"A lot of women have opted out and have gone on to be very successful entrepreneurs," explains Barbara Corday. "They look through that glass ceiling now and say, 'Please, I don't want to do that.' They see men being sick to their stomachs and having ulcers and worrying about heart attacks and quadruple bypasses and all that and say to themselves, 'Oh, if that's equality, maybe you can have it. I don't want to become that. I don't want to be one of them.' "

Recognizing the limits within the corporation, some women have left in order to use their talents more fully, to find their own style of doing business. They have become entrepreneurs.

10

THE WOMAN ENTREPRENEUR

ACCORDING TO THE White House Conference on Small Business, presented in 1995, 40 percent of all businesses in the United States are owned by women. In Los Angeles, 80 percent of all new businesses are created by women. Although most new businesses fail within the first two years, women tend to have a higher success rate than men. This is partly because they seek out support from others, partly because they often build their businesses slowly before going full-time.

The film industry is no exception. Many small businesses in financial planning and management, marketing, script consulting, and business planning have been created in the last ten years—and most of them are run by women. The film industry is unusual because it is fed by independent contractors at every level.

"Since the death of the studio system, many jobs in film are for-hire," says Los Angeles–based career consultant Judith Claire, who has worked in this business since 1978 and helped create successful businesses for many men and women. "I teach people that, if they're writers, directors, editors, costume designers, cinematographers, script supervisors—they're all entrepreneurs. Whatever the job, it eventually comes to an end and they need to find another client, another project. That means they don't have the luxury to just be creative people or tradespersons. They have to operate as a business and do all the functions necessary for a business to survive—including public relations, marketing, sound financial planning, and having a good lawyer."

Many women, looking for more freedom to define their work, find that creating a small business gives them an opportunity to create their own style while also filling an important niche. With the growth of independent filmmaking, there is a recognition that there are many tasks that can be done much better by specialists and consultants. These businesses cover all aspects of the film industry, including the creation of special effects; international consultants who develop, help finance, and distribute films abroad; attorneys and managers; consultants who help people develop their careers, hone their scripts, and market their work; and instructors in everything from writing scripts to shooting the low-budget film to breaking into the business.

These entrepreneurs—myself included—do not exist in isolation. Many of us use a team model to support one another, believing that there's enough to go around, that together we can form a team to help clients through every aspect of their work, and that each of us can't be an expert at every aspect of the business. A number of women in the consulting field have gone out of their way to meet other consultants, learn about their specialties, and when appropriate, refer clients to them. Even with jobs that seem to be competitive, many women use a supportive model, believing that there's an advantage to having more than one person as an expert.

Judith Claire sees that what may seem competitive actually need not be. "The more of you there are, the better it can be, because what you do becomes more accepted. If there are lots of script consultants, career counselors, or marketing experts, then using them doesn't seem unusual. It becomes part of the process. They are integrated into the industry."

Through the teamwork model, women can also share experiences, discuss strategies, call on one another to figure out how to handle a difficult situation. This support makes it easier for them to make their contributions to the industry.

IDEALS AND CONTRIBUTIONS

What are women trying to do with their businesses? Make lots of money? For most women, there needs to be a stronger motivation. It's the personal goals that drive them.

"We are trying to raise the standard of the art of film and television by teaching people the skills they need to create better work," says Judith Claire. "I want to raise the level of artistry, confidence, power, and ability to succeed of the people I work with. I'm there to help them manifest who they really are, not just to make a living."

"I feel like I'm helping the independent film," says Sydney Levine, president of Film Finders, a company that tracks independent dramatic features worldwide for film buyers. "I'm providing a service by showing that many of the nonviolent independent films are doing well. I can tell producers, 'Are you aware that this film that came out of Quebec is a top grosser?' And maybe that information will lead others to realize that a nonviolent film can do well. Or maybe a large company will buy it for a million dollars to remake it for the English-speaking market."

Levine wants to bring some order to chaos. "I feel the film business is one of the most chaotic, badly managed endeavors in the world. For me it's helping to make something flow a little more easily. I want to help create a standard that people can use."

International coproduction consultant Wendy Carrel sees her goals globally: "My biggest interest is in bringing cultures together, getting people to communicate well with each other—sharing perceptions, and finding solutions so there is a basis for durable and long-lasting alliances."

Several women entrepreneurs mentioned that they felt they were trying to make information more accessible, so that people can concentrate on other areas that are more important. Marketing consultant Donie Nelson says, "I see us as doing business by setting up a different kind of model that is actually much more efficient, and that if the larger companies and studios begin to see that our model is workable, they are going to be more efficient and run better."

PART OF THE BIG TREND

The entrepreneur is part of a larger trend in society. Through a ripple effect, small businesses have the potential to change the way business is done at other levels.

"We are part of this social change," says story consultant Natalie Lemberg. "We read about it everywhere—toward home-based businesses, outsourcing, new technology that connects us without having to leave our homes. In the course of a day I often feel as if all the decisions I make are very individual, but I also recognize that I'm part of a huge trend, I'm helping to break new territory. What feels biographical to me is really historical."

Since so many small businesses are run by women, and because women have integrated work and home for years, they are in a position to create and define many of the models which will serve business into the next century.

And what makes for a happier life may also make business more efficient. "So much of the work of the larger corporations could be more effective with specialized work," says entertainment attorney Susan Schaefer, who started her own firm in 1984. "Studios don't make films anymore, they invest in people who make films—such as the stars, producers, directors. Consultants could be of more help if they would recognize it. They can work more efficiently by farming out part of the work to a script consultant, or computer consultant, or through outside public relations people to sell and market the film, or outside attorneys for the legal work, or to track music rights and the success of the films, or track finances—all of this could be done more efficiently through outside specialists."

WHERE ARE WE NOW? WHERE DO WE WANT TO BE?

Although women in the film industry are doing slightly better than the national average as executives and entrepreneurs, they are not doing nearly as well in defining the product. Only three women have won Academy Awards as producers of the Best Picture: Lili Zanuck. Julia Phillips, and Wendy Finerman. Out of more than three hundred films produced every year in the United States, fewer than 5 percent of those are written or directed by women.

Television fares better. About 50 percent of all prime-time series have at least one female producer, and about 25 percent are written or cowritten by women. But women directors still make up only about 15 percent of all television directors.[5]

If we're doing better than the national average, do we have a right to complain? Is the moviegoer missing out in some way because of the lack of diversity in films? Does women's presence really matter?

Since the media is considered one of the most influential of all social structures in the world—some say it's even more influential in some homes than the family, education, and religion—the entertainment industry is one of the few businesses that has a product capable of impacting society. If Ford Motor Company or Hughes Aircraft or General Foods have women in their corporate offices, it may not make a big difference in terms of what the car, the airplane, or the breakfast cereal looks like. But the entertainment industry has a product that affects all countries, all cultures—male and female, young and old.

If women do tell different stories, create different characters, and give a voice to people that we may never meet, then the lack of their voice diminishes knowledge and removes potential role models for women as well as men.

Do women affect the product? Do stories look the same whether they're told by men or by women? Will female writers and directors really create better female characters? Will the presence of greater numbers of women in this industry really make a difference where it counts—in the movies that we see?

11

CASE STUDY

Lili and Richard Zanuck

LILI AND RICHARD ZANUCK won the Academy Award for producing the best picture of 1989, *Driving Miss Daisy*. They have been married for seventeen years and have been working together since the early 1980s.

How does their partnership work?

RICHARD: There isn't a clear-cut definition of responsibilities. There's a great deal of overlapping. There are certain things that one is more inclined to do than the other.

LILI: Dick gets more into the mechanics of a production—like budget and scheduling and deal making.

RICHARD: She's very good at casting. The main roles are always a collaborative joint effort, but she has a better knowledge of the subsidiary and unlikely casting. She can bring faces to my attention and to the director's attention that I probably wouldn't know of or hadn't seen.

We're both obviously very much in sync in the choice of the script, the choice of the writer and the director. All major aspects of a project are a total joint collaboration, starting with "Should we make this story in the first place?"

LILI: Dick will develop projects that I don't like, but I don't think we have any projects in development that he doesn't like. But we have never made a picture that I didn't like. I think, Can you make a movie out of it? Is it a good story? Good stories find audiences. But I don't have that ability to know what an audience wants to see.

RICHARD: I've had a lot of experience as a studio head where we had to make twenty pictures a year, and a lot of experience of what works and what doesn't work.

LILI: Dick has it in his DNA to understand material and what is a movie and what makes a movie and what is dramatic. Dick would be a gold mine if somebody just stuck him in a room and let him read scripts all day and go yes, no, including fixing them. I like the darker stuff more than he does. Dick has a kinder, gentler perspective. He'll say, "This is very interesting but look how dark it is." Dick will like a scene that I think is too sentimental. He likes to make sure you feel something. Yesterday we were shooting a scene in a Western movie. Our leading man had a guy holding his leg, dragging him across the floor. When he couldn't shake him off, he shot him. I thought it was pretty cool.

RICHARD: I thought it was pretty cruel. I won.

LILI: On the big things, we agree.

RICHARD: Many of the pictures we've made that were successful for us have been ones we've had to fight for—*Cocoon* and certainly *Driving Miss Daisy.* We're not going to do the *Die Hard* pictures or blatantly obvious commercial fare. Once we get into subject matter that is more specialized and dealing with emotions rather than action, it creates a bigger struggle to convince the powers that be to put up the money.

LILI: We've had to fight for many of our films. I don't shy away from a fight and I don't care about doing the safe thing. I don't like middle-of-the-road anything—middle-of-the-road writer, middle-of-the-road director. I want the A-team or somebody who has the ability to shine because they're a new talent. Dick will say, "We could get so-and-so," but I don't really care if we can get so-and-so because it's not interesting. I'm far crueler in my evaluation of somebody than Dick will be. He will be more generous.

RICHARD: Sometimes I like to take someone who has been great in the past but who has perhaps had a nonproductive time of it, and sometimes I'm able to get the best out of them. Sometimes that works and sometimes it doesn't.

LILI: Nobody wanted to do *Cocoon* because nobody wanted to make a movie starring Don Ameche in those days. And nobody wanted to do a film about older people.

RICHARD: *Cocoon* had a lot of heart and it had a lot of comedy. One of the wonderful things was the fact that these people had spirit. While their bodies were ancient, their minds were still forging forward. It seemed to me so touching and yet full of compassion and humor.

LILI: In my youth I had a real fixation and fascination with older people. Older people and children are in exactly the same position. They're constantly trying to get their independence. Up until *Cocoon,* older characters had been either cute or curmudgeons, but in fact, no matter how old we are, internally we think we're younger. The characterizations I had seen in movies were wrong. It wasn't the way people really feel. When we did *Driving Miss Daisy,* that was a real fight. We had to fight for Morgan Freeman and for Jessica Tandy—they weren't hot then.

RICHARD: We had a Pulitzer Prize–winning piece. We had a budget of $7.5 million, so it wasn't a crazy thing. We were willing to finance whatever overages there would be over and above the $7.5 million ourselves. We had a wonderful cast. We loved the material. The relationship between these two people touched everyone—that very unique relationship of two people coming from totally different cultures, totally different backgrounds, totally different colors, who were thrown together, who through the years developed a great love and dependency upon one another.

LILI: I loved how smart it was done, how subtle it all was. It was really like a puzzle. You need every single piece of this to tell the story. It was beautifully balanced storytelling and incredible writing.

RICHARD: But it reached the point where it was becoming an embarrassment to be turned down by the people to whom we were going to hat-in-hand. I never lost enthusiasm, but I really thought we had reached the end of the line. I thought that maybe the project would be best served by taking time out, letting it sit, than to make it with some kind of a company whose distribution and financing and everything else might be very suspect. It was insulting to us. I think pride came into it. I said to Lili at that point, "I don't want to talk to these people anymore. I don't want to pitch to people I don't even know who they are." I felt at that point in my life I had gone beyond that. But Lili hung on and she didn't have those feelings of injured pride, of insult that I was feeling by all of this rejection.

LILI: I'd get discouraged, obviously, but I was just determined, I guess. Dick doesn't even know about some of the dentist groups that turned us down!

I didn't want it resurrected at some time in the future because I didn't think we would have Jessica and Morgan and Bruce Beresford, who was a great director—it was this perfect situation. A lot of times, if you don't make it that minute, you can resurrect it, but it's a whole new party. I knew that *Daisy* was a great movie, but the *Cocoon* sequel, which we didn't like, wasn't having trouble getting made, and it was a $17.5 million movie. Here we were, spending $17.5 million to rip ourselves off and we had an opportunity to spend $7.5 million to do something new that was really wonderful. The conflict for me was, if we couldn't have made *Daisy* and the sequel had happened, I would have had to reevaluate for myself why I do this at all because it says there's no room to do your best work.

RICHARD: Finally, Warner Bros. and Jake Eberts saved us.

LILI: I remember feeling very strongly that if you can't make this, who cares, because obviously you can only make something mediocre. Mediocre's easy and great is hard.

Dick has a great sense of fairness that applies to every aspect of his life. It permeates every decision he makes, whether he's making a deal, dealing with the children, or when he felt I was qualified to produce and that overrode for him what somebody might say.

RICHARD: Lili has great instincts. Her intuitive judgment of practically everything is very correct. She has a great deal of common sense. She gets right to the bottom line of whatever the issue is. She's not afraid to voice her opinions. Sometimes people are shocked before they get to know her. At first she can come off as rather abrasive—her ability to dissect the thing and not tolerate any BS. She's not as diplomatic as I tend to be. I'm known for directness, too, but I don't quite go at it in the way that Lili does, which is really a no-nonsense, let's not screw around with any of this, let's go right to it kind of way.

LILI: Dick has real temperance. He never cries wolf or screams. I cry wolf all day.

RICHARD: Lili has great persuasive abilities because she's smart and she's funny. That's a tough combination to go up against—she can be a very formidable opponent. But she's very likable. People admire her for what she's been able to achieve. She proved on *Rush* that she could direct a picture, take a very tough subject and make a compelling picture out of it. She got great performances. She had the courage to direct. I've always admired her for putting herself out there because she didn't have to do that. We had done well without that kind of exposure but that just added to her accomplishments.

LILI: I have the most incredible organizational skills that I've copied from Dick.

RICHARD: I have a lot of organizational training, probably developed when I went to military school. I'm very much on time. I'm exacting, almost to a fault. Lili has her own sense of organization that confuses me because I don't quite understand it. But she does get things done.

LILI: I'm not as compulsive as Dick. I'm far more comfortable spreading myself thin than Dick is. If the desk is full and I have a hundred meetings, then that's the way that day went. If Dick has a hundred meetings and there's paper all over his desk, he literally has an anxiety attack. There's no way it can wait until tomorrow. There's no ease to it. He will limit the amount of activities because he knows at some overload place he'll hate it. I think this is because I'm a woman. The idea that it can all be compartmentalized in a comfortable way isn't even an issue with me. It cannot be as a woman. You cannot have a house, have a career, have all of these things and think your desk is going to be clean. I do think being a mother and wife trains you for that because you know there is no end to your day; there's the day-to-day maintenance—orthodontics, new clothes, going to camp, and sewing labels. My kids got the iron-on kind. There would be no Christmas if women went on strike. Nobody would get a tree. There would be no presents. There would probably be crappy birthdays. All of these occasions in our lives work because we take the responsibility to keep them going. There's none of this if there isn't us. That's the luxury only a man has.

There's no doubt that for me a driving force has always been I want the whole package. I want to try. I don't care how tired I'm going to be when I go to bed. It doesn't matter. I don't have any problem running my house and working and doing all these things. The time and interest would have to be taken up with something, so it might as well be taken up with something I can do well, that I love to do.

PART THREE

WOMEN AS STORYTELLERS

SOME IMPORTANT BREAKTHROUGHS FOR WOMEN

1920s: Lois Weber is the first major writer-director to work consistently with socially conscious themes.

1923: Twenty-four-year-old producer Lotte Reiniger begins work on *The Adventures of Prince Achmed,* the first fully animated feature.

1930: Frances Marion creates the prison genre with *The Big House.*

1930–1947: Zoe Akins focused on strong women's roles and strong stories for the great stars of the 1930s and 1940s.

1939: *The Women,* from the play by Clare Boothe Luce and the screenplay cowritten by Anita Loos, is one of the first female ensemble films.

1946: Leigh Brackett writes one of the most important film noir scripts, *The Big Sleep,* for Humphrey Bogart.

1979: *Alien* proves that a woman action hero (Sigourney Weaver) can carry a picture.

1992: Penny Marshall directs *A League of Their Own,* an ensemble film about women and baseball, which goes on to gross over $100 million.

1995: *Waiting to Exhale,* the first mainstream black female ensemble film, is a surprise hit.

1996: Emma Thompson is the first person nominated for an Academy Award for actress *and* screenwriter, for *Sense and Sensibility.*

1996: *Antonia's Line,* from the Netherlands, wins an Academy Award for best foreign film; it's the first time that a feature directed by a woman (Marleen Gorris) has won the honor.

12

FINDING OUR VOICES

Although some use stories as entertainment alone,
tales are, in their oldest sense, a healing art.
Some are called to this healing art, and the best . . .
are those who have lain with the story and found
all its matching parts inside themselves. . . .
In the best storytellers I know, the stories grow out
of their lives like roots grow a tree.[1]
—*Clarissa Pinkola Estes*

WHAT IS A WOMAN'S STORY? Ask many male executives and they'll say it's about relationships and emotions. It's character-driven. They might mention the ultimate derogatory term: "It's *soft.*" And, they might add, they don't make money.

What is a man's story? Conflict. Explosions. Killing. Guns. Special effects. A strong, heroic, nonemotional man doing physical action. Dinosaurs. Monsters. And, men might add, "They make lots of money."

That's the stereotype, and there's some truth to it. Who writes these films? Although today almost all the guy films are written by men, until the 1950s women wrote every kind of film—mysteries, science fiction, Westerns, animal stories, Biblical epics, and in more recent times, such action films as *The Empire Strikes Back* and *Romancing the Stone.* The male-oriented film, with male protagonists who conquer, overcome evil, make the world safe, has always been around, whether written by men or women.

Movies about women, with female protagonists, told from a women's point of view, have a different history. Although they were prominent in the 1930s and 1940s, and there are a few stellar examples of great female-oriented films in any period of history, this type of film is more apt to be found in television than in film. But even in television, it's not unusual to see the female as victim, in jeopardy, or mainly as the love interest.

Women who try to break out of these limits encounter another stereotype—that there are human films and woman's films. Executive Laura Ziskin says, "We all grew up believing men made this world we live in. We were told men write universal truths, universal themes. Women write women's stories."[2]

Most women I interviewed don't want to censor the men's stories, but they do want more diversity, an opportunity for their lives, their experiences, their identity as women to be expressed on screen. But writing, selling, and marketing these films is still difficult. Why? Because many executives still believe that movies about women don't make money. And because the woman's voice has not yet clearly emerged in the art of screenwriting. Finding the woman's voice in storytelling can be just as difficult as finding her voice in management. The woman first has to create the story. It seems simple enough, yet often women have few other films as models about how to tell their stories and express themes that have not been shown before. If she's found her voice, even if it's considered by most to be a great script, she knows that many of the executives will probably consider it not commercial because it's unlike the other films on the market. Or they can devalue it by calling it a woman's movie. "If it has a female audience," explains writer Callie Khouri (*Thelma and Louise*), "then there is always a somewhat derogatory connotation to a so-called woman's picture. I'd like to see that done away with."[3]

Writer-director Amy Holden Jones (*Indecent Proposal, Beethoven, Maid to Order*) noticed this attitude and turned to writing "as a way around what I believe was very real discrimination against me as a director because I was a woman. And it was not in the form of meanness or anything like that, but it was in the form of not wanting movies that I wrote which centered around women, and not trusting my opinion when I think they might have trusted some twenty-eight-year-old guy's opinion."[4]

Discovering her voice as a storyteller, and having it accepted, becomes even more difficult for a woman writer when she realizes there is little help from those who have gone before.

ALL THE ROLE MODELS WERE MEN

Finding the woman's voice begins by trying to figure out where to look for it. Almost all of the great dramatic works have been created by men. Think of the Greek dramatists: Aristophanes, Sophocles, Euripides, Aeschylus. Think of the great medieval dramatists: Shakespeare, Marlowe, Ben Jonson. Think of the beginnings of modern drama: Henrik Ibsen, August Strindberg, Anton Chekhov. Not until the twentieth century have there been a few—a very few—great women playwrights whose works can compare with those of men, such as Lillian Hellman, Wendy Wasserstein, Beth Henley.

In order to understand the woman's voice historically, there is a better source than drama: the novel. The first novel was written by a woman—*Tale of Genji,* by Lady Murasaki Shikibu in the eleventh century. The first English-language novel published was about a woman—*Pamela,* by Samuel Richardson in 1740. Some of the greatest novelists were, and are today, women—Jane Austen, the Brontë sisters, George Eliot, Louisa May Alcott, Toni Morrison, Alice Walker, Harper Lee, Agatha Christie, Carson McCullers, Doris Lessing, Ursula K. Le Guin, Ayn Rand, Amy Tan, and Margaret Atwood, to name just a few.

What do these stories tell us about female storytellers? Basically, women are more apt to write stories about women, just as men are more apt to write stories about men. Writer Catherine Turney wrote a number of the great women's films of the 1940s and is well versed in the woman's novel. "The Brontë sisters and George Eliot paved the way for strong women. Women like to read stories where the woman is able to control her life. They are looking for something that's going to take them out of their own, somewhat pedestrian life, to see a woman who does something positive." This model paved the way for the female characters in the films of the 1930s and 1940s. "The women were self-directed, able to stand on their own feet, had guts, gumption, and very clear wants. They want something—and go after it."

If you made a list of the great films from the 1960s through the 1980s, your list might include *Midnight Express, Raging Bull, Platoon, Midnight Cowboy, The Wild Bunch, Jaws, Apocalypse Now, The Deer Hunter, Lawrence of Arabia, Taxi Driver,* and the *Stars Wars* and *Godfather* films. The change in subject matter is obvious.

Although a list of what might be called contemporary women's films is not long, there are now enough films written, sometimes also directed and produced, by women to begin to form some conclusions about what women are contributing to storytelling.

WHERE IS THE WOMAN'S VOICE?

The search for the woman's voice is a process that women filmmakers are going through all over the world—in Australia, New Zealand, the United States, Canada, Denmark, Germany, Great Britain, and elsewhere. Over and over again I was told by the women I talked to that women don't need to and shouldn't tell stories the same way as men.

"Today you can't tell the difference between something produced by a woman and things produced by a man," says Roseanne Barr, "and that disturbs me. When women's voices sound like men's, then women have effectively been censored."[5]

It isn't just individual women writers looking for the woman's voice, but also companies who are dedicated to finding and nurturing the woman's perspective. Some companies have been astute in recognizing the problem and have responded to pressure from women filmmakers who believe women's lives need to be portrayed more accurately on the screen. For that reason, in 1974 the National Film Board of Canada established the pioneer Studio D in Montreal, a studio which is still the only government-funded women's filmmaking group in the world. Working with women filmmakers across the country, Studio D's mandate has been to fund documentary films produced, directed, written, and as much as possible crewed by women. What do they consider a woman's film? "A woman's film—as contrasted with a man's film!—puts a woman's story front-and-center of the frame," says Ginny Stikeman, current executive producer of Studio D. "Whether the subject is racism, pornography, sexuality, or humor, our films look at it through women's eyes and experience, and we look for stories that we don't find in mainstream media. We've tried to challenge stereotypes and assumptions about our lives, and most of our films—whether about famous people or ordinary/extraordinary women—have been successful in doing that."

Sometimes the search for the woman's voice begins by defining what it's not. Lifetime Television was created as a woman's channel. Vice president Judy Girard says, "There are many films we don't air here, such as violence-against-women films; not because we're on a social mission, but more because women aren't interested in violence against women. We don't do films that exploit women, or 'my life as a doormat' or women-as-victims kind of stories, because they don't appeal to our woman's demographic."

There's one common denominator in all these films: The main character is a female. Susan Seidelman has written and directed *Desperately Seeking Susan, She-Devil,* and *Making Mr. Right.* "Our stories start with a female protagonist. That's the simple answer. It doesn't have to be a sensitive story about a housewife who's struggling with raising a family. It could be a story about female fighter pilots in World War II. Of course, when you do have a female-driven story, the studio executives say, Let's change them all to men because then we'll get the seventeen-year-old boys to come in and watch the movie three times."

Having female protagonists doesn't seem like a revolutionary idea, until you look at the number of films at any one time that are male-driven. In the fall of 1995, more than two-thirds of the films had male protagonists, and almost all were written by men. The remaining films, with female protagonists, were written by women. And most of the female-driven films center on the love relationship, whereas the male-driven films are about drugs, killing off the enemy, their lives on the job, and their lives in society.

Many of the films with female protagonists tend to be character-driven rather than plot-driven.

German filmmaker Katja von Garnier is preparing to direct her first American films. She says, "I look for characters and relationships. But I have trouble finding stories that are different, that match my spirit. I feel that my first American movie should reflect something that I want to do. In so many cases, I can wrap my mind around it, but not my heart." Australian director Gillian Armstrong says she wants to make films "where human beings are observed and where we as the audience learn something about human behavior."

Character, behavior, emotions, and relationships are emphasized over and over again by women filmmakers. Some say this is a stereotype. But gender research continues to indicate there is a difference. Women's experiences tell them that they are more emotional and relational than men. The latest research on the brain says they are. Since women think differently and experience their culture differently, their films deal with different issues.

Meg Ryan's company, Fandango Films, has a number of scripts in development—comedies as well as dramas, historical pieces and contemporary scripts. But there is a consistency in subject matter. "What unifies the material for us is that all of the material is examining or addressing in some way the contemporary questions that women of our age are dealing with, whether it's how we live our lives, how our spirituality is manifested, how we have our families, how we are with our friends, our connection to nature, our social orientation and morality, or how our professional identities are formed or impressed upon by the world around us."

In Mexico, writer Alma Rossbach says, "Women's scripts are different because there are different themes. In my country it's often the story of a family—their habits and conflicts, the thoughts that women have about sexuality, or confronting men in relationships, or about children, or about being mothers."

Lifetime Television deals with women's issues. Vice president Judy Girard says, "We were the first, to my knowledge, to do a movie about a heterosexual woman with AIDS [*And Then There Was One*]. There's one about a husband who realizes he's a homosexual and how his wife deals with it. We do films about important women, such as Margaret Sanger, birth control advocate of the early twentieth century, and Jessica Savitch, one the first women broadcasters. I think women as a whole are more interested in social issues, partly because they're more interested in relationships."

Women's films are personal. Subjective.

Dawn Steel says that the movies she makes as a producer will be much more personal than those she made as a studio executive. "I feel a responsibility to create positive, female pictures, and there are all sorts of female pictures that need to be done."

Writer-director Patricia Rozema says, "Our voices, our representations of ourselves, have been in the hands of others, namely men, since the beginning of the mediums of film and television. My main character in *I Heard the Mermaids Singing* videotaped a confession that is used through the film. It's her way of having control over her definition of herself. It's her way of controlling her voice. I think of my films as subjective—taking all of those sensations, all of those wishes, all of those hopes, all of those disappointments that we feel and somehow giving them visual representation. I want my films to be a very intimate experience."

Women's films value women's experiences. "Many women filmmakers are saying that the big things in life, such as war and violence, have been overvalued and the small events that create the true texture and value of life have been undervalued," says New Zealand producer Robin Laing.

Producer Sarah Pillsbury, who has done a number of films that feature women, including *How to Make an American Quilt* and *Desperately Seeking Susan,* says, "Women tend to honor and validate daily life and human transaction and recognize that within the mundane the miraculous often exists." She adds, "There are many ways to show that in films."[6]

"We've grown up believing our stories aren't interesting," says actress Marlo Thomas. "We learned to be listeners, not talkers. Maybe we learned this in our families because men did a lot of the talking, or because the movies we saw were mostly men's stories. Or sometimes we learn this because we tell a male executive our stories and we see their eyes glaze over, whereas a woman executive understands and then helps get that story on the screen. And when somebody does make one of those great movies—like *Thelma and Louise* or *Fried Green Tomatoes*—everyone cares. We have to learn to believe that what we have to say, what we've experienced, is interesting. And not just to other women, but to everyone."

LESS ACTION, MORE EMOTION

Women's films change the focus, often emphasizing the character's emotions, behavior, and psychology above the character's actions. But this can present problems in terms of telling the story. New Zealand producer Robin Laing, who works with director Gaylene Preston, understands this challenge. "When you don't tell an action story, you have to find the connections of events by digging deeper. Emotion is harder to write down than action. If we have to see emotion, we need to turn it into some kind of physical event for the film. But we have to value it and trust it."

Simone Halberstadt Harari from Tele Images, a women-run production company in Paris, focuses on films that are "sensitive to the psychology of characters rather than action-adventure. Movies where women form strong bonds. Period pieces where women try to assert their autonomy. We do family programming, psychological, romantic comedies, movies that help people live, based on emotions."

Harari also recognizes that culture and history play a part in the kinds of stories that women want to convey. "I'm perfectly aware that in our images, presentations, and goals, we are also part of a generation. I know and feel as a woman that fifty years before and fifty years from now the perspective will be radically different. It's my perspective, but it's my perspective as a woman in Paris in the 1990s. We have to know that this is not the universal truth. It's my belief here and now. As a women at this point in history, we want to find ways to bring everything together. We don't want to sacrifice our jobs, or love life, or family life. Women are about giving birth, love and romance, having free choice. We want to do films that can get at these layers."

Many women filmmakers emphasize both the human experience and the transformation of women. According to Australian producer Sandra Levy, "When we make shows that we want to make, we make shows about what it feels like to be human—about the essential humanity of us all."

Actress Anjelica Huston, who recently directed her first picture, an adaptation of the novel *Bastard Out of Carolina,* says, "I've got a great story. It's about people. I've never been interested in special effects, in explosions, except human explosions."[7]

Producer Polly Platt (*The Last Picture Show, Paper Moon*) feels there's "no point in making a movie unless it talks about what's happening to us. I don't see what else there is to talk about except the human condition and what stories help us to cope or understand or better live our lives."

In Germany, film director Vivian Naefe sometimes does action films on assignment, but she is more interested in other types of films. "I'm trying to do films about women heroes too. But I see women heroes as often quite normal women. I want to do films about their lives—about women who have a dream, overcome something, are different in the end and have learned something."

Barbra Streisand says, "I am committed to making films about positive transformations and unlimited growth. I want uplifting, life-affirming films, films not only about life as it is, but life as it can be."[8]

Some women do films about subject matter that has traditionally been considered male, but by changing the focus they change the point of view. *For the Boys,* produced by Bette Midler's company, was an antiwar story. "It was a way of telling a story we felt was a message about men," explains Midler's producing partner, Bonnie Bruckheimer. "But it was told from a woman's point of view."

FINDING THE WOMAN'S VOICE

Finding the woman's voice begins with the question, Why even look for it? Most women artists, like male artists, create films to share their individual truth. They want to emphasize their artistic uniqueness, not their gender. Some women filmmakers are uncomfortable with the idea of gender as part of their artistry. "I don't think there will be any real equality until the first thing you say is that women are individuals and we're different as artists," says director Gillian Armstrong, who wants to be known only as Gillian Armstrong, filmmaker, not as a woman filmmaker. "I'm proud to carry a woman's vision but I don't like that label at all. It's like putting women in the ghetto. It limits women because it says, 'Oh, you can make women's films, but you can't make other films.' "

Labeling the woman's voice in any form may be dangerous, according to director Victoria Hochberg. "It's a form of marginalization. Telling a director she has a 'woman's voice' is telling her that her experience is unique, but in the movie business that usually means it's not good unique, it's who-cares unique. Can you imagine how absurd it would be to create other 'voices,' or categories, like 'short-male voice'? No matter how you rationalize or justify it, being called a 'woman' anything in this culture is not a compliment. I have a director's voice. That's it."

Looking for the woman's voice can remove women from opportunities to do action-adventures, thrillers, science fiction. It can also stereotype men, leaving relationship stories as women's domain.

That's all true, and even discussing the woman's voice can be problematic, but many women feel it should be discussed, in spite of the possibilities of new stereotypes emerging. Saying that we don't want to talk about it does not remove the woman's voice. It simply makes it harder to find, to acknowledge, to value. Women do have a point of view, just as men do. Dismissing it, pretending it doesn't exist, or devaluing it doesn't negate it, but it does mean that a large realm of experience is not up on the screen.

Finding the woman's voice in the film industry also demands finding her commercial voice. That can mean adapting to the extent that the woman loses her unique point of view. Anne Milder, vice president of production at Universal Studios, says, "Adaptation and compromise are part of being an individual within a larger system. No matter what your position in Hollywood, whether executive, producer, director, or writer, you must find the delicate balance of clinging to your own voice and making compromises. For example, a writer, even a male writer with an action voice, probably thinks, How do I take my voice and fit it into the marketplace in such a way that it's commercial, so that it makes money and I can continue to write? The same is true for the rest of us. The danger for all of us, not just women, is twofold: adapting too much by giving up ourselves and our voices, and adapting too little by insisting on individuality and separatism to the point of exclusion."

For women or men, adapting their voices to the commercial voice often removes originality and authenticity from their work, which begins to look derivative, predictable, and all the same. It also limits the kinds of films that are made—another voice never emerges.

WHAT HAPPENS IN THE PROCESS?

The woman's point of view is rare because, as we've seen, executives over the years have not wanted it. Robin Swicord, who wrote *Little Women* and *The Perez Family*, wondered whether it was her writing, her gender, or her point of view that was the problem when she was told that her scripts were wonderful but nobody would make them. "One day I looked down at the Writers Guild ballot and I noticed they numbered the movies. I turned to the very end of the ballot—there were 122 movies that were eligible for the Writers Guild Award that year. That's a lot of movies. I counted up how many women writers were represented. There were about four movies written by women that year. Suddenly it was as if somebody had turned the light on inside my head. I realized I don't have to take this personally. There's a kind of trend, a definite bias toward not having them made."

When the script is finally bought, then what happens? "When I was trying to finance *The Perez Family*, a story with a female protagonist, the story notes I heard for several years were, 'Why can't it be about Juan Raul Perez instead of Dottie?' There's a mindset within the industry that overwhelmingly favors male protagonists. As I have tried to analyze it, I think this exists in part because women are skilled at projecting themselves into male characters. We did it in school—if you couldn't imagine yourself as Thomas Jefferson, you were going to end up as Betsy Ross. So who would you choose? Thomas Jefferson, that's clear. Women learn very early to do this kind of projecting trick. But it's very hard for many male executives to put themselves into a story that is not centrally about a man. So women who write female protagonists are one down."

Writer Linda Woolverton (*Beauty and the Beast*) also struggles with the balance between accommodation to the powers that be and originality. She wonders if there is another way. "Men's stories are simply easier to put up on the screen because we've been doing it for years. Our emerging voices are still in that amorphous stage."

Since the woman's voice is devalued, writers and directors are very careful about how they discuss a project. "There are buzzwords," says director Victoria Hochberg, "like *sensitive, feeling, soft.* These are 'women's words,' and unfortunately I need to be very careful to avoid them when selling a project."

"But how will the culture change if more and more pictures that are out there desensitize us as human beings?" counters director Nancy Malone. "I think those are wonderful words, and I don't think the value in pictures is to desensitize, but to sensitize."

Women are caught in a catch-22. Hochberg struggles with this artistic bind. "When you talk about taking away words like *sensitivity* and *feeling,* it frightens me as a member of the human species. If—or hopefully, when—the culture changes, these words will be deemed valuable."

Some women believe in this woman's voice—enough to put money into its development. Producer Sara Duvall has obtained financing to do two to four films a year that will be written, directed, produced, and in a large part crewed by women. Duvall believes that the woman's voice has not yet emerged, and she wants to help it. "I've convinced my investors that films with a woman's point of view have a built-in audience of 53 percent of the population, and that men want to know what women want and what we think." Sara should know. Her *Fried Green Tomatoes* was one of the one hundred most successful films of all time, among both female *and* male moviegoers.

But finding the woman's voice isn't easy. "I'm going to have to cultivate the writers of these scripts," says Duvall. "I'm going to have to convince the women writers that I really mean it, about the woman's point of view. Women have written so long for the male audience that for them to believe I really want a script with the woman's point of view is going to take a lot of work."

Where is Duvall getting these scripts? "These are the scripts that agents wouldn't even send to the studios, because they don't think they're commercial. Or they are scripts that women have written just for their own satisfaction and put away five years ago, knowing that no studio would ever buy them."

WHAT IS THE WOMAN'S POINT OF VIEW?

The difficulty may not just be finding the scripts. Women may not yet be sure what their voice is saying, and how it's saying it. Women live in a world defined by men. Finding our way begins with trying to find the truth about ourselves, as women, and then creating stories built around these perceptions. It's an identity problem.

To find the truth, where do we look? Actress Mary McDonnell feels we have to look to other periods of history. "Change is happening so quickly in our lives that it's hard to stay grounded on the earth, in history, in family." To find the truth, we may have to go way back. "What were women at the beginning of time? What is her-story, as opposed to his-story? I want to tell women's stories that aren't about being victimized or having to fight men. What I'm really interested in is how we've been misinformed as human beings and how we've been living in a sort of darkness. I'm very interested in where the light went out. That means going way back to reconstruct our past when we were powerful. I'm interested in how we've been separated from our spirituality as women, which is a place of power for the feminine. It's a tough thing to do emotionally because you don't want to constantly focus on the gender problem. It's really more about when feminine power was abandoned, because men also have great feminine power within themselves that has been abandoned and covered up and said no to. They've also been robbed."

To find the truth, we may need to reevaluate the myths that we live by, or create new myths that better reflect who we are as contemporary women.

CREATING NEW MYTHS

A myth is a story about our deepest aspirations. They're often heroic stories that tell us something about the human condition, stories we tell ourselves about the world around us and within us. As our lives change, the myths that define us and guide us, also change. The fairy tale about finding Prince Charming is no longer the only guiding model for our lives. Part of finding the truth involves redefining the myth.

Actress Meg Ryan sees this as a necessary but difficult process: "If we don't redefine the myths, that's our own problem. But it's hard to find a language for a lot of this. It's hard to even get women together to find a common language and talk about what it is we're missing. I often talk to my girlfriends about this—we're trying to figure it out together."

Karen Barnes, vice president of the Fox Children's Network, believes the answer lies partly in deeper storytelling. "There isn't a lot of really good storytelling on television. We don't have the kinds of myths and legends that are not only giving the kids an adventure on one level but are dealing with their subconscious on a completely different level. We've gotten away from myths and rituals in our culture. But there's a purpose to myths, and it's to stir up feelings, to add another layer in order to help us understand our lives."

Adding the deeper myth demands writers who can think more deeply about the stories they tell. Barnes is concerned about this problem because she has writers who didn't grow up on books, they grew up on television. "Their idea of a story is *Scooby Doo.* If I talk about writing a myth, they ask, 'What is it?' They don't understand it. We look at fairy tales, stories from other cultures, Arthurian legends—these speak to us about trends of early civilization, about a collective unconscious, about what children have to conquer, about a sense of empowerment."

Myths seem so much easier to find for men. There are thousands of years of them, with male heroes in fairy tales and religious stories and folk stories. Writer-producer Lindsay Smith wrestles with the problem: "I look at stories with men as the primary characters and I see a mythos that has been created, for instance, around the cowboy or the action hero. This male myth is so rich and communicates very quickly. There's really a romance, a glamour about maleness. It's very powerful, and I think, What's the female equivalent? Our mandate, as women writers, is to identify and develop the female myth, which is as big and as compelling as the male myth."

Writer-director Susan Seidelman sees that women's daily lives demand a different mythology. "Traditionally women haven't gone off and fought in wars or had adventures, slayed dragons or commanded troops. We just don't have that history. There's always been some exceptions, but in general that's not part of the female mythology. Up until fairly recently, they've been at home with their kids or working at jobs because they need to earn some income to take care of their kids. They've had less outlets for yearning for something more, for bigger territory, for a larger life."

Writer-director Caroline Thompson works with the mythic dimension in many of her films, such as *Edward Scissorhands, Black Beauty, The Addams Family,* and *The Secret Garden.* The latter is a myth about awakening. "There's a garden and it's enclosed and safe, but it's dead. The child finds it and is afraid of it and brings it back to life. It's a way of discovering herself and her own sexuality and her own powers of creativity. I suspect as a woman I can understand that journey in a way that a man can't necessarily understand."

Some of the myths are about cooperating rather than destroying. "I remembered Black Beauty as a female and started writing her that way, and then realized that in Anna Sewell's novel he was male. But I gave him a kind of generosity and spirit that I generally reserve for women. Mostly, I've always been intrigued with the otherness, such as with animals like Black Beauty. We look into an animal's eyes and see something there—their urge to communicate with us, a generosity. I've always been drawn to their spirit and appalled by our need to dominate instead of cooperate. It's an obsession of mine."

As women find their mythic stories, they can resonate not just with women but with men as well. Thompson sees that the metaphors underneath all of these stories are about the human condition. Still, the perspective she brings to her work comes out of her own perspective as a female. "I really do work out of my guts, and my guts obviously are female. One is always working in gender politics whether one is conscious of it or not.

"*Edward Scissorhands* was written very much about my perception of my own childhood. But if you talk to the director of that film, Tim Burton, he would also claim the myth. With a good myth, we can both claim it. It's universal." Thompson adds, "Our mythologies are our mythologies for a reason. They resonate with us. These ideas are part of our collective unconscious. Writing from a mythic viewpoint is the strongest way to get at reality."

13

WOMEN IN ACTION

THE MYTHIC JOURNEY of a woman can begin in any number of places. Within the last ten years there have been several strong women protagonists in heroic stories. Sigourney Weaver played Ridley in *Alien, Aliens,* and *Alien*^{3}. Later, Linda Hamilton played Sara in *The Terminator* and *Terminator 2: Judgment Day.* In 1994, Meryl Streep played in the action-adventure *The River Wild.* Holly Hunter, in *Copycat,* played a role originally written for a man.

Although there are plenty of strong women archetypes in myths (the goddesses, for instance), in dramatic literature there are few female heroes. Aristotle, in his *Poetics,* made it quite clear that woman was not a worthy subject for heroic stories, partly because she's an "inferior being" and partly because the hero demands "manly valor, but valor in a woman, or unscrupulous cleverness, is inappropriate." And since he felt that drama needed to be true to life, obviously the woman hero was not a role that was viable.[9]

Women, however, don't want to leave the hero myth to the exclusive domain of men. This myth is the easiest one to translate dramatically. It's active. It's physical. It's dramatic. It's exciting. Put a woman instead of a man into the lead and allow her to react to the action, and the female character automatically comes alive.

The woman-as-hero story is not outside women's experiences. As children, plenty of our fantasies are about doing heroic acts, being part of adventures. Given the chance, women choose to be part of heroic actions. Women producers, writers, and directors are no exception. Gale Anne Hurd, who produced *Alien, Aliens, The Terminator,* and *The Abyss,* says, "I've always loved action-adventure, partly because I've always been athletic and active physically; at the age of thirteen I was *the* athlete of the year—I beat out all the boys."

Janet Scott Batchler, who cowrote the story and screenplay *Batman Forever* with her husband and writing partner Lee Batchler (Akiva Goldsman also received second-position screenplay credit), loves writing action but knows she would not be hired to write action-adventure if she weren't paired with her husband. It's Jan who writes most of the action sequences. "I love to think that the action that had teenage boys all over the world cheering was actually written by a woman," she says. "I often write the first drafts of the action scenes. People assume that Lee, the man, writes those, and that I, the woman, write the emotional stuff. It's often the reverse. In particular, I'm better at writing visuals. I think of an action sequence as serving much the same structural function in a movie as a song does in a musical. The story's moving along, one plot-beat at a time, with character interaction, dialogue, et cetera; then all of sudden the story seems to come to a complete stop as we move into an action sequence. The action sequence should in fact be able to stand on its own as a minimovie, just as a song can have a life independent of its purpose in a musical. But when the action sequence is over, the audience should find that the story's taken a quantum leap forward, either in terms of story points or a character's emotional development or, hopefully, both."

Even within the action genre, women are making different kinds of contributions. A number of them find the usual kind of fighting—hit, fall, hit some more—a bit of a snore. Women seem less interested in the conventional fights and gravitate toward other approaches. Janet Scott Batchler finds straight fight scenes boring: "He punches him on the jaw. He falls back. *That* anyone can write in their sleep. I'm interested in more unusual action situations." What does she like instead? "In *Batman Forever* we had the Batwing submerge under water and turn into a Batsub. I like the expensive action sequences that have not been done before."

Karen Arthur says she likes to "exercise and stretch as a director and look for opportunities to do action. But I'm not going to lobby to try to do a film where somebody's going on the lam and everybody's chasing him. I'm not going to lobby to do a television Sylvester Stallone, because I don't find all those Uzis and explosions interesting. But I do think I have something to bring to the genre—emotionality, of course. But also a certain kind of rhythm and movement. I used to be a choreographer and dancer. As a director I'm used to movement. Everybody moves all the time in my films. Consequently, that's part of my style—to understand the movement of it."

In action-adventure, it isn't just the female character's physical ability that is emphasized. "The heroine is able to think on her feet," says Hurd. "She can overcome the limitation of lack of strength through her imagination. It doesn't have to be about who's got more muscle. There are more creative solutions as a result. In both *The Terminator* and *Aliens,* the weapons the heroines used were very unconventional. Sara Connor terminated the Terminator with a stamp press, and Ridley in *Aliens* used a blowtorch."

Another skill the female hero brings to the story is intuition. Myth consultant Pamela Jaye Smith defines intuition as "knowing without any so-called factual evidence. It's listening to the little voice inside of all of us, paying attention. It's a kind of internal sight, the ability to read a situation. Intuition has been devalued, yet many men in the military have said that the quality they always use in combat is intuition. It's a big, big thing for the warrior."

HOW WOMEN DEAL WITH VIOLENCE

Although some women question why there is a need to show violence at all, violence is sometimes used in woman's films. When it's used, however, different aspects are often emphasized.

"Our concern is that movie violence have consequences, as it does in real life," says Janet Scott Batchler. "I think the most jarring violence in *Batman Forever* is the death of Dick Grayson's parents. But that action has profound consequences. It's what causes Dick to become Robin, Batman's partner in fighting crime." Gale Anne Hurd thinks about violence in a similar way: "If I'm going to do a film in which there is action and violence, I want it to be the last resort."

French director Agnes Varda confronts the issue of violence and emphasizes its emotional impact. "I'm not so convinced that the audience wants violence and rape and killings. Some like it, but little by little, producers, directors, and writers have captured the audience to like it more and more. I don't think we do good for our society to bring out all the stories of prostitutes, pimps, gangsters, serial killers, and perverts as if they are typical figures. The more you put them into films, the more you give credit to them in society. I'm not saying hide the problem. But don't create them as heroes. I don't want to fall into the trap to show a good little rape and then say I'm against rape. That's hypocritical. You need space in films for people to be shocked, moved, touched."

Jan Strout runs a workshop on women's resistance to violence in the movies for students, women's centers, and others. She's studied a variety of approaches within films such as *Thelma and Louise, Fried Green Tomatoes,* and the New Zealand film *Once Were Warriors,* all written by women.

"I've noticed that there's a profound difference in these films in terms of how the resistance to violence is portrayed. Many of the ways that violence against women has been depicted have focused on women as victims. Yet when I look at these films, in all cases women resist the violence. That is a radical concept. These are not victims to be pitied. The ultimate ending is one of affirmation."

Strout notices that in many of these films, the violence comes out of something that is wrong in a traditional relationship, whether in a male-dominated marriage (*Once Were Warriors* by Riwia Brown, *Fried Green Tomatoes* by Carol Sobieski and Fannie Flagg, *The Color Purple* from the novel by Alice Walker and screenplay by Menno Meyjes); in male-female relationships (*Thelma and Louise* by Callie Khouri); or in society (the Australian film *Shame* by Beverley Blankenship and Michael Brindley).

"These films also challenge the underlying assumption about why violence against women happens," explains Strout. "The stereotype is that the woman is the source of violence. If she weren't so titillating or so seductive, she wouldn't be victimized. But these films relocate the source of violence within the male perpetrator who inflicts it on the woman, and also portrays women actively doing something about it." They show women resisting.

These films and some others show another element of women who have been victims of violence. They show friendship and support by other women and some men as crucial to supporting the victim's resistance and her healing. "We women do not exist in isolation," says Strout. "The relationships that are central to women's development is a very different model than the isolated, strong, alone, individualistic male models that have been so important to literature and film. It is crucial for women's full development to be in relationship with others, and her success in resisting and overcoming violence is about relationship and support."

Although most woman's films do not focus on violence, some women writers and directors are interested in exploring it and do it very well: Hilary Henkin wrote and produced *Romeo Is Bleeding*, Alexandra Seros wrote the blockbuster *The Specialist*, and Kathryn Bigelow directed *Blue Steel*, *Point Break*, and *Strange Days*. Many would consider them exceptions to everything that's been said before. And to some extent they are. No idea is completely gender based. There is a feminine and a masculine side in all of us. However, when discussing these ideas with these women, a particular point of view emerges that moves away from gratuitous violence and puts its emphasis elsewhere.

"I'm not inherently intrigued by movie violence," says Hilary Henkin. "In *Romeo Is Bleeding* two people are killed and a guy loses a toe. When Rambo drops out of a plane with a machine gun and opens fire, there is an enormous body count. There's a question here about whether the violence is personalized or not. In my films it's personalized. By that I mean it's not like in a funhouse where some guy walks in with some sort of machine gun and starts picking people off with it. My question about violence has always been the same: Where does it become an interesting issue and where is it merely more carnage? I don't like to see films with a lot of carnage because it's not interesting to me as a storyteller and that's my main bone to pick with violence."

Alexandra Seros put her emphasis in *The Specialist* on behavior, not action and violence. "I have always liked big emotions—love, hate, revenge—and then between the lines you have the chance to be subtle. Characters are really the plot. I'm interested in Jungian psychology and in archetypes, specifically in *The Specialist*, the puer, or eternal youth figure. Ray Quick [played by Sylvester Stallone] is such a puer who happens also to be an explosives contractor. He is lonely, frightened of his dream, without intimacy in his life, and therefore, like a bomb, ready to explode.

"However, when *The Specialist* was reworked, it was in that inevitable process that the emotional and thematic underpinnings were deemphasized and the overt action emphasized," says Seros. "I was using the action to personify Ray's inner world, and I made him a bomber as a metaphor for a guy who is pent up, ready to explode."

Seros, like Henkin, is not interested in violence that's gratuitous and separate from character motivation. "Gratuitous violence is violence for its own sake," says Seros. "It comes out of nowhere. It's perverse. Violence needs to serve the story. I always begin with the psychology of the character and, if that's truthful, then I don't have a problem with the violence."

RETHINKING CONFLICT

If action is one of the essential elements of great drama, conflict is the other. Much of male drama is about external conflict, but with women it's more personal. They rethink conflict by looking at their own lives.

Documentary filmmaker Johanna Demetrakas sees that conflict traditionally has to do with "the ego thing. Losing face isn't much of an issue for women because one, we never had face in the first place, and two, we tend to deal with the situation itself rather than use it to prove something about ourselves. Less ego and more problem-solving oriented. Men are trained to compete, and you need a lot of ego for competition. They're also trained to respect big male egos."

Some women look at their own lives to decide how they'll deal with conflict. "As a woman, when I think of conflict I look at how I can diffuse it because I want harmony," says director Karen Arthur, emphasizing a win-win situation. "If there's a conflict in our house, my husband would confront it, which seems to me makes it build more. Either it has a violent end or the two parties walk away but nothing has been solved. I think that the male has a need to confront. There's aggression, someone has to win. But as a mother, you want to separate those two boys and try to keep them from killing each other, and try to help them come back and say you're sorry and let's work this out. I think that's part of our nature."

Danish producer Lise-Lense Moeller also looks to the family to understand how conflict seems to work in real life. "Conflict is complex. A lot of male conflict has to do with a sense of honor, a sense of status. This is something you rarely find in women. Women tend to get less immediately involved in the conflict. They are more interested in seeing how to get through this and how to deal with it. I think we smooth it out more. With women, I think conflict is solved. Maybe it takes a longer time. It goes deeper. Very often you are foreseeing the conflict before it comes because you're so used to knowing what your child wants, being aware of everything before it happens. You see it coming and deal with it even before it becomes a conflict. Sometimes I see it on the crew and I see it coming between two male persons much before they realize it could be conflict."

How does this translate into film? It's not a matter of removing the conflict, but of approaching it differently. "I'm dealing with the emotional side of the conflict," Arthur says. "If I have a shoot-out, I don't just want to see the guys rolling on the floor. I want to know who's afraid, who's the person who is trying to get out of the situation, the emotions behind why people are fighting, the emotions behind why people are standing their ground. I want conflict to give me insight into human nature and what that conflict has cost the character."

Many women ask, Do I have to use violence and conflict in my films? To what extent do my stories have to conform to high-drama, high-concept stories? Could I use dramatic conventions and reshape them? Can I make other themes and storylines work, even though the stories are vastly different from what I see on the screen?

When the subject matter of the stories change, the shape of the stories also changes.

14

STRUCTURING THE SCRIPT

IN MOST HOLLYWOOD SCRIPTS, the story is relatively direct and linear. The male action hero solves the crime, stops the bomb, wins the trophy, gets the girl. However, women are looking at other models for shaping a story, believing that the way we see our lives, even live our lives, might lead to new structures.

The idea of a female structure for scripts was first introduced to me in Denmark, where I was told that one of their writers, Ulla Ryum, was exploring this idea, using male and female sexual rhythms as a metaphor for the movement of a story. As I talked to other women around the world, similar ideas emerged.

Documentary filmmaker Johanna Demetrakas is intrigued with this same structure. "One of the things that interests me most is gender and how it manifests itself. When I started writing screenplays, I began to see the subtle differences. Structurally, men seem to work in an Aristotelian way. I didn't invent this idea of comparing or associating male and female sexual rhythms with artistic modes of expression. From a male point of view, conflict is essential. Their stories have one conflict, which is always a clear piece of action that triggers everything and has to be overcome. There is one climax, and of course one denouement. That isn't necessarily so from a female point of view. That is a huge, fundamentally different approach. With the female approach, there are many conflicts, it's multiclimactic, and often has many endings. Soaps and some of the best hour-long dramatic series work this way with a feminine kind of structure."

"The influence of the American narrative structure on film worldwide has made people expect that we're going to have very linear kinds of stories," says Sara Duvall. "Women don't dwell on the action moment. They consider everything leading up to it as the story. Women want the buildup, the tension, that's what's exciting. The process, how you get there, is more important than what happens when you get there."

The linear model may not even be the best model to describe how we operate as human beings. "We receive information through the pores of our skin and in our heart and in our gut and through our eyes," says Janet Yang. "It isn't focused through a linear, logical pattern initially. We reconfigure it and adjust it to fit the demands of storytelling. I think as women we tend to blend mind, heart, spirit, and body in our work."

If the structure is different, less linear, what does it look like? Women have used a number of metaphors to imply these nonlinear structures.

"It's like a circle," says African-American filmmaker Julie Dash. "In *Daughters of the Dust,* I told the story in the way an African griot, an African storyteller or keeper of the historical records, would tell a story. Things keep revealing themselves and unfolding like an onion. Unfolding and unfolding and unfolding." New Zealand aboriginal writer Riwia Brown (*Once Were Warriors*) uses the circle image too. "The circle can show the importance of the community, and the identity of the characters within their community."

Some use the spiral or helix metaphor rather than the circle. The spiral combines the line and the circle. It is also the image of DNA—the basic building block of life. French director Noemie Lvovky (*Forget Me*) uses another metaphor. "I think men's films advance more with a narrative. I tend to look inwards, more like a whirlpool."[10]

This particular model is process oriented rather than climax oriented. Not everything is neatly sewn up at the end. Danish filmmaker Bente Clod studied this model. She explained, "The circular spiral structure asks *how*—how is the villain a villain, rather than focusing on the result. With the spiral model, the story often has no natural ending; it could continue and it often presents a difficult decision for the writer where to stop it. The scenes often seem carved with a knife, cutting still deeper into the wood."

Marjorie Beaucage, a Canadian aboriginal filmmaker from the Metis nation, sees her stories as a helix. "We think about films as just like life," she explains. "We think of a story as an actual event that happened in history, that gets re-created and then called a 'dramatization.' But films are not just like life. Films and storytelling are the process of taking a moment of life and reshaping it, reflecting on it, adding to it. That is the gift of the artist, to provide new insights, to help us remember ourselves.

"Indian time is not seen only in a linear way," continues Beaucage. "Every moment contains a past and the future within it. If you're not driven by a linear narrative, you can cross time and space anytime you want. You don't have to see how fast you can drive time forward. If a narrative is driven by one line of thought, it doesn't make room for everything else that is happening in that story. So that a film, or a storytelling tradition, gives you an opportunity to stop the story and say, 'But first, in order to understand this next event, I have to go back to tell you something that happened with this person before.' If you focus on relationships rather than conflict, you don't have the same formula of driving the story toward a resolution, so there's not as much a sense of direction. Instead you're focusing on character and relationships, on what's happening at this moment, at the different layers of the event. So there's a focus on the unfolding of events, and the complexity of the event."

American screenwriter Naomi Foner uses a ripple metaphor. "We all exist in contexts and they interrelate. They grow out, like ripples, connecting, overlapping, causing dilemmas. You're in the context of your family, the context of your work, the context of your friendships, the context of your morality, the context of your politics. If you don't see yourself that way, what are you here for? What's the point?"

Australian writer-director Monica Pellizzari calls it a mosaic. "Women texture their films in different ways—by the way they use sound, image, color, design. I would term it as a mosaic structure. I've gone left and right and up and down and around and back. I use elliptical flashbacks, as part of layering the dimension of the character. It's a method for seeking the depth and the truth."

Pellizzari also emphasizes the details, because they lead to the big things. They're a microcosm. "I'm not saying that women are made to do microcosms. We have to be careful not to be stereotyped that we knit and sew and let the men build the bridges. But I would say that microcosm leads to big ideas."

"I structured *How to Make an American Quilt* like a patchwork quilt," says writer Jane Anderson. "I saw it as a compilation of stories so that when you stand back and look at it at the end, you see this huge canvas and realize what the story is about. The flashbacks, which are designed to have an emotional impact, are essentially a panel in a quilt. Finn, Winona Ryder's character, has a storyline which is more linear and is the border of the quilt."

Producers Yang and Duvall both use the image of layering to express what their films are trying to do. "A person's emotional life has this separate stream running through," says Yang of *Joy Luck Club*. "As women, I think we're often willing to take more time to rest in that stream, to flow in that stream. On the surface it may look like not that much is happening, but if we allow ourselves to delve into that deeper emotional layer, it has its own forms and shapes and movement. Look out your window. You see layers upon layers of activity, very different entities which are somehow blended together. It's a question of where you want to focus, and for how long, but a full recognition is that it's all happening."

Duvall sees a similar structure with *Fried Green Tomatoes*. "The structure of a script is kind of the skeleton. In itself, that's not very interesting. The only thing that makes that skeleton come alive is the layering of character, the layering of the complexity of the story."

Duvall sees that this metaphor of layers reflects our lives. "Thematically, we have themes that we address and that we keep coming back to whether we want to or not. They keep circling us, and we grab them and finally figure them out."

What does this structure look like in films? Australian writer Margot Nash used it in a script about Holocaust hero Raoul Wallenberg. "I wanted the audience to keep looking at aspects of the narrative from different points of view. So I would keep coming back to the particular moment when Wallenberg was abandoned to the Soviet Union, and look at it from the point of view of another person, or another country, or another group."

The spiral structure gave Nash an opportunity to "talk about what was important, to talk about the level of complexity, to show the layers and show the interplay of historical forces and the psychology."

What is the effect of the film when it's a circular structure? On the one hand, it sometimes takes some getting used to. "The circular story often seems boring to an audience that is used to the fast-action style, which has an immediate impact," says Bente Clod. "It's a new way of thinking that we have to get used to. We might compare this to the difference between living in the city and living in the country. In the city, we go for a climax, a result. In the country, we don't necessarily go out to get anything, but we *feel* what it's like to be out. It's more subtle. But it still feeds our life, or heightens our quality of life in a way that the linear results do not."

This structure does not abandon the idea of a beginning/middle/end. There still remains some linear narrative that keeps moving the story forward but without the rapid pacing of the action film. The proportion of emotion and psychology becomes greater. Action is de-emphasized.

Writer Jane Anderson sees that this linear line is essential so the audience doesn't get lost. "The more emotionally based your film is, the more abstract it is, the more careful you have to be as a writer to give it a backbone."

None of these writers are saying that this is the new structure for all films in the future. "We need to be able to see a lot of different ways of telling a story and not just the Western way, the tall tale, based upon Western literature," says Julie Dash.

The approach is risky. Dealing with a new structure needs time to figure it out. Some women who are trying to tell different kinds of stories may not yet have the craft to make these different models work. Although these kinds of stories can be done for a much lower budget than the more action-oriented models, if they fail, women know they usually don't get another chance. If they compromise, they feel they aren't truly telling their stories.

This model demands a willingness to change on the part of producers and executives. Writer Linda Woolverton has a system for trying to do that—the nudge-it-a-little-at-a-time system. "Now we may have to operate within the male view, within the system as it stands right now. And then we need to slowly add our own thing. But do it slowly. Stay within the rules. Don't scare anybody. Just nudge it. Kind of nudge it over here. Nobody is going to panic. Push it that way a little bit. And then stop. And then wait until that is acceptable. Then you try again. Push it a little bit more."

With enough nudging, the opportunities may be there. But when they are, women need to be ready—ready with the well-crafted story, ready with their own clear voice, ready with the skill, the creativity, the ability to create successful stories about women that can meet the demands of the market.

Even with the good stories, the market has to be ready. Is it?

OPENING UP THE WORLD TO MEN

Women want more diversity in films. We don't want to remove the male action film, but we ask for the opportunity to create different kinds of films *in addition to* the usual. Most films are marketed for teenage boys, because there is a perception, which is incorrect, that this audience is what determines the success of a film. But market research is discovering new information, and executives have not all caught up with how the market is changing.

The fastest-growing segment of ticket buyers are women, up 19 percent in two years. Women represent more than 60 percent of the even more lucrative video market. Women are apt to choose a movie on a date, or to go to films with their girlfriends. A film marketed only to women can now be successful.[11]

Anthy Evergates-Price is the senior vice president of media at the Universal Pictures marketing department. Universal has produced and/or distributed a number of films that have a female focus, such as *Fried Green Tomatoes, The River Wild,* and *How to Make an American Quilt.* Is the market changing? "I think the focus has changed a lot from when the baby boomers were teenagers. During the last ten years there has been a little less emphasis on a teenage demographic and a shift toward older product. By older I mean eighteen to forty-nine, not fifty-five-plus. Now all of a sudden family films have been quite successful, and there seems to be a rush by many of the studios to produce family product. I think to some degree it mirrors population. As the baby boomers get older and have kids, there is an increase in the need for family product—basic supply and demand. However, it always varies by studio. I can remember a few years ago, certain individuals would be reluctant to market a film toward females only, in particular young females. Some would even say you can't open a film to young girls only. However, look at the success of films like *Mannequin* or, more recently, *Clueless.*"

Is the moviegoing audience shifting? "It's not so much a shift," says Evergates-Price. "I think there has always been a market for female-driven movies. Look at *The Sound of Music, Steel Magnolias, Sleepless in Seattle,* and *Fried Green Tomatoes.* All female-driven." But Hollywood has not always recognized this as a valuable market. Often these are considered flukes. "There was a time that if we had a female targeted movie, we would work like crazy to find a way to make it appealing to men. I can remember some of us saying that no matter what you do, guys are not going to want to see this movie, but we would still rack our brains for a way to get them. Now it seems people accept a film for women and agree that that is who we should target. We also know that a decent percentage of these women are going to bring men to the film. I'm not saying 50 percent of the audience will be male, but a good 30 to 40 percent will come as dates, dads, or friends."

Why is this female audience growing? "Women have gotten more financial power," says Evergates-Price. "They're no longer dependent upon somebody else to take them to the movies." With increased financial independence, women expand the market of moviegoers to other segments of the population. "For *Little Women,*" says writer Robin Swicord, "we believed there would be a large, multigenerational audience. We felt that there had not been movies that grandmothers could take their grown daughters and their great-granddaughters to. We theorized they would come if we made it. What we found with *Little Women* was that we were absolutely right. Almost 70 percent of the audience for that film is female."

If a film doesn't cost the entire budget of a small country, it's all right for it to be a moderate success. Those moderate successes add up; but there's still the problem of studios backing the female-driven film through both production dollars and marketing dollars. Some do, some don't. *Little Women* and *Legends of the Fall* came out at about the same time, one with a predominantly female cast, the other with a predominantly male cast. *Legends* cost more, but according to Sid Ganis, president of marketing at Sony Pictures, the same amount of media marketing dollars were put behind both films.

Redefining a commercial success means redefining the relationship between cost and profits. The blockbuster is any film that makes over $100 million; a commercial success is a film that makes over $50 million. But many of the blockbusters, which are often action films with male protagonists, costs $60 or $80 million to make. With many of these female-driven films costing less than $20 million, even some less than $10 million, it leaves room to take some risks.

How the market works, and how some think it works, may be quite different. "The men ranked *Fried Green Tomatoes* even higher than the woman ranked it," says Sara Duvall. "It tested higher than any film since *Star Wars*. They loved the main character and saw this as a different kind of filmmaking. It was a surprise, it was honest, people felt fulfilled by this film. They felt like something was added to their lives. They were with people they wished they knew."

Success builds on success. One agent, who asked not to be named, says, "As more women are writing, as more of that energy and perspective is brought to the screen, the more the market will be expanded. That has an effect upon all of us as individuals working in the industry. And it affects the consumer, and the audience, too."

Creating change doesn't end with the story. Women filmmakers also want to change the characters who inhabit these stories. What are the new characters they'll create? Will they be able to better portray our lives, to move us, to touch us, even to dazzle us?

Director-producer-writer Alice Guy-Blache, the creator of the first fiction film *(Courtesy of Gaumont)*

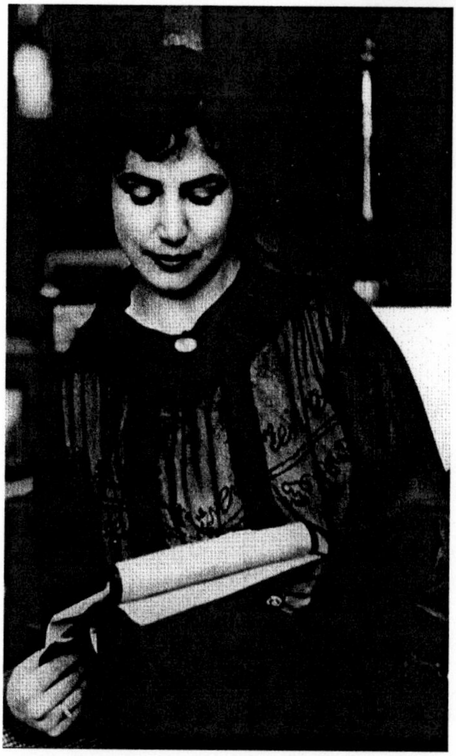

Writer-director-actor Lois Weber, who pioneered social issue films *(Courtesy of the Academy of Motion Picture Arts and Sciences)*

Frances Marion, one of the most successful and important writers in the history of film *(Courtesy of the Academy of Motion Picture Arts and Sciences)*

Dorothy Arzner, the only woman studio director from 1927 to 1943 *(Courtesy of the Academy of Motion Picture Arts and Sciences)*

Ida Lupino, the only woman studio director from 1949 to 1966 *(Courtesy of the Academy of Motion Picture Arts and Sciences)*

LEFT: Sherry Lansing, formerly President of Production at 20th Century Fox, now Chairman, CEO of Paramount Motion Picture Group—the first woman to head a studio

RIGHT: Lucie Salhany, President and CEO at United Paramount Network, the first woman to head a network

head of distribution at a studio

RIGHT: Barbara Corday, co-creator of *Cagney and Lacey*, and the first female vice president in prime-time television

LEFT: Betty Cohen green-lights for the Turner Cartoon Network. (Photograph by Andrew Eccles)

RIGHT: Barbara Barde, programming head of the Women's Television Network in Canada

Randa Haines, the first woman since Ida Lupino to direct a feature film and a television film which were critically acclaimed and commercially successful; at right, actor Richard Harris *(Photograph © 1993 Warner Bros.)*

Director Lee Grant, whose films on social issues have heightened consciousness and helped change legislation, seen here with cinematographer Tom Hurwitz and sound recorder Maryte Kavalauska *(Photograph © Mariette Pathy Allen)*

Television director Karen Arthur, the first woman to direct a miniseries.

Writer-director Caroline Thompson brings mythic themes to her work. *(Photograph by Keith Hamshere; © 1994 Warner Bros.)*

Myth consultant Pamela Jaye Smith (left) helps writers, producers, and directors develop myths in their films. Production designer Cynthia Charette is at right. *(Photograph by KASSA)*

French director Agnes Varda is the mother of the French New Wave. *(Photograph by BORREL; © 1994 by Ciné-Tamaris)*

Television series director Victoria Hochberg likes shooting in wild, barren places.

Writer-director Maxi Cohen helped pave the way for independent production and distribution.

LEFT: Writer Linda Woolverton changed the concept of the Disney heroine in *Beauty and the Beast. (Photograph by Molly Moore)*

RIGHT: Writer-director Julie Dash uses African storytelling patterns in *Daughters of the Dust. (Photograph by Molly Moore)*

Writer Hesper Anderson brought new images of sensuality to *Children of a Lesser God. (Photograph by Molly Moore)*

Writer Hinda Brooks, a strong advocate for employing writers over forty *(Photograph by Nomi Isak)*

Janet Scott Batchler (left), cowriter of *Batman Forever*, and Alexandra Seros (right), writer of *The Specialist*, bring emotion, psychology, and strong visual sequences to the action film.

Interactive Media. *(Photograph by Molly Moore)*
RIGHT: Comedy writer Treva Silverman brings a fresh sense of romance and love to her work. *(Photograph by Molly Moore)*

Gale Anne Hurd, a producer, has proved that the female hero can be a big box office draw.

LEFT: Stuntwoman Linda Fetters-Howard is an expert at fire stunts. *(Courtesy of Pat Solomon)*
RIGHT: As the trainer for Meryl Streep for *The River Wild*, Arlene Burns brings the female perspective to adventure.

Editor Carol Littleton brings her powers of observation and emotion to the task of finding the right visual moment to tell the story. *(Photograph by Molly Moore)*

Lili Zanuck, shown here with her partner Richard Zanuck collecting their Oscars for *Driving Miss Daisy*, is one of the three women producers who have won Academy Awards for Best Picture. *(Courtesy of the Academy of Motion Picture Arts and Sciences)*

Marcey Carsey and her partner Tom Werner, the top comedy producers in television

Emmy award–winning producer Marian Rees (left), with producing partner Anne Hopkins, creates quality, socially conscious programming.

Producer Denise DiNovi has produced action, children's, fantasy, and ensemble films; here, she is seen with the cast of *Little Women.*

Writer Robin Swicord (center) created the strong ensemble films *Little Women* and *The Perez Family.*

Actress Nancy Kwan (pictured with her son, Bernhard) proved that casting Asians could be commercially successful.

Actress Julie Carmen, one of the most successful Hispanic actresses in film

15

CASE STUDY

Barbara Barde

ON JANUARY 1, 1995, the Women's Television Network (WTN) premiered in Winnipeg, Canada. It was the first television network to be programmed by women, about women, focusing on woman's stories. Although New Zealand is testing a woman's television network, England has U.K. Living, and in the United States, Lifetime decided to focus on women in 1995, WTN premiered a different kind of approach to programming. According to a national survey of Canadian women, television wasn't meeting the needs of 84 percent of the female viewing audience; WTN responded to these needs. Out of fifty-two employees, fifty were women. The vice president of programming for the year of the launch is Barbara Barde, formerly an independent television producer and chair of the board of the Canadian Film Center, founded by Norman Jewison on the model of the American Film Institute.

"The idea for the network came from two men, Ron Rhodes and Michael Thnat. They realized they couldn't carry this off themselves, so they hired me and Linda Rankin, former president and CEO. Since there had never been a woman's network, we set out to do research about what women wanted. We sought to establish that in fact there was a thing called a women's media market and that it was definable.

We asked women, 'Where do you get your information for your lives as women?' They didn't say television. They said they got it from magazines, they got it from friends, and they got it from family.

"I started from the premise that it mattered who made programming, and that women told stories differently than men did, and that they developed characters differently. When our researcher started the research, she didn't believe it. The results absolutely turned her around.

"We've discovered that women writers tend to do many more character-driven stories. They care more about people, the dimension of the people. They care more about the characters than they do about the action. They don't care about cars leaping off bridges, or as much about cop shows, mysteries. They want you to understand the motivation in the character and the circumstances the character came out of.

"I think women fundamentally tell stories differently. It's empowering for women to have the voice to tell the stories they want to tell. That's what we have the power to do. In other channels, 75 percent of the staff can be female but it doesn't make a difference in terms of the kinds of stories that are chosen to be told, because the women are not ultimately making the decisions. It's having control, having input, being taken seriously. You can have women on camera, you can have women reporters, women researchers, women producers, but if the ultimate authority in terms of what that show looks like is a male, it won't make much difference.

"The motto of our channel is 'For women, by women, about women and their worlds,' because women have different worlds.

"There were certain groups of people who had a hard time understanding what a woman's channel was. Some men asked, 'Why isn't there a men's channel?' I said, 'They all are.'

"When we first got licensed, a lot of guys would call up and say, 'I've got a perfect show, a cooking show, a gardening show or a makeup show or a fashion show.' I would answer, 'We don't do cooking. We don't do gardening. I'm not doing fashion shows. We don't do makeover shows.' They'd ask, 'What do you do?' Now that isn't to say women don't watch those shows. But there are plenty of these on other channels, and this is only a very small percentage of what our lives are about.

"We aren't trying to program for one kind of woman. What we want to do is to create a channel. I always say, 'It should feel like home.' You can turn away to other channels but you can always come back and you know there isn't going to be gratuitous violence. There isn't going to be horrible sexual stereotyping. There aren't going to be those awful beer commercials.

"I think we are fundamentally trying to change what television is all about and the way it's put together. We try to have our programs produced, directed, and written by women. When we give money to new projects, it matters to me that we try to give it to projects where women have creative input and creative control.

"Sometimes women don't have the experience necessary to produce an ongoing series. I have to make sure the product's going to be delivered and that it's going to be high quality, so we will look for more experienced men to mentor them through the process. But it's important to me that the story be either driven by a woman or it be codriven by a man and a woman and that they drive it equally. With a lot of channels, this wouldn't matter, as long as it's a good story. But it matters to me. When we were doing the research for the channel, a lot of women and men said, 'Our children, whether they're males or females, need good role models and they need to see that women actually drive the stories and they don't always end up as victims.' They're not dead, raped, murdered in the first five minutes of the story. It's also important to me that you see all kinds of women, that you see good women and bad women. There are women with stories that you're not going to like. That's OK. At least you have the depth of experience to show all those things.

"Besides producing programs, we buy a lot of product that's already been made. Even in this case, I want to have all different kinds of women so we have many shows with women of color. But we don't marginalize them by having the aboriginal hour, the black hour. They are simply part of the story.

"Much of our programming is informational. We have a car show about everything you should know so you have control over the car. One show is about how to change your oil, another about what you should know when you go to a mechanic. It's very practical, with a high male viewership.

"We have a money show. When it comes to money, most women are terrorized by the institution. They think the institution thinks they're stupid and they don't know what to do. Most women don't have a lot of money and all those other shows presume you have a lot of money. In our show it doesn't matter if you have $20 or if you have $2,000 or if you have $20,000. It's the same principles you have to take into consideration. This is particularly important because the majority of women outlive men and end up living poor when they're over sixty-five.

"I bought some movies from the Lifetime Channel, including a series called *Intimate Portraits.* These included a story about Martina Navratilova, one on the Kennedy women. We also have *Herstory,* which presents the biographies of Australian Olympic champion Betty Cuthbert, who won the track-and-field Olympics in 1956, Wilma Rudolph, who won track and field in 1960, and others.

"We put money into a pilot called *Unforgettable Romances,* about such couples as Princess Grace and Prince Rainer, and Rita Hayworth and Ali Khan. They're going to be documentaries with all the old footage and the stories of their lives.

"We want to do a current-affairs show that doesn't look like every other news show on TV and which tells those stories that often get dropped from other channels. We're doing a show called *Jane Taber's Ottawa,* which tells the woman's point of view about what happened in a particular week in the nation's capital.

"We're doing this show *Girl Talk,* aimed at teenage girls. Sony donated Hi-8 cameras for them, and we train them to produce their own stories. We teach them about how to find a story, how to identify a story. They shoot the stories themselves. The camera work is MTV kind of style. The first show was on body piercing. There's one section called 'Rants.' In each show, somebody rants for a minute about things. One show they all sat around and talked about their breasts and how they feel about them. Another one has them talking about are they or are they not feminists. We also do *Change of View,* a half-hour show each week where we feature young Canadian women directors whose work hasn't been seen before.

"World Film Festival shows the work of female directors from around the world and stories with strong female protagonists. Our first one was directed and cowritten and produced by Aparna Sen from India. It's a story of a woman who had been raped in her little village. The family was shamed and they knew that she could never get married, and in India, if she couldn't marry, nobody else in the family could ever get married again. So they married her to a tree. It's the story of this woman and the tree. Wonderful stuff.

"This week we have a Chinese one by Huang Shugin. It's the story of a woman who becomes a star in the Beijing Opera Company, playing male roles. On the stage she gets to be accepted as a man, but once she comes off of that she goes back to being a woman. It's all the problems this creates for her as she struggles between having this incredible acceptance being in the opera versus not having this same acceptance in society.

"We do an interview with the director and we look at her whole life, how she got into it, how she started doing it, why she started doing it, and then look at her various films. We started with Jane Campion talking about *The Piano.*

"We buy British sitcoms, which often have strong female protagonists. We've done *Birds of a Feather* by Esta Charkham, about two sisters whose husbands are in prison and who end up living together. And a thirteen-part series called *Rides,* about a group of women who own a minicab company, produced by Lavinia Warner in London. She owns a company called the Warner Sisters, as a contrast to Warner Brothers. We have a show called *Shameless Shorts*—over 180 short films, all directed by women.

"We do a number of films about social issues. When we were doing our research, many women said that when they watched social issue stories on television about such subjects as wife abuse or child abuse or incest, that the film wasn't over when it was over and that they wanted to talk about it. Women want closure to stories.

"We have a show on Tuesday night called *Open for Discussion* and the first week we did families and AIDS. We showed the British film *Sweet as You Are,* with Liam Neeson and Miranda Richardson, where he had slept with one of his university students and he gets a little note saying I think you should go for a test. He goes for a test and he's HIV positive and he has to tell his wife. It's an incredibly strong movie. At the end we did a half-hour of talk with women who have gone through this. We didn't have counselors on the phones but we did have an 800 number and we had a referral service. We had people who do AIDS counseling, on the line referring people across the country for more information. The next week we did families and aging. We dealt with Alzheimer's. Last week we did special-needs kids. We also did eating disorders. This week we have one of our strongest, called *Why Blame the Mother?* It's stories of the mothers of children who commit crimes. As one of the mothers says, 'All of our kids' friends want to be lawyers and doctors, but my son's a rapist. What do you say, Hello, my son's a rapist?'

"Women want to learn from movies, to integrate them into their lives. A lot of women like sequels. They want to know the next stage of the life of the characters. Or they like those long credits at the end of the film: 'So-and-so married so-and-so. So-and-so are now divorced. They have three kids but they don't live together anymore.' That to me is closure.

"We also program the overall channel differently. We honestly do not look like any other channel on television. We have channel hosts because one of the things that came through in our research was that a lot of women have the TV set on all day and they never turn it off. So they view television as a companion. So we decided to make it a companion and have somebody host it. One woman hosts the morning, one woman hosts the afternoon, one woman does after school and late nights, and one woman does prime time. Over time these women become your friends. You like them and you will write letters to them. You'll ask them questions. There's an interaction, back and forth. These people are honest enough to talk about their own personal lives. They're not just performers.

"That's what our role is, to make sure those voices are heard. The calls that we get from women across the country say, 'I didn't know what I was missing.' The women feel empowered by these stories, by these people.

"But we aren't just successful with women. Many men have called, saying, 'I loved the shows. It's dynamite TV.' They say it's refreshing, different. And we feel, in spite of the long hours, the stress of starting a new channel, all the difficulties, that we are having an impact."

PART FOUR

CREATING WOMEN CHARACTERS

SOME IMPORTANT BREAKTHROUGHS FOR WOMEN

1939: Hattie McDaniel wins best supporting actress for *Gone With the Wind;* she's the first African-American to win an Academy Award.

1951: Lucille Ball creates one of the longest-running shows with one of the most memorable characters in television history.

1966: Diana Rigg stars in *The Avengers* as a sexy, smart professional secret agent.

1966–1971: Marlo Thomas stars in *That Girl,* the first sitcom about the independent working woman.

1970: Mary Tyler Moore portrays a single, happy professional woman on the *Mary Tyler Moore Show.*

1970: Diahann Carroll stars in *Julia;* she's TV's first black female with her own series.

1971: Ruth Gordon in *Harold and Maude* proves that an older woman can be charming and sexy and eccentrically wise.

1974: Writer Treva Silverman wins an Emmy Award for her work on the *Mary Tyler Moore Show;* she is the first woman to win the award for a situation comedy.

1976: *Laverne & Shirley* brings a new kind of woman to the screen—the working-class single woman.

1982: Sharon Gless and Tyne Daly star in *Cagney & Lacey,* one of the first cop shows where women are not defined by their sex appeal.

1984: *Murder, She Wrote,* about an older woman (Angela Lansbury), premieres and becomes one of the longest-running series on television.

1985: Whoopi Goldberg and Oprah Winfrey make their first screen appearances in *The Color Purple* and go on to become two of the highest-paid performers in the business.

1986: Marlee Matlin (*Children of a Lesser God*) is the first deaf actress to win an Academy Award.

1988: *Roseanne* (Roseanne Barr) shows that a working-class woman with a smart mouth can be a commercially viable character.

1989: Euzhan Palcy is the first black female director to have a major production deal at a Hollywood studio, to direct the film *A Dry White Season*.

1991: Callie Khouri creates the female buddy film *Thelma and Louise* and wins an Academy Award for best original screenplay.

1991: Helen Mirren stars as Inspector Jane Tennison in *Prime Suspect,* a realistic cop show that gives the woman's view.

1994–1995: Margaret Cho appears as the first female Asian-American lead in a sitcom, *All-American Girl.*

16

EXPRESSING OUR IDENTITIES

What am I supposed to do . . . walk around
like a puppet or use my intelligence?
—Katharine Hepburn in Stage Door *(1937),*
RKO Radio Pictures

IF YOU LOOK AT females in real life, you see the bad and the good. The gangly and the beautiful and all the in-betweens. The powerful and the insecure. The wise and the foolish. You see women in traditional roles—as mothers and secretaries and nurses and teachers—and in almost every nontraditional role, from airline pilot to rabbi to engineer.

If you look at females in most films, one kind of character is consistent—young, beautiful, and sexy. The media limits women, drawing their models from a very small slice of life, in fact a slice of life which may only be found in a small number of Hollywood parties and some photography sessions.

As Kate Capshaw said at the 1995 Women in Film Crystal Awards, "Even today our colleagues are more interesting than 90 percent of the characters we see in the movies."

It seems obvious that female roles need improvement, and logical that having more female writers and directors would help solve the problem. This is not to say that men are unable to write strong female characters. A writer's creativity and research can often transcend gender.

"In order to write the other gender, you have to observe," says British television producer Grace Kitto. "It's much harder to write the other sex, but you can do it if you pay attention to that character, if you research. Obviously you don't have to be a murderer to write one, but you have to know your trade very well and you have to be working in a supportive environment that allows you to go after the truth."

But the great female characters written by men are far too few. If the portrayal of females on screen were only limiting, it would be unfortunate. Many portrayals of females, however, are degrading, insulting, and unrealistic.

Writer Linda Bloodworth-Thomason created an entire episode about the portrayal of women in the media for her television series *Woman of the House.* Within her "Women in Film" episode, film and television actresses talked about the roles they've played:

"I've been asked to play a topless secretary, a topless doctor, a topless judge," says Loni Anderson. "Well, you get the picture—the standard female role models we see everyday in our society."

Joan Van Ark (*Knots Landing*) has played "a woman who's stalked, a woman who's raped, a woman who's kidnapped, carjacked, and skyjacked. Frankly, I'm exhausted."

Shirley Jones, who won the Academy Award for *Elmer Gantry,* says: "I've played hundreds of decent, caring woman over the years, but it took the role of an exploited, used, and abused prostitute to win me an Oscar."

"As far as I know," says actress Brett Butler (from *Grace Under Fire*), "the only woman who's been allowed to be consistently independent, adventurous, and unmolested is Lassie, and they used all boy dogs to play that part."

Roseanne Barr asks for a disclaimer. "I notice that at the end of those Black Stallion and Flipper films they have a little card that says 'No animals were hurt or exploited in the making of this film.' They should have one of those cards for women."

Linda Bloodworth-Thomason says, "We accept these portrayals as a way of life. Men think this is sexy, and it's everywhere—it's on cable, on the computer, on the Internet, in our mainstream theaters. Right now, in 1995, there are five films being made about striptease—five mainstream movies. You can't do on film to any other group what men do to women!"

Why do men continue to do it? They say it's in the name of artistic expression. Linda Bloodworth-Thomason voiced her response to that excuse through the mouth of her main character, Representative Suzanne Sugarbaker. "We've seen women raped, beaten, kidnapped, killed, and tortured. That's been expressed. Now, let's move on to express something else. What about women who are friends, women who have adventures, women who wear clothes, women who aren't in jeopardy, women who are, in fact, doing just fine. At some point it's got to stop because it's just plain wrong and it's hurting your wives, your girlfriends, your sisters, your daughters, and if you say it can't be proven that it's hurting them, let's just say it's not helping. OK?"[1]

While trying to address the years of stereotyping, women writers sometimes find a whole new set of problems. New Zealand television writer Judy Callingham expressed her frustration: "Political correctness is killing us. It's gagging us as storytellers. You can't write a story about a woman who isn't a feminist. You can't write a story about Maori women or about victims. You can't write stories about bad women, which are often the most fascinating because they open up those areas we've been never allowed to explore. You can't show violence of any kind, even though the violence may be absolutely essential in order to show a character transforming."

Writer Linda Woolverton agrees. "We're pendulums swinging so far away from the sexist stereotype. I'm starting to feel like every time I write a woman character, I have to be so worried that it's going to please everyone. I'm nervous that every woman we're going to see has to be perfect."

Women writers feel caught between trying to create more dimensional female characters and trying to make up for past wrongs. The issue is complicated because the search for a more realistic depiction of female characters is also a search for the female identity.

FINDING OUR IDENTITY, FINDING OUR FLAWS

Women filmmakers—writers, directors, producers—do want a say in creating women characters. They feel they are in the best position to know the intricacies of their psychology and to help formulate the character of the modern woman.

They also feel that as their own identities emerged through the radical social changes of the 1960s to the 1990s, they were still finding their way. Women were discovering aspects about themselves that were dramatic—discoveries that would perhaps even make good films. They began to define what it was they wanted to see on the screen. Some common ideals emerged from our discussions—beginning with the need to show the complexity of human beings.

Writer Naomi Foner finds that "good-guy, really-bad-guy stuff is useless. It's much too simple. It's not how people really are. In terms of character, I'm always trying to make people who are much more complicated. The compelling villain is much more dangerous, the flawed hero more likely to create tension in a story. If heroes are too good, we can't identify with them and that defeats the entire purpose."

Part of that complication includes expressing the nuances that mark gender differences. When Foner first started writing, she thought men and women were alike. "I thought if we weren't, it was just some political issue or social law that made us different. But I see now that's not true. We are different. And more and more I feel it's my responsibility to be the voice of women. Part of the message to women is: Define yourself, not in terms of someone else but in terms of yourself. Look for your own integrity because that's part of your self-definition. For years women had to work through men. They shouldn't have to do that anymore."

Meg Ryan's production company, Prufrock Films, is developing projects with competent, complex women. Ryan says, "Many times we see scripts where the man's story is much more complicated and defined and the woman character feels appended or tacked on. She doesn't have equal weight in the story. For me, everything comes down to this process of complicating a female character like we, as women, are complicated. We don't exist in the broad stroke. We are interesting because we are subtle."

Actress Susan Clark (*Webster*) wants ambivalence. "Few women are allowed to have that expanse of gray that a male character is allowed. We have to be either all good or all bad."

Roseanne Barr doesn't want perfection. "I never want her to be perfect," she says, referring to her character from the hit TV show *Roseanne*. "I want her to be flawed. And all the characters on the show are flawed, as are all women and all human beings."[2]

Sometimes the process begins by drawing the woman as not beautiful in order to get at reality. Although the U.S. film industry is driven by the star system and by the beauty myth (with a few notable exceptions, such as Roseanne), the business in other countries is far less so.

Muriel's Wedding went beyond stereotypes, says one Australian writer. "She's such a lumpy girl. She's got thighs." The New Zealand/Australian coproduction of *Alex*, about a champion swimmer, also broke stereotypes. "Alex is a tall and gangly girl, even somewhat awkward when she's not swimming," says director Megan Simpson.

Flaws. That means not perfect. It means real. Sometimes it also means seeing the dark side, the shadow—without exploiting it. For some women, this becomes a danger signal—does this now mean that women, once again, will be painted bad instead of good?

Being imperfect need not be a negative. Actress Mary McDonnell sees that "it's very important to portray the shadow so we can get it out and see it. I want to play women we might not like, women who are carrying the shadow and acting from the shadow."

What is the shadow? "All the great stuff that we carry within us that goes along with being a woman and feminine in nature," says McDonnell. "Everything from storms to earthquakes to hurricanes to floods—these things happen inside the feminine. That means expressing rage and passion. When I say rage I see it as a positive thing. I don't mean rage as mad. Women are capable of experiencing incredible rage that helps motivate them to overcome injustices."

Writer-director Johanna Demetrakas recognizes that women may not want to see this side of themselves. But she sees it as important to portraying well-rounded characters. "Many women have a real resistance to seeing their dark side. Maybe it's because we've been brought up to regard ourselves as the pillars of morality, so if a woman's behavior comes from an amoral place, she's immediately shot down."

"This is about multidimensional women," explains writer Lindsay Smith. "It's not about depicting saints, because we're not saints. Too many characters have dealt with the veneer of the woman, not the reality. We want to pull up all these layers."

This does not negate the possibility of seeing the good woman in films. One only has to watch a film like *Sense and Sensibility* (from Jane Austen's novel, screenplay by Emma Thompson) to see that goodness can be richly nuanced and include vulnerability, sorrow, fear, and anger.

But good doesn't mean idealizing the woman. Susan Seidelman tries to make her characters real, "with a combination of flaws and virtues. I've never felt the need to glorify women. That can be just as negative. Making overly idealized women is the flip side of the bimbo coin. Making women too perfect or too virtuous is unreal."

She sees that the great male icons "like James Dean or Marlon Brando or Robert de Niro have been so memorable, not because they're perfect but that they've been confused and flawed. To me, that's the kind of complex female characters I would love to make and love to see."

McDonnell agrees: "We have a lot of great films out there about absolutely despicable men, about losers. These guys are so interesting. They have so much to say about being a loser and what's wrong with it and what's funny about it. Within these loser roles, there are insights and perceptions."

But it can be dangerous to put this interpretation of women in the hands of men, since so many films by men that have dealt with the dark side of women have exploited the character, made her sexy and an object and a victim. It isn't that women haven't been victims. Jodie Foster says that "it's real important to go and see the reality of our vulnerability and our precariousness on screen. . . . The truth is that a good percentage of women's history is about being victimized, and we shouldn't forget that. It's not like you sweep it under the rug and say it never happened."[3]

But playing her victim status again and again is not what women want. There are other aspects to explore. Some companies, such as Lifetime Television, are trying to address this directly. "Women have often been portrayed as ancilliary characters or as reactive," says Sheri Singer, vice president of movies and drama series. "We're trying to create really meaty roles for women. Most of the time they're the active character."

The executives at Lifetime also look at the woman character in relationship to the male character. Having a great female character at the expense of the male characters is not desirable. "We try to be just as sensitive about the way we portray men. Because Lifetime is a service that targets women, we are held up to a pretty heavy barometer in terms of whether we are bashing men in order to make women look better."

Creating the flawed and complex female character is a beginning to creating great female characters. But it's only one step in the process. Women also want to have strong, heroic female characters and to see an active rather than passive female. To do this, some women writers are rethinking the mythic heroine.

17

WOMEN AS HEROES

THE SEARCH FOR women characters sometimes begins where men begin—looking for the strong, capable, powerful hero. Although we've rarely seen them on film, there are plenty of heroines around. Almost every heroic action that men have done, or historic role men have played, women have done also. Sometimes they've done it first.

"Heroics are not unnatural to women," says stuntwoman Linda Fetters-Howard. "There are female astronauts, there are female firefighters. And it's changing more and more in the movies. Sharon Stone plays a gunslinger in *The Quick and the Dead.* Geena Davis plays a pirate in *Cutthroat Island.*"

Since drama has often been defined as action, violence, and conflict, it presupposes a heroic story, a form that some think is essentially masculine. "The reason why men's stories lend themselves to such drama and excitement is because men tend to grow more by doing," says writer-producer Lindsay Smith. "I think we tend to grow more by reflecting and feeling and maybe even analyzing. The outer versus inner processes makes it easier to dramatize the male than the female. Men's stories are more dazzling. It's more interesting to see a guy do something big and broad in terms of storytelling."

Does that mean that women can't be heroes unless they follow the male model? What is our heroism about? Is it possible that we can dazzle, excite, and engage audiences through our heroism? To find the answer means redefining the myth of the heroine. Linda Woolverton had to do just that when she wrote the Disney film *Beauty and the Beast.* "I realized you couldn't make Belle a throwback to Snow White," says Woolverton. "I felt responsible about this character as a role model. And I felt responsible because I was the first woman to have ever written a Disney animated feature film. In the meetings, it was clear that I was looked on with some suspicion. So I went in and just fought for what I believed Belle should be."

And what should she be? "She's an active heroine. She uses different reasoning. She's motivated. She does something. Boys get to do action all the time. They go out and affect the world, but the girl has to stand around and wait for the world to come to her. I wanted to change that."

The active heroine has been seen in a number of successful films. The *Alien* and *Terminator* films, *The River Wild, Tank Girl, Gorillas in the Mist, Annie Oakley, The Wizard of Oz, Mata Hari*—all overturned the stereotypical view of women as submissive, passive, defined by the man.

Woolverton mentions another stereotype that has to be changed to create the heroine. "It was important to me that Belle was not a victim. She has the courage to stand up to the Beast." Belle's activity does not defeat the beast but brings about a different ending. "By not being a victim she changes him."

The ending for the heroine may not mean vanquishing evil, but transforming it. Many films focus on overcoming evil as the climax. But to do this the hero has to do the evil that he would like to overcome. He kills, fights, explodes, destroys, conquers. For a woman to create the climax of the film, a new model is emerging. Since evil stifles the life force, rather than destroying evil she embraces and even transforms it. In the process, she is also transformed.

Myth consultant Pamela Jaye Smith emphasizes the importance of this transformation. "Whether you come back with the elixir for the tribe, or never go back and go on to other adventures, the heroine is changed in the process. At the end of the film, she has always learned something about where she should be whether or not she made it there. If she gets there, it's a happy ending. If she does not, it's a tragedy. But regardless of the physical ending, the vision is still insight."

For Smith, this transformational model seems to fit the female journey and leads to empowerment. "I think our transformation in the last twenty years has been far more profound than male transformation," says Smith. "But this may happen because we have had something to fight against. I think men are trying to change, but since the world belongs to the men, they haven't had that obstacle that has forced their transformation."

Gale Anne Hurd, producer of both *Alien* and *The Terminator*, also emphasizes character transformation for the heroine. "The qualities I personally like to see is someone who doesn't start off already imbued or endowed with those abilities. I like to see a heroine who questions her own ability to handle the situation. She's a reluctant heroine—an ordinary person thrust into an extraordinary situation. You want to see that person grow and find the skills within them, as opposed to having them at the beginning of the film. It allows the audience to identify with the central character."

The transformation may be not just for the character, but for the world that she inhabits. If the antagonists are seen as flawed or wounded but not objectified as evil, the ending of the story changes. The work of the heroine might then be about overcoming obstacles in order to create, nurture, heal, or empower. She gains the power to not only transform herself but to transform adversaries, whether they be specific individuals or a society.

To do this heroic work demands different qualities. Gale Anne Hurd has long been attracted to the rich possibilities inherent in changing the focus from hero to heroine. "Just about every emotion and every conceivable conceit has been used with respect to male action heros. With women you get an entirely new canvas. You can explore new territory that people haven't seen on screen before."

Hurd does not look for the same image as the male action hero. She wants flaws. "They should have problems. I find that superheroes are not that interesting. All the range of emotion from A to B."

The creation of the female hero does not mean writing a male role and giving it to a woman. It means looking at the differences between how a man might approach a challenge in the adventure and how a woman might approach it. A 1995 action-adventure film was *The River Wild,* with Meryl Streep as an expert river rafter. Journalist Laurie Werner explored this male-female difference in an article for the *Los Angeles Times.* "When it was announced that Meryl was doing the movie, the take that everyone had on it was Meryl Streep doing a Bruce Willis part, an Arnold Schwarzenegger part, like it was sort of a gimmick, shooting her in an action movie. And Meryl smiled and said, 'It wouldn't be appropriate to have Bruce Willis as a mother from Boston.' "[4]

"At first they referred to the film as a fish with feathers, neither here nor there," says director Curtis Hanson in Werner's article. "Because they're so used to feeling that action movies appeal to young males and Meryl Streep movies appeal to females and the two can't cross. But they can, if the movie is really good." And did.

"When I first read the script," says Streep, "the possibilities of who the character might be in terms of a multidimensional person, someone recognizable to me, weren't as obviously there. She is a bit of a cipher, more plot-driven. Things happened and she fought back. Curtis was willing to listen to what I felt were the shortcomings. I was interested in the interior lives of the characters and what they were grappling with beyond their physical challenges, and Curtis was kind in letting me help shape that."[5]

The woman who trained Streep for the role was Arlene Burns, considered one of the best rafters in the world. She sees a clear difference between the approach of women and men to heroics and adventure.

"Men tend to rely on sheer strength to power their way through a situation, such as the rapids of a river. Women, perhaps lacking in muscle mass, tend more to use their mind to actually 'read' the water, comprehending the subtle energies within the current and tuning in to a force that is already there. Women don't have as much to prove. I can run a rapid or I can walk around it—and it won't make me feel less about myself."

If the woman is not depending on her muscles, what does she rely on? "Technique. Brains. Intuition," says Burns. "For a woman to do the same thing a man can do, they're going to need to use a more creative approach to accomplish the same objective."

How does this translate into character? In *The River Wild,* Streep played a strong character, feminine; a mother, a wife, a woman not easily frayed. "She obviously had emotional reactions to what was happening around her but she had a creative, problem-solving mind," says Burns. "She wasn't taking a passive role, just letting whatever happened happen and being a victim. She was always trying to think of creative ways to overcome the situation, even within the interaction and conversation with the bad guy."

One can find similar capable, confident, and complex heroines in a number of films and even in strong supporting roles.

"I'm very proud of *Batman Returns*," says producer Denise Di Novi, who helped create the Catwoman character. "She is a really historic character. It's one of the few mega-action movies where you don't just have the girlfriend as an appendage to the man. She was a complex character. Dan Waters, who wrote the script, and Tim Burton, who directed, are two of the least sexist men I've ever met. It was important to them and to me to make her a feminist character."

To Australian producer Sandra Levy, who created an action show called *Rescue,* physical action was an important part of her female characters. "Our main character, Georgia, is strong, athletic. She swings off ropes. She sails off huge buildings. Climbs down cliff faces. It's unusual to see women playing characters where they have a chance to be equal to men physically. In real life, there weren't women in Police Rescue in these roles. But our research told us that this was possible. And in our rescue story women are just as successful and important as the men."

Creating the strong, heroic character not only reflects the reality and the possibility, but changes it. "Our show has been running since 1990," says Levy. "Now the police force has many women in positions of importance, more than in 1990. And they now have women in these highly trained specialist squads. Many of the women on this force said they watched the show and it helped them decide to go into it. They see the blokes do it and they say, 'We can do it too.' "

But this does not mean that the woman wants to do her heroics exactly as the men do theirs. "I'm not sure women have a desire to be the female Rambo," said one studio executive who expressed the sentiments of a number of women. "We don't want to see women doing the indiscriminate violence that male stars engage in all the time. Sometimes when scripts come in with a woman action hero, we ask, 'Is this really a strong woman character or is this just a role written as a man and, for the sake of marketing, they made it a woman?' You can make a character a female without making her a real woman."

Meg Ryan sees that "women's strengths are different than male strengths. It takes longer to see strength in a woman. It's not that it's not there, but it's in the person's character a little more obliquely. Our strengths are not always immediately apparent. They're often more internalized and less externalized in the world."

Some writers redefine heroism by looking at female models. However, because it's still a new concept, women writers struggle with how to express it. Linda Woolverton sees the most heroic act as mothering. "But I can't yet figure out how to put my experience of motherhood on the screen. I came to motherhood very late—at the age of thirty-eight. I had no respect for mothers. I had an idea that said you just stay home with your kids, but I wasn't going to let a child stop me from competing in the world. But now when I look at the true heroism of mothering, I realize the mother is the most influential person in American life. Of course, idealized motherhood is in many films and television shows, but motherhood as I see it isn't there. When I became a mother, my whole viewpoint changed. I suddenly had something in common with women from the dawn of time. Suddenly I felt I could relate to a woman in Zimbabwe, starving women and children all over the world. I had never felt this before."

Writer Caroline Thompson, like Woolverton, sees the importance of these heroics. "The world of the house is the strongest world there is. It's where everything starts and ends. It's food and shelter and clothing and warmth and comfort. The politics of the world, the money and power of the world, that all happens outside of the house. But it's not the basic stuff of life."

Many women writers start with a heroic model but put the heroine into a female context, with issues that may be quite different than a man would encounter in the same situation. British writer Lynda La Plante broke new ground with the creation of Inspector Jane Tennison in *Prime Suspect.* "When I first created her, I didn't realize I was breaking barriers. But I thought she was fascinating because she was a new creature."

What was different? The issues were different. Issues of domestic life, balance, romance, all affected the women differently. "For these women, you realize that this is an all-consuming job, so they have very little domestic life at all." The physical description of the woman was also different. "A woman doesn't have to have a great figure, an amazing face, to be attractive. Jane Tennison, for all her problems and tiredness, is still a very attractive, sexual woman. But she's a real woman."

As a real woman, she's got other real qualities that are rarely seen in female characters. La Plante defines some of them: "She's very observant, intuitive. A woman's mind is different than a man's. There's a nimbleness in the mind of a woman which I don't believe is the same with the male. A woman's mind can hop from one thing to another. A woman can be putting everything in various departments in her brain and run them all at the same time."

Do the men like her? La Plante has a theory about that. "I think there are many male viewers who don't want to see a *Playboy* pinup. I think they see her as a real woman and they like her. They can also say, 'At last there's somebody like the woman I love.' "

The dimensional female character has been proven time and again to be commercially viable. *Prime Suspect* has "been sold to about fifty-nine countries and has opened up the world of realism for other detective shows," adds La Plante.

Other women are looking to different models for female characters. They see no reason why we need to follow a male model to create strong women. The strong female character need not be heroic or an action hero. To create the true-to-life female character, we only need to look to our lives, as women in relationships.

18

BREAKING STEREOTYPES

WHEN WOMEN FILMMAKERS choose to express their lives in films, it's not unusual for them to concentrate on friendship or ensemble stories. One of the most successful friendship films was *Fried Green Tomatoes,* from the book by Fannie Flagg, with a screenplay by Flagg and Carol Sobieski. The film was executive-produced by Sara Duvall. "Women have endearing friendships, which are different from male buddy-film relationships." says Duvall. "Women confront issues, they influence. They change each other. They take each other seriously, even at the minutiae-of-life level."

What is the nature of women's friendships? Sharing. Vulnerability. "Women are not as afraid to bare their souls as men are," says Bonnie Bruckheimer, producing partner and longtime friend of Bette Midler. "Women's friendships may be based on vulnerability. If you've been hurt or you're insecure, you can tell your best friend. I find in my friendships I can let everything out, scream and yell and have a fight like Bette and I have done, and once it's over, we get over it and go back to our appreciation for each other."

Women recognize that friendships can be liberating and transforming. Susan Seidelman explored this theme in *Desperately Seeking Susan,* seeing it not just as a female friendship movie but a kind of love story. "The film turned the traditional romantic comedy on its head. In the traditional film, the girl ends up getting the free-spirited guy. The man liberates her from the stuffy marriage she's about to enter into. This film is the story of a suburban housewife who felt her whole life was a little bit boring, like there was a much more alive person inside her. She felt that she was stifled creatively. In all of this there's this longing for something more, whether it's for adventure, romance, scaling new heights, whatever it is."

Desperately Seeking Susan explores the problem between imagination and reality. "Women's imaginations are quite free, but the ability to actualize what we imagine can be harder. Roberta [Rosanna Arquette] represented the kind of female character who is determined and energetic. But she's confused about something. She doesn't have her life totally together. Roberta's journey allowed her to become a better version of the person that she already was."

French director Agnes Varda explored another aspect of this theme in her film *One Sings, The Other Doesn't,* a story about a long-term friendship between two women who help each other cope in a man's world. "I wanted to make a film about the energy of women, about the friendship of women, about their connection to life. Women have a basic energy that I love."

Varda's film empowered women who watched it. "Years after I made it, women said they saw the film and felt so strong. It gave them hope, inspiration."

THE WOMAN'S ENSEMBLE FILM

Sometimes this energy between women is translated into the energy between a community of women. This is explored in a number of female ensemble films, including *The Joy Luck Club, Chantilly Lace, How to Make an American Quilt, Enchanted April, Steel Magnolias, The Women, Now and Then, Waiting to Exhale, Little Women,* and *Moonlight and Valentino.*

"I think both men and women like these kinds of films," says producer Denise Di Novi. "They deal with feelings and conflict and human emotion and very sensitive issues as we did with *Little Women.* The guy ensemble films like *Diner* often have each guy character represent a different type of person or different experience. It's the same thing with a woman's ensemble. It allows you to explore many different character types and different human experiences. In *Little Women* you have the vain, pretty sister, the shy one, the ambitious one—each one a different aspect of being a female."

A number of actresses seem attracted to these films because of the opportunities it affords them. Meg Ryan says that "there are so many really great women in their fifties and sixties that I'd love to work with, whether as a mother or a friend. These include Anne Bancroft, Joan Plowright, Joanne Woodward, Ellen Burstyn, Gena Rowlands."

The multigenerational relationship suggests the multidimensional relationship. "The ensemble film may be particularly well suited to showing the lives of women," says writer Robin Swicord (*Little Women*), "in part because it isn't unusual for a woman to spend the greater part of her life mostly in the community of women. Also, a good number of women experience their own lives in terms of relationships, with parents, their children, lovers, mentors, coworkers, rather than being highly focused on external rewards. It's character over plot."

Working with the ensemble film creates possibilities to explore other aspects of relationships. "I love the possibilities within it," continues Swicord. "It's not a straight line. There's something egomanically obsessed about some movies because they deal with what a single protagonist wants. But the ensemble film deals with what different people want and how those different desires play off each other."

Swicord thinks the form itself may have something essentially feminine about it. "The linguist Deborah Tannen talks about women seeking consensus. If she's right, there's something hardwired into us that works for consensus, that wants to get all those points of view home to a finish line at the end of a film."

Producer Janet Yang (*Joy Luck Club*) sees that the ensemble fits into the "cooperative nature of women, so no one voice has to dominate. They can all flourish and can create a nice stew. It's a different dynamic." She also sees another reason why the ensemble film represents woman's character. "There's something about women that is rounder, with fewer sharp edges. We can adapt to the space in between. We are more like water, men like rock."

By bringing in multiple points of view, multiple wants and goals, the ensemble film rounds out the different aspects of being a woman. It creates diversity. Women want the whole diverse range of female experiences to be opened up in films. This means breaking stereotypes for all female characters.

WHAT ARE THE USUAL STEREOTYPES?

Everyone is stereotyped in films at one time or another—white women, ethnic women, ethnic men, disabled men and women, even the white male. But white male actors have far more choices; they can choose what kind of character they want to play. White women actors have fewer choices, and ethnic women's choices are almost nil. Although minorities have traditionally been stereotyped, women minorities suffer from a double stereotype—the cultural stereotype and the gender stereotype. Sometimes there's also a class stereotype; the ethnic woman is often portrayed as lower class and poor. Many women filmmakers, whether white or ethnic women, want to see a broader spectrum of women's lives on the screen. As the recipients of this stereotyping, ethnic women are trying to use whatever clout they have to make changes, or at the very least to voice an opinion about what needs to be done.

"Historically, we were the whores and the slave girls," says African-American actress Vanessa Bell Calloway, who has appeared in such films as *What's Love Got to Do with It?* and *Crimson Tide*. "Then we graduated to prostitutes. Either you were big, bad, and a tough and foxy mama, or you were some whore being abused."

"Films about Native Americans have gone back to the John

Wayne–type films," says Doris Leadercharge of the Lakota Sioux nation, who was the consultant on *Dances with Wolves.* "They're always fighting and always killing and always scalping. They're portrayed as fierce fighters and the women are slaves."

"The Hispanic stereotype is the Chiquita Banana role, where the ethnicity is the joke," says actress Julie Carmen, who has appeared in such films as *The Milagro Beanfield War, In the Mouth of Madness,* and John Cassavetes's *Gloria.* "Or she's the hot mama."

"Asians were seen as the exotic-erotic Asian woman," says actress Nancy Kwan, who was the first Asian actress to star in a major role, in *The World of Suzie Wong.* "Or the femme fatale, the shady woman," adds retired agent Bessie Loo, now in her nineties. "Or passive and submissive," says producer Martha Chang (*Teenage Mutant Ninja Turtles: The Movie*).

The disabled come in for their share of stereotypes—when they are seen at all. "The dominant images of disability are male," says documentary filmmaker Bonnie Sherr Klein, who suffered a congenital brainstem stroke after she had completed filming *Mile Zero.* "There's the pitiful or tragic image, the Tiny Tim prototype, and what we call the macho 'supercrip,' as in *Coming Home* or *Waterdance.* The dominant female image is still the saint—a woman stricken with some kind of disability or terminal illness sacrifices herself for the good of her family. Then there's the brave and triumphant woman in what we call the Triumph over Tragedy, or TOT, genre. It seems we are either seen as a burden for whoever loves us and cares for us, as sad and unhappy, or unrealistically brave and triumphant. People think we shouldn't have been born, or that we should have blown away. They don't see our humor. They rarely see us in groups. They don't realize we have a very rich culture that has never been tapped for the screen."

What needs to change? Do women want to simply change the character name of "Judy" to "Lupita," or cast an African American as Mary Smith? Do they want to say everyone is human underneath and make sure their character is just like all the other characters? No, said these women, who emphasize that characters need to be both universal and culturally specific. They need to express the full range of humanity and at the same time illustrate that ethnic background does add important details that have the potential to create fascinating, original characters.

Doris Leadercharge brought cultural specifics to *Dances with Wolves* and was pleased that director-actor Kevin Costner and writer Michael Blake took her role as consultant seriously. She was able to influence the authenticity of the film. "On the set, if Kevin or Michael would say 'Do this,' and if I would say 'No, that's not how we'd do it,' then we wouldn't do it. They didn't want to do anything to offend the Lakota. I taught the language to the actors. I tried to show how the women are held in high esteem, they are not treated like slaves. Caring is important. Because we've been exploited from day one, we don't like to exploit anybody else. They wanted to show sweat lodges, but we don't like to show anything that's spiritual, it's not to be filmed, so they didn't show that. I clarified that the painting of the faces only happens when they're going into battle—they paint their faces, their horses. There was only one time when they didn't go along with my recommendation. In fact, they got quite mad at me when I told them that making love is very private. You wouldn't ever see a man and wife touching in public. They wouldn't be making love in their teepee with others present. But they didn't change that."

Actress Julie Carmen emphasizes the importance of the authenticity of a role, which comes from having more minorities in influence. "The more Hollywood is influenced by Latin or other ethnic writers, the more inside the culture the writing will spring and it will have more of the specifics. If the accents, mannerisms, point of view is not from the inside, the role loses its cultural authenticity."

Director-writer Julie Dash (*Daughters of the Dust*) believes that the "tiny specifics, the cultural nuances" need to be portrayed in the character. Those specifics may not be understood without drawing on the understanding of a black director, black writer, or black actress. What are they? "Motor habits for one," says Dash. "The way you move. The way you stand. The whole hands akimbo thing, which is African and comes from carrying the baby on one hip. The way you walk with the rhythm, which can be African, Brazilian, Caribbean. You learn this from your mother and father—everything is rhythmized, it's part of the religion. Everything is in motion."

But Dash also sees the need to move past the cultural specifics to also seeing ethnic minorities doing much the same things that everyone does: "I'd like to see African-American woman traveling the world, showing that we're citizens of the world, that we perhaps grow up with a desire to be a trapeze artist. that we have shops, that we desire perfumes, that we have a zest for life, and that not every confrontation in our lives is racial. So much media bears little resemblance to what our lives are about. It confuses other cultures about us."

Nancy Kwan agrees. "Although an Asian can bring another flavor to the role, if the only flavor you're bringing is your Asian features, it's not enough. We're Americans. We eat hamburgers, talk like Americans, go to college. We should be able to go for any role, regardless of the color, and be judged on our acting ability. Although some roles are written specifically for an Asian, or Hispanic, or white, many are not culturally specific, like a lawyer or a doctor. Those should be open to all."

Producer Martha Chang clarifies, "It's more about individuals than about ethnicity. It's not about ethnicity, it's about equality."

When the roles have been open to all, many of the ethnic actresses in nonspecific roles have been hits. Rosie Perez appeared in *White Men Can't Jump,* written and directed by Ron Shelton, who saw her potential and saw no reason why the main male character couldn't have a Hispanic girlfriend. She later went on to play in *Fearless,* again in a role that was not written for a Latina but that could be filled by an actress from any culture.

In both these instances, Rosie brought her ethnic flavor to the role, influencing its interpretation.

BEYOND HOLLYWOOD: STEREOTYPING OF OTHER CULTURES

Women are not only stereotyped in Hollywood, they are stereotyped all over the world.

Nandini Pressad from New Delhi, India, has studied the depiction of woman in Indian cinema. India is one of the largest producers of films in the world, creating about eight hundred a year. But more doesn't mean better.

The stereotype begins by defining women narrowly, as bad or good. "If women smoke and drink and wear trousers, they are bad," explains Pressad. "If they conform to what is socially acceptable, they are good. A woman's place is within the four walls of the home. If she steps out, then she's bad."

Pressad adds, "The majority of our women live below the poverty line, in the rural areas. They are invisible where the media is concerned. They are never depicted in the films. It's only the middle-class, urban-based women who are shown in the films."

Are these narrow depictions of women changing? Pressad sees some small changes, as more women begin directing, writing, and producing. But the change is limited, "because most people do not go to see films about women. So these films are in the alternate cinema. Most of the mainstream films are violent; the woman is very often looked upon as belonging to the man."

Dr. Rasha Al-Disuqi gives workshops on the image of Muslim women in the media. Egypt, like India, produces a great many films and television shows, with 90 percent of families being reached by television. Al-Disuqi says, "Media is a major cultural tool that leaves its imprint on the eyes of people, and shapes the attitudes of an entire society. We don't see women in media as mother, as a woman raising good children, nor as women who can influence society."

Dr. Amany Aboul Fadl Farag gave a workshop with Al-Disuqi at the fourth United Nations Women's Conference, held in Beijing in 1995, sharing statistics that show that the greatest proportion of female characters in films from Muslim countries are dancers or prostitutes; some show her as the love interest but not identified with any job, and a few showed her as a nurse or humble worker.[6]

In Egypt, as in India, many of the images of women are influenced by Western culture. They not only see the stereotypes of women in their own culture, but see the stereotype of women in Western culture through the many American films exported to these countries. "In Muslim countries, 52 percent of the females in advertisements are Caucasian," says Dr. Farag. "We see the Western model of beauty."

IF IT MAKES MONEY, EVERYTHING'S OK

Although many male and female writers and directors affirm their support of seeing more minorities on the screen as part of their overall desire for greater diversity, they also understand that Hollywood perceives a problem in giving them this opportunity. The stereotype is that films with minorities don't make money. The stereotype has been proven wrong—again and again.

"*Daughters of the Dust* has a large crossover audience," says Julie Dash. "When it was playing downtown, there were little old ladies with mink coats waiting in line next to the blacks dressed in African style."

"Everything bottom-line is monetary in this business," says Nancy Kwan. "If it does well, if it's a success, then there's going to be a bandwagon, and others will make a similar film." And they did. The studios followed *The World of Suzie Wong* with *Flower Drum Song*, a film with an all-Asian cast; it also made money. It still took more than twenty years for another Asian studio film to be made, *The Joy Luck Club*, which also made money. Minorities can be marketable, both in front of and behind the scenes.

When the market is tapped by doing films that include minorities, audiences find their lives touched by the universal story and by insight into another culture. "Had I not been a Chinese-American woman, would I have been so passionate about *Joy Luck Club*?" asks producer Janet Yang. "It was an almost spiritual awakening of sorts to read for the first time something that so accurately reflected my own life. But other people had gotten excited about the book who aren't Asian-American and aren't women, thereby proving that you don't have to be from that culture to want to see the film."

Dash sums it up: "Everybody needs their lives affirmed on the big screen. The dominant culture has a great many films. We're inundated with the macho male film. But as women, we don't have those same choices available."

EXPANDING THE VIEW

Women filmmakers are expanding the view of characters by recognizing the vast diversity of women. In the mid-1980s, Donna Dietch wrote the script for, produced, and directed *Desert Hearts,* one of the first films to deal with lesbians. In the 1990s, a number of films from a lesbian viewpoint have been produced, including *Sister, My Sister, The Incredibly True Adventures of Two Girls in Love, Bar Girls, Bushwhacked,* and *Claire of the Moon.*

Another of these films is *Go Fish,* written by Rose Troche and Guinevere Turner, directed by Troche, and produced by Christine Vachon. "I think that there have always been films that dealt with lesbian sexuality or alternative sexuality," says Vachon. "*Go Fish* was a breakthrough to a certain degree because it alerted Hollywood that enough people would go see such a film to make it a modest art-house success."

But is Hollywood homophobic? "No," says Vachon, "because money is not homophobic. And ultimately I don't think they really care that much about how the money is made and what audience is going to see it, as long as there is one."

What do lesbian films have to tell us about women's lives and women characters? "We're seeing women on screen having a life. *Go Fish* presupposes a lesbian space, so that the film really begins after the coming out has ended. And it's not about women discovering their sexuality, it's just about them living with it in a place where they feel comfortable. That's very, very revolutionary. So this is a film where that fight is over and people are living their lives. It's about whatever heterosexual movies are about."

Grace Kitto is the producer, Jayne Chard is the originator and director, and Bryony Lavery is the writer of the first episode and synopsis for a lesbian detective series, *Headley*, funded by British Channel 4. "Lesbian and gay relationships, like heterosexual relationships, are not homogeneous," says Kitto. "It's partly this variety and color that we want to show in this series."

These filmmakers see the importance of creating a series with lesbian main characters. "In lesbian films we play the center stage," says Bryony Lavery. "We're not pushed to the edge. Some people have said to us, 'Why is she [Headley] a lesbian detective?' I say, 'Why isn't she?' " By creating a lesbian role for mainstream audiences, they see that they can break certain stereotypes about women. "We're creating clever, sassy, funny women, some of whom are lesbian," says Jayne Chard.

THE YOUNG AND THE OLD

Diversity covers the broad spectrum of female characters, including the young and the old. The woman over forty has to look carefully to find any woman her age on-screen, any women that reflect her own issues.

Actress Susan Clark says that television is somewhat better "because the audience is women, and there are more powerful women in television in positions of power, but we are still under the aegis of the male. Women over fifty are usually playing the neurotic mother or grandmother, the victim."

Russian actress Inna Churikova contrasts this with how men do over fifty. "The interest shown in male actors is almost the same, regardless of their age, whereas interest in an actress starts to fade as soon as she crosses that frontier between youth and maturity. It is replaced by a melancholy and sadness. This is the usual reaction of directors and scriptwriters when they see before them a woman whose face shows the mark of time. But why? Why? A woman is interesting in her youth and in maturity. And it's interesting to know how she has acquired her wrinkles."[7]

Sophia Loren also attests to the difficulty of good roles—anywhere. "A good movie is hard to find not only for women of my age, but also younger than me. Because I think that men write for men—and they don't write for women."[8] Another actress over forty defined it even more forcefully: "We've been relegated to the sexual trash heap."

Although some male actors over fifty, sixty, and seventy—Paul Newman, Sean Connery, Al Pacino, Robert de Niro, Jack Nicholson, Dustin Hoffman, Anthony Hopkins, Alec Guinness, Sir Laurence Olivier, Clint Eastwood, Brian Dennehy—have no trouble finding great roles, most actresses over forty find they are no longer wanted.

But the myth—that no one wants to see the woman over forty—is not the truth. Older women have appeared in many successful films. Jessica Tandy appeared in *Driving Miss Daisy, To Dance with the White Dog, Nobody's Fool,* and *Foxfire*; Katharine Hepburn in *On Golden Pond;* Shirley Maclaine in *Terms of Endearment. Murder She Wrote,* with Angela Lansbury, has been one of the longest running and most successful television series. But, according to writer Ann Gibbs, there's a difference. "Jessica is written as an active working writer—they don't make a point about her age. Executives think that at sixty you're walking with a cane and your hair is white."

Whereas the woman over forty is rarely seen in films, and the woman over fifty is rarely seen in television, the older woman in many cultures is one of the most important female characters in fairy tales, in literature, and in real life.

Producer Renée Missel (*Nell*) sees this character as "the one that you come to with your troubles. She's the one who settles disputes. She's the one who heals. She passes on wisdom and tells stories to the children. She's useful in most cultures, but she's not useful in American society." In literature she's called the Crone.

Missel explains why the woman over fifty is not wanted. "She's postmenopause. In Hollywood that's considered over the hill. She's no longer fertile. She's no longer defined by her sexual function. She no longer fits a sexual stereotype."

Writer Naomi Foner agrees. "The movie industry has an unwritten law that says when your body is no longer perfect, you're not a suitable subject for films." Yet for many women like Foner, the most interesting women are over forty. "I think many of the stories we're telling aren't worth telling about people who are under forty. They're too predictable and boring. There's no wisdom. After the age of forty we're caught up with things worth paying attention to. By the age of forty we've accumulated enough wisdom so that our choices about what we do with it are more interesting."

"We're third-act people," says writer Ann Gibbs, who began writing for television in the 1970s. "We've been through major crises, major diseases, the big life situations have happened to us at least once or twice. We have endurance, a sense of hope and continuity, a sense that these little petty issues that are driving the world crazy today are not important. We're survivors. We're fighters. We have buoyancy."

Gibbs believes there's definitely a market for stories about women over forty because these women are leading the kind of exciting lives that make for good drama. "There are women who are divorcing after twenty years and dating for the first time and finding romance. There are stories about women, now freed from the care of children, who are pursuing new career dreams, expressing themselves through art. They're traveling, going on adventures, opening up their lives to new possibilities. There's a big audience living these stories who would love to see them on the screen. Unless television matures as America grays, the large aging baby boomer audience will find other ways to spend their evenings. Think of the impact on advertising revenues!"

Whatever age the character, the scripts are not written by older writers. "I think the executives have convinced themselves that their audience is younger and you have to be younger and have younger characters to write for that audience," says writer Hindi Brooks. "They don't want to feel as if they're dealing with their parents by hiring an older writer. I've actually heard a producer admit that he didn't want to hire anyone who has more experience than he did. And agents were told on *Golden Girls* not to bring in any gray-haired writers."

What is lost by this attitude? "There's no question that the young simply do not bring to writing the same level of craft and life experience as those of us who have been doing it for many years," says Brooks. Both Brooks and Gibbs admit that younger writers may work better for a hip show that demands up-to-date youth language and a particular mind-set, but they affirm the importance of their own contributions. Ann Gibbs considers the best solution to be to "blend young and old to get the best from all of us."

So how do writers respond under these circumstances? Some begin working with younger male partners. Others put a man's name on the script. If a writer has many credits, such as black-and-white credits which imply their age, "We just lob off the first twenty years of credits," says Ann Gibbs. But there's a problem: "Those were my best credits, so I had no résumé left because I haven't been able to work for a few years." Others will do the occasional charity script. "That's when a writer or producer brings in a senior writer who can no longer sell but needs to sell one script a season to keep her Writers Guild insurance current. The senior writer does most of the writing, but the younger one takes the credit—and more money."

Women writers are working on this problem. They're changing awareness by founding woman's advocacy groups and age-awareness committees at the guilds, including the Screen Actors Guild, the Directors Guild, and the Writers Guild. The Academy of Television Arts and Sciences did a one-day seminar on ageism in 1995. Women writers have written articles and completed an eighteen-minute film, called *Power and Fear,* about ageism, and have formed a production company made up of people over forty.

THE GIRL-CHILD

Just as you rarely see the older woman in films and television, you rarely see the girl under thirteen in feature films and as the main child character in television. Most girls, when they are portrayed in a film like *Clueless* or *The Babysitters Club,* are seventeen or eighteen, and thereby are portrayed as sexually attractive, sexually interested, and sexually aware.

If you made a list of the family and children's films of the last five years, most of them have boy protagonists: *Home Alone, Home Alone II, Honey, I Blew Up the Kid, Angels in the Outfield, Lassie, The Adventures of Yellow Dog, Man of the House, Pagemaster, Tom and Huck, Black Sheep, Blank Check, Toy Story, The Santa Clause, Angus,* and *Black Stallion.* A few have several children as protagonists: *Honey, I Shrunk the Kids, Mrs. Doubtfire, Now and Then.* Only a few feature a girl protagonist: *Casper, The Secret of Bear Mountain, The Little Princess, Beetlejuice, The Secret Garden,* and *The Secret of Roan Inish.*

"This all starts in childhood," says one television director. "Little girls want to be little boys, but a little boy would rather die than be a little girl." It also happens when most of the decision makers were boys rather than girls.

There are not enough films for girls for anyone to know what kind of crossover audiences are possible. *Casper* did well, but *The Little Princess,* in spite of some of the best reviews of the year, did not. Although there was much conjecturing around Hollywood about why it failed—whether the title didn't attract boys, or because it sounded too sentimental—each of these failures convince the powers-that-be that little girls are not a commercially viable market.

Some girls, such as ten-year-old Zoe Erwin (a young aspiring writer and daughter of producer-writer Ellen Erwin), are refusing to "see one more film about boys." Why? "It's not fair," says Zoe. "Why is it always a boy and a dog having incredible adventures? I don't get it! Why can't it be a girl? I think girls are just as powerful and as brave as boys. They shouldn't be denied. Besides, all the movies about boys are the same movie over and over. All boys, same topic. I'm not a boy. And if I were, I'd feel the same way."

Women executives believe there is a need and a market for girls and are tapping it. Margaret Loesch, president of the Fox Children's Network, says, "We have two strong girls in our show *The Mighty Morphin Power Rangers. X-Men* has three women and three men. The women are equally powerful, and the men accept the women in the shows as equal. And boys watching the show are totally accepting of the females because they, too, are powerful."

Geraldine Laybourne, formerly president of Nickelodeon and now president of Disney/ABC Cable Networks, also confronts the issue of the girl-child. "In general, the things that are unique to us are the fact that we include kids in the process, so we are making sure that what we do is not some adult view of what is cute or what is groovy for kids. We continually try to strive for creative innovations. We basically respect kids' intelligence and don't fall into dumb and dumber kinds of ideas.

"We do have girl heroines," continues Laybourne. "Our most popular show on Nickelodeon, which is popular with boys and girls, is *Clarissa Explains It All.* It has a girl right in the center of it."

Feature-film writer Caroline Thompson and others would like to change the world for children through the stories they write and by giving girls strong role models. "I want to give children the opportunity to be compassionate," says Thompson. "Get them to see they're not alone and that there are other people who feel the way they feel. On a more personal level, I want to provide a role model for the girl-child, in terms of profession for when she grows up. I hope young girls naturally assume that they can do anything they want to when they grow up."

Linda Woolverton feels a similar mission, because she recognized that Belle in *Beauty and the Beast* would be a role model for girls. "When I was creating Belle, I received some pressure to have her manipulate, or be tricky and sneaky, or boss Gaston around. But I wanted Belle to be feminine, to be a lady. Belle manages to get what she wants without being insulting or combative. She's smart enough to work the situation, strong enough not to be nasty. Belle is not influenced by looks; even though Gaston is handsome, it's the Beast she falls in love with. She's not swayed by public opinion. She's lonely and a bit eccentric; the only way she can live in that town is through her books. And she's not a shrinking violet. There's a lot of Belle in me—a lot of me in Belle, but she's nicer than me, I think."

INTERACTIVE—THE NEW TECHNOLOGY

In the new emerging markets, such as interactive, girls are also stereotyped, if not invisible. Women, like Laura Groppe, founder of Girl Games, are looking for ways to make interactive computer games more appealing to girls.

The interactive market has been almost exclusively male dominated. There are more than nineteen million girls between the ages of seven and seventeen in the United States, and female video-game players are increasing at a rate of 25 percent a year. Yet there is a 13–1 ratio of males to females pictured on game covers. In the forty-seven top-selling video games of 1994, one-third of female characters were treated as victims. According to *Sex Roles Journal,* 85 percent of young women say they would play more computer games if there were more titles designed with them in mind.[9]

Laura Groppe has studied this market and agrees girls want something different than the boys. "Girls like some of what boys like, such as action games, but the action games that are out there are limited in terms of what they can do. You can't do much with the characters. For the girl, the game becomes redundant and repetitive and boring. She seems to require, on the whole, more stimulation and more challenge than the boys do."

What kind of challenge do the girls want? "They want to have their intuition challenged. So we need to build intuition into the design. The girl will bring a different point of view to the game. She'll figure it out differently."

Writer Carolyn Miller, who has worked on the highly successful *Carmen San Diego* CD-ROM series, is in the forefront of the rapidly growing field of interactive "edutainment" products, which combine games with educational themes. She too has seen the difference between boys and girls, and between the male and female writers who create the games. "Boys have generally liked the twitch games—where you move your thumb and operate a mouse or a joystick. There has been very little plot to these games, and virtually no dialogue. Mostly things killing things. It's men who create those games. But when you get into the more story-driven games, there are more women creating them."

One element that Miller adds is character. "Many of these older games had a very rudimentary idea of character. But as the technology improved, both in terms of animation and live action, it became possible to add more dialogue and develop more well-rounded characters. I've been hired a number of times to work on characters, either to dimensionalize the stick figure characters or to work on new characters. I've added personality and emotions and reactions."

She also had to fight, often with an otherwise all-male development team, to include more female characters. "Men don't even notice when all the major characters in a story are males; they are simply blind to it. In one case we were adapting a children's book, turning it into a CD-ROM, and the only female was the mother of one of the boy characters. This mother not only played a minor part but was also fairly negative; shrill and bossy. I managed to convince the development team to change one of the boy characters to a girl, and to add a new female character. We also modified the mother character to give her more dimension."

But just substituting a female for a male character is not enough. "You need to ask girls what they're lacking, what they want," says Groppe. "Girls want some sort of identification with the character.

They don't always need a girl character—it could be a boy or an animal—but they need to be able to relate to the main character."

Groppe's staff is mostly female. "We're developing and designing content for girls, so it's critical that women are the creators. If you put together a competent team of women—a female programmer, a female designer, a female writer, a female art director, a female sound artist—they will naturally and intuitively hone in on what is needed and weave these layers together more readily than if you have men involved. There's a sensibility from women. We put a lot of faith in our intuition."

This female point of view in the creation of Girl Games is changing the technology. Says Groppe, "Technology has evolved up to this point with very little input from females. Think about the directions that technology will take once women start to say, 'This would be much cooler if this box did this or if I could do this from my car.' This will bring about some radical new innovative hardware and software. When we brainstorm with girls, they come up with outstanding, creative ideas about what they want from technology in the future. We are thinking of entirely new concepts about games. These games are not about point and click, get a clue, move forward. They're not about running around and shooting. It's entertainment and activities and tools and puzzles and social interaction—but it's not games as you know them right now."

ADVOCACY

Women recognize that female characters need to be improved. Many are trying to do that—in any way they can.

Casting directors Jane Jenkins and Janet Hirshenson have their own company and have cast such films as *The American President* and *In the Line of Fire*. "When a script comes in for casting, many of the roles are nondescript, such as judge, doctor," says Jenkins. "We can suggest that maybe the judge could be a woman or a black or an

Asian. Frequently we go through the script and there are several supporting roles that we could make women's roles or ethnic roles. Usually the producer and director are open to that. When you change casting, it has to be for the benefit of the piece." And it often is.

Hirshenson adds, "Frequently, having women in some of these parts adds to the richness of the piece. And it's a truer reflection of what the world is about, since there are now many successful female doctors, judges, and most other professional roles."

Women are leading the way toward opening up opportunities for themselves, but also for others.

Some women activists are very vocal about what they want to see changed and have been for some time. In the late 1970s the Association of Asian-Pacific/American Artists was founded to try to change hiring practices and increase the presence of Asians. There have been some breakthroughs. The first Asian-American series appeared on television in the mid-1990s, *All-American Girl,* with Margaret Cho.

Blacks have had stronger characters on television and have played in breakthrough roles in films, such as Whitney Houston in *Bodyguard* and the successful black ensemble film *Waiting to Exhale.*

UNICEF (the United Nations children's fund) produces a television show called *Meena* for India, Bangladesh, Pakistan, Nepal, and Africa, to change attitudes about the girl-child in these countries. This UNICEF series is working to change the portrayal of the girl-child in the media, thereby changing the behavior toward her in society.

There is some evidence of changes in consciousness in female roles. By the mid-1990s the captain of the Star Trek flagship was a woman. Even James Bond's women were going through some subtle changes. Casting directors Jenkins and Hirshenson cast the James Bond film *License to Kill,* and in that film and also in *Goldeneye,* they see an attempt to move away from the babe image. "There was an attempt to make the woman less of a Bond girl, more of a character, more in charge," says Jane Jenkins. "This is partly because a woman, Barbara Broccoli, is now producing the Bond films. Certainly in the last Bond movie James did not jump in and out of bed quite so blithely. There is a consciousness about the AIDS epidemic and female sensibilities."

Television actress Donna Mills sees that roles have improved. "When I was first starting out as an actress, there were few roles. You could play someone's wife, someone's mistress, or someone's secretary. I'm less limited now. I've played a doctor, a policewoman, a teacher, a mogul, and an executive."

Some of this has changed because "women have much more power," says Mills. "We're not going to be glamorous and perfectly coiffed because we're playing real women and that's not the way it is. Glamour still sells, of course, but it's not the only thing anymore."

Actress Sharon Stone believes that "the power of women in film is now accelerating like it was in the 1940s. Women just weren't bringing people to the theater in recent years, primarily because the roles weren't there for them. People are bankrolling films where women are the central characters. More and more we can voice ourselves. Until recently, these characters that were written were a man's idea of a woman, his idea of how he wishes a woman was, but very rarely did they actually demonstrate anything to do with a real female personality. . . . As women we have to recognize that we are equal to but not the same as men, and demonstrations of power can take different forms. It's up to women to define themselves as powerful."

The clout of female actresses such as Stone can do much to nurture better roles, and roles written by women for women. Stone says, "I try to find some pictures that support my soul. Scripts have to be written that support the female character . . . they have to be written and they can be written by women for women. . . . What we have to do is write inspirational material that supports and embraces the female spirit. I have a pro-woman agenda."[10]

Nandini Pressad in India sees the potential for great changes in the future. "We now have a lot more television channels. Unfortunately, since we do not have enough product, a lot of them are clips from Hindu songs and dances and stereotypical Hindu films. But this could change. Because of so many channels opening up, there is more opportunity for women now to make programs that might change their portrayal."

There is far more work to be done. What we see in films directly influences us in our lives. It either empowers us or diminishes us. But it's not just in story and character that the woman is limited, but in the area of sex, love, and romance. This too has to change before females are represented fairly in the media.

19

CASE STUDY

Liv Ullmann

SCANDINAVIAN ACTRESS Liv Ullmann is known for her strong and deeply layered women characters. She has appeared in many films, including *Scenes from a Marriage, The Passion of Anna, Cries and Whispers, Persona,* and *Autumn Sonata.* She is now writing and directing. Two of her own films have appeared in Europe and in film festivals.

What is needed to create great women characters?

"I played so many different characters in film and theatre in Hollywood, on Broadway, in Scandinavia. I grew up working with maybe the best director for women, Ingmar Bergman, who also writes about women. Many men can capture a woman character. Ingmar Bergman did it with *Scenes from a Marriage.* In theater I've done Henry Ibsen; like Ingmar Bergman, he saw women very clearly. But they don't capture the woman with the absolute closeness that only a woman writer or director can do. It's seen through the experience and the frustrations of a man in terms of a woman. What is missing is that they have to see through their emotional language, which is different from a woman's because they live in a very different world.

"Men and women are both complex, but it comes out in different ways. So many men can't reflect on their lives because they've put on the uniform, they've put on their breastplates. Their armour is so deep within them that they don't know about themselves. That is why often when they write, the writing comes from somewhere in the armour but it's not from the very depths of them. As long as they are experiencing that, how can they describe a woman? When playing these women's parts written by men, you have to add a lot of your own interpretation.

"I am now directing my own scripts, which gives me enormous joy. I know I can depict the woman in a very different way. What I really want to say is what we feel. As women, we come from a different land and we express a different kind of language. I've done two films. The first one is *Sofie,* about a woman who had many dreams about what she wanted to do with life, with love, with work, but she doesn't get what she wanted. At the end, she reaches some understanding; she has found that life was all right.

"The second movie, *Christine,* is based on the book *Kristin Lavransdatter* by Sigrid Undset. It takes place in the Middle Ages and is *the* love story. It's the love story between two middle-aged people. It's the love story between man and God. No man could have written this story. It was written about everything she knew about being a woman. It's her blood in it. I understand her blood because I'm a woman. These kinds of movies have to be written by women who dare to say, 'That's how I feel.'

"We need great artists to write and direct this kind of more feminine material, great actors to play it, and great producers to embrace it. We need to do it in such an artistic way that the audience will connect with it, even though it's unusual. I hope these kinds of films change how people see women. You can't always change how people look at things, but you must hope for it, and that's why you continue to do this work.

"As women we have to feel that we are strong and able. We have to stop being the victim. That's how we're brought up to be, 'poor me.' We are brought up to think that men will feel sorry for us and want to be protective. But victim women frighten men and in the end they hate her. We have to get away from that.

"We have to feel good about ourselves as we age. We don't age in the same way as men. They become wiser and more wonderful and we become middle-aged and invisible. That's what men say. We mustn't say that. We must feel we are growing. We are wonderful. We are better at fifty than forty, at sixty we're better than at fifty, and we must take pride in that. We must not let men take away our dignity and self-respect. We fought so long to feel good about ourselves.

"As more women get our souls on the screen, I hope more people will see that's where the beauty is. I'm worried about the women in the States. I'm seeing more and more actors and actresses I admire and they look strange to me. So many of them have had plastic surgery. I'm thinking, In ten years' time, are people going to forget what a middle-aged woman looks like? It's terrible. I don't know how it's going to be reversed because little children are starting to buy into that. I believe a face is beautiful when it's four years old and when it's seventy, but what I love about the face is the expression, what comes from the inside. On the whole, European actors have kept away from the beauty myth.

"For me, the creative process has been to start to understand what I should write about, or reasons why I shouldn't write. I shouldn't write to be loved. I shouldn't write to be admired. I should write because I want to express something.

"I don't know if anything I will ever do will change a little thing in the world, but I feel responsible to myself, to what I truly believe. That's the only way that one can live. If you live for the box office, if you live to be understood by a big mass of people, it may give you something in the moment but in the end it gives you nothing. There's only one true voice—what you feel inside."

PART FIVE

SEX, LOVE, AND ROMANCE

SOME IMPORTANT BREAKTHROUGHS FOR WOMEN

1896: May Irwin and John Rice share the first on-screen kiss, in the short film *The Widow Jones*. This led to a demand for screen censorship.[1]

1914: In *Hypocrites,* directed by Lois Weber, actress Margaret Edwards performs the first nude love scene.

1914: Theda Bara introduces the vamp role, in *A Fool That Was,* giving rise to a genre of vampire films.

1920: Gloria Swanson introduces the bathroom scene, in *Male and Female,* presenting the inherent sexuality of a woman taking a bath.

1926: Mae West's play *Sex* lands her in jail for obscenity; she is later signed by Paramount, where she writes and controls her own work, saving the studio from financial ruin and revolutionizing notions of sexuality in America.

1927: Clara Bow introduces the definition of sex appeal when she becomes the girl who has "it," in *It*.

1934: Frances Goodrich and Albert Hackett write *The Thin Man,* showing that romance and professional equality can go together.

1970s: Mary Richards of *The Mary Tyler Moore Show* implies that she's on the Pill; it's the first time a "nice girl" admits it on a network show.

1976: Lina Wertmuller writes and directs *Swept Away,* a film where the rich woman and the deckhand switch roles.

1983: Barbra Streisand directs, acts, and produces *Yentl,* the first sound film where a woman has performed all three functions, with a story that combines romance and a woman's search for an equal opportunity to learn.

1984: Candida Royalle begins Femme Productions, creating adult sexual-themed films from a woman's point of view.

1993: Jane Campion is nominated for an Academy Award for best director of *The Piano,* a sensual love story from a woman's point of view.

20

CHANGING THE POINT OF VIEW

Sex is an emotion in motion. . . . Love is
what you make it and who you make it with.[2]
—*Mae West*

TO SOME MEN, women are sexual objects. Women regard themselves as sexual beings. Rarely is the woman's image of herself seen in films—and women would like to change that.

Sexual object. What does that imply? The sought-after object that is pursued, won, conquered, overcome, and possessed. She's the trophy wife, the glamorous girlfriend who is there to serve the man, define the man, and be defined by him. She is his.

The idea of the sexual object also implies manipulation of—or often by—the coquette. Distrust. Sometimes betrayal and deceit. And it implies passion, excitement, tension, and a grand climax—all the elements that make up good drama.

So what's the problem? Some sex does involve control and possession. Some relationships involve deceit and manipulation. The problem is that this approach is limited, one-dimensional, often offensive, and a misinterpretation of who women are, what they feel, what they want, and of their complex sexual responses.

Many woman filmmakers not only want to expand the view, but

they believe that their viewpoint has the potential to be more erotic, at least as passionate, and at least as exciting to men as it is to women. They suggest that creating the sexual being demands a different view of the female character. It demands mutuality, not an unequal relationship. The emphasis would change from the focus on the sex act to a focus on the sensuality and intimacy and love surrounding sex. Sexual issues would be explored in greater depth. The complexity of women, in both its negative and positive aspects, would be more fully expressed.

What is a sexual being? "A sexual being is someone who has pleasure and delights in her sexuality, in her own sexual life. Sexuality is part of her relationship to the world," explains writer Naomi Foner. "If you want to engage with a sexual being, then you're engaged with someone whose sexuality is equal to yours and is as full of energy as yours. It's a mutuality."

What is a sexual object? Foner sees a sexual object as "something you use. It's almost inanimate. It has no energy coming from itself. It's a toy."

As women write and direct more sexual scenes, the images of sexuality will change. The differences in approach will become more apparent. What can we expect to see? How are women directors, writers, and producers thinking about sex? They begin by thinking about what is erotic.

EROTIC IS . . . ?

A number of woman filmmakers are exploring the erotic in film and television. Marilyn Vance-Straker created *Erotic Confessions* as a television series. German producer Regina Ziegler produced a series of short films about erotica, *Erotic Tales. Erotique* explores the erotic through four short films directed by Lizzie Borden, Monika Treut, Clara Law, and Ana Maria Magalhaes (although Magalhaes's film was cut in postproduction). Candida Royalle produces adult films from a female perspective. Susie Bright writes and consults about the erotic, and her books and speeches have become hot sellers. If *sex* is the word emphasized by men, the word emerging in the female's vocabulary is *erotic*.

Elizabeth Engstrom gives workshops on writing the erotic scene. "Eros is, of course, the god of love. So 'erotic' implies a love-based arousal. Sexual, of course, but one can find sexual overtones in everything. We are spiritual beings locked in animals' bodies, so everything we do is motivated, I believe, by our baser natures in conflict with our spiritual yearnings. There is a broad range of sexuality, but it's only when we add love that everything can be erotic."

Producer Ziegler explores the erotic through her *Erotic Tales*, shown at the Cannes Film Festival in 1994 and on German television. "Erotic is the whole of life," she says. "Erotic means fantasy and imagination; it warms the heart; it brings joy to human beings and to the human condition. Erotic draws upon a partnership or relationship between a man and woman. It's about loving life, giving of yourself, being open and spontaneous. A voice can be very erotic—just talking on the phone and listening to the voice of another can create an erotic feeling, an erotic experience."

A female view of the erotic in film is elusive. It's rarely seen in Hollywood movies. Few mainstream female writers or directors have explored this topic, with the exception of Jane Campion in *The Piano* and Martha Coolidge in *Ramblin' Rose*. Films such as *Witness, The Big Easy, The Thomas Crown Affair,* in which strong erotic images do exist, are written and directed by men, with the male protagonist as the main character and the overriding viewpoint. In order to understand the female view of sexuality, we have to look to the art-house films, foreign films, and the adult films.

Marilyn Vance-Straker, formerly a costume designer, has now turned to producing. She is focusing on erotic subject matter for a series on HBO called *The Erotic Confessions*. "Erotic involves the viewer, not just as a voyeur, but with the sensation that you are close to the action, that you are there. From the male vision, everything erotic becomes voyeuristic. Through the woman's eyes it becomes more participatory. We want to draw the audience into the experience without embarrassment, without titillation."

Candida Royalle is a writer, director, and producer of adult films—clearly a problematic area for many people, especially women. Of all views of sexuality, the pornographic has been the most degrading and harmful to women. But it's not the traditional pornographic view that interests Royalle. She has studied psychology and physiology and has made her own observations about the difference between male and female erotica. Her work emphasizes sex, of course, but takes a very different view of sex than the usual X-rated, NC-17–rated, or even most R-rated films. She emphasizes sensuality, caring, and love as part of the sexual act. Many experts agree with her approach. Her work has been endorsed by some feminist groups and by medical practitioners for using safe sexual practices and promoting positive sexual role-modeling in her films.

She began her company, Femme Productions, in the early 1980s, feeling that the way sexuality had been portrayed on screen was exploitive and untruthful. She felt that the sexually explicit film could have a positive function. "Originally people looked at adult films to just get off, but I think a lot of people use it to learn something," explains Royalle. "We really have had very little sex education until now. I saw that men would look at pornography and it did not teach them anything about the way women work. It was perpetuating a lot of misinformation." Hollywood often reinforces this misinformation by ignoring or diffusing the current issues around sexuality or by pretending they don't exist because it's just fantasy.

"Every year or two there's a big Hollywood movie that somehow conveys the nature of sexuality in America," says director Lizzie Borden, who has explored sexuality in *Love Crimes, Working Girls,* and *Erotique.* "There's been *Fatal Attraction* and *Indecent Proposal* and *Disclosure.* So often these movies either present young women as commodities or show this culture's fear of unbridled women's sexuality."

To Borden, these films ignore the sexual issues. "In my films I don't want to exploit sexuality, but to explore it."

She gives an example of exploring sexuality in her film *Working Girls*, about prostitutes. Part of that exploration means recognizing that how the woman feels may be quite different than how the man feels. The woman's issues around the act may be quite different than the man's issues. "What I want to do is to show sexuality in a way it hasn't been shown before. In *Working Girls* I was trying to show what a woman feels in the bedroom if she's taking money for sex. At what point is she just going through the motions? At what point is she disgusted? At what point is she vaguely turned on? All of these things go against the current mythology of prostitution."

Adding emotions, exploring issues, means broadening the palette of how film looks at sex. In 1995 a number of films dealt with strippers, showgirls, and prostitutes, including *Showgirls*, *Leaving Las Vegas*, *Jade*, *Mighty Aphrodite*, and *Casino*. Actresses Elisabeth Shue, Mira Sorvino, and Sharon Stone were nominated for Academy Awards for their roles, continuing a long tradition that began when Janet Gaynor won the first Academy Award for her role as a prostitute in *Street Angel* in 1928. However, all these actresses appeared in films written and directed by men, from the male point of view.

Lizzie Borden sees this view as limiting. "In Hollywood films, sexuality is either rape or romance. There's nothing in between. Healthy sexuality is about whatever makes a person what they are. It's part of the character. That's the kind of thing that has to be presented."

Exploring sexuality cinematically involves using different images. For many women, sensuality is emphasized above sexuality. These women begin by paying attention to the context in which sex occurs.

21

IN THE REALM OF THE SENSES

FILM IS A sensual media. It paints its story through the use of visuals and sound, by showing touch, and with the capability of implying taste and smell. It's a particularly good medium for communicating the woman's emphasis on sensuality.

"Women are much more subtle and much more sensual," says Candida Royalle. "The high level of estrogen in our bodies makes our entire body an erogenous zone. It causes us to be a lot more sensually aware. We do like the soft touch and a variety of touch. The real importance in my films is the sensuality. I try to deemphasize intercourse and highlight all the other wonderful things that we tend to rush past and forget about." What are these things? "Women are the ones who bring in the beauty, the texture, and the different aspects to the love act."

Women see part of sexuality as setting up a sensual context, creating private rituals which nurture themselves. They often involve touch, sight, smell.

Writer Laura Esquivel (*Like Water for Chocolate*) uses images of cooking in her novel and film and discusses how the act of eating converts into the act of love where "the man becomes the passive receiver and the woman the active giver. A woman's energy, blended into the smell, the taste, the textures, penetrates the body of the man, sultry, voluptuous, turning the pleasure of eating and the pleasure of sex into one and the same."[3]

Writer Hesper Anderson chose sensual images in *Children of a Lesser God* to communicate Sarah's sexuality. These were reinforced by the work of director Randa Haines. In the film, Sarah swims by herself, nude. "The pool was Sarah's space," says Anderson. "It was all her own. It was her world. It was her free, silent place, and because of her deafness, her other senses were heightened. We wanted to show the sensual quality of moving through water, of practically doing a ballet. There are many sensual images in the film—there's a lot of water. It starts right away, when James [William Hurt] arrives on the ferry. There's the mist and the water, the fog, the wind and the rain, a storm. There are the sensual images of the autumn leaves after he gets off the ferry, Sarah's cat, her dancing. She can't hear the music, but she can feel the vibrations on the floor, and she starts doing this really sensual dance—in her own world, not caring what anyone's thinking or what she's doing, just moving to the vibrations. That was sensual. But she's not doing it for him."

Setting the stage for sex can mean also setting the stage for intimacy. What happens in that space can be quite different when mutuality is emphasized above just getting the woman into bed.

"I think for women that sex is just one aspect, one form of close communication," says Anderson, "but it's really not any more important than any of the others. It's a really close way of expressing love, of sharing the body with another person, but there are times when you share your soul with another person and it's just as intimate as sex. Intimacy is basically really, really close communication in whatever form it takes.

"In the script of *Children of a Lesser God,* I wanted to show the variations of intimacy—sometimes sex is quieter, interspersed with laughter, playfulness, so it's not just sex. Much of this was cut from the film, but some of it was preserved, such as when she plays with shadows on the wall. I wanted to capture some of the gentleness, the vulnerability, those levels of feeling that are more natural to women than to most men in our society."

Any good director and writer thinks visually. Many writers also think sensually and bring those sensual images to the page. The director expresses them and the editor's choices make a film more or less sensual, more or less sexually explicit.

Carol Littleton edited one of the hottest Hollywood films, *Body Heat,* written and directed by Lawrence Kasdan. "One of the reasons why Larry Kasdan wanted a woman editor was that he felt he wanted the built-in censorship that a woman could bring to sexual material. I felt it was teetering toward the pornographic. In fact, we were both aware of how important it is to keep sexual material suggestive and erotic. Isn't it more powerful to show the spark, to capture the chemistry between two people, to imply the erotic connections?"

What does Littleton emphasize? How does she find that spark? "Essentially we're all voyeurs. As an editor, I'm helping influence what we are watching on film and when. I want to emphasize emotion. There are many ways of looking at human emotion, of bringing sensitivity to the characters, of looking at the intricacies of their behavior. Perhaps it is a subtle look, a gesture, a tiny moment of trust that tells us everything. Images can be more powerful than words. I am thinking of the moment when Ned Racine, played by William Hurt, gathers the courage to tell Matty Walker, played by Kathleen Turner, that they are going to murder her husband. They are standing in his office. They embrace in the dim afternoon light. Ned smells her hair, which gives him the courage to make the decision that will change his life forever."

Television director Karen Arthur faced similar choices when directing the television movie *The Rape of Richard Beck.* She recognized that the film could easily be exploitive if the brutality of rape was shown fully. To get around the problem, she resolved it in some of the same ways as Littleton—focusing on emotions and behavior and psychology, not just on the actual act itself. "I was more interested in taking a man who was powerful, totally sure of himself in every realm, and see his fear, helplessness, and impotence, which he never thought he would feel in any situation, and ultimately the humiliation, the pain, and the degradation, and the fact he couldn't forgive himself."

When approaching the sex scene, Arthur focuses on character, not necessarily the event itself or the mechanics. "I'm not interested in how much skin can we show, how turned on can I make the audience. I want them to understand something about the character or something about the relationship if we are exploring two people together. Is she passive? Is there joy or violence in their lovemaking? Is this a give-and-take or just take relationship? How a character makes love tells us who they are."

Arthur looks at all the sensual details to build up the character's sexuality. "The use of music, how somebody undresses, the use of mirrors, how the woman is bathing herself, perfuming herself, getting herself to a place she then offers herself—all the different elements. How much touching do the characters do? How free are they with their bodies? I'm always looking at what helps us understand more about the character at that point."

FLIGHTS OF FANCY
SECRET FANTASIES

In their desire for more realistic images, women do not forget that many films are about fantasy—men's fantasies about themselves, women's fantasies about themselves, men's fantasies about women, women's fantasies about men. In many films women are depicted as men's fantasies, with little exploration of their own fantasy life. Men presume that the woman's fantasy male is Michael Douglas, Harrison Ford, Tom Cruise, Kevin Costner, Brad Pitt, Keanu Reeves. Sometimes they're right; often they're wrong. Men were surprised to hear that women considered one of the sexiest films of the 1980s to be *Witness.* They were puzzled to hear that the fantasy males in 1993 for a number of women were Harvey Keitel in *The Piano,* Tommy Lee Jones in *The Fugitive,* and Anthony Hopkins in *Shadowlands.*

According to research, women's fantasies are different than men's. "Women's fantasies emphasized touching, the partner's feelings, the woman's physical and emotional responses to what was going on, and the mood and ambience of the encounter."[4]

The difference in male and female fantasies can lead to different casting choices by female directors and producers. This is no better illustrated than through the casting of *The Piano.* Producer Jan Chapman discusses what kind of actors they wanted for the film. Their choices were not according to type.

"The traditional casting would have been Sam Neill as Baines, Harvey Keitel as the unwanted husband, and perhaps Michelle Pfeiffer as the beautiful new wife," says Chapman. "But for Baines [Harvey Keitel], we wanted somebody who was not refined or controlled. We considered men who were sometimes taller and younger, but they were not wild enough or driven by their instincts. It was always our idea that Stewart [Sam Neill] would be more obviously attractive, conventional. The studios suggested all sorts of the most marketable actors. But it was never going to be right for us to make the film casting in that kind of way."

Even their casting for Ada changed when they saw the different dimensions that a woman could bring, beyond a particular physical type. "Ada was originally thought of as very tall with a cool beauty. Holly Hunter is of course quite petite," says Chapman. "Holly heard about the part and tested for it. She brought an intensity, a passion to the test that made us change our view."

Fantasies also deal with escape, what women or men want to escape from and escape to. Susan Seidelman explored this idea in several of her films. "Maybe it's a theme I'm obsessed with, but we have our ordinary workaday life and we fantasize. Within all of us there's this feeling of, Wouldn't it be great to escape into another reality? In the case of *Desperately Seeking Susan,* Rosanna Arquette's Roberta was able to escape into a freer world through her obsession with the free-spirited Susan [Madonna] character. In *Dutch Master* there's this dental hygienist who escapes into another world—into a seventeenth-century Dutch painting where she has an erotic adventure."

Whereas *The Piano* and *Desperately Seeking Susan* were films greatly respected by many men and women, other fantasy films are much more controversial.

"*Pretty Woman* shows the knight-in-shining-armor notion," says Lizzie Borden. "If the right man comes along, the woman can be bought and taken out of her life and transformed." Borden calls this a false fantasy rather than a true fantasy. "It's a false myth. It's the same fairy tale that women have been conned into believing for so long, which has prevented women so often from being realistic about what's there, what we want, how to make it happen. It's the old romantic tale that allows you to think your life will be saved by a man. That myth is as alive today as it was twenty years ago. That's part of the reason people were outraged. The realists were saying this doesn't happen to hookers. It romanticizes being a hooker. Certainly Julia Roberts was nothing like any hooker you would ever see on Hollywood Boulevard."

Many women filmmakers are outraged about other films that do not clearly and realistically tell the truth about women. "*Fatal Attraction*, for one," says Monika Treut. "The main character is simply a wimpy female, basically neurotic. And deep down she's quite weak because she has nothing else to do but to pursue this impossible relationship." Women add others to the list: "Many of the films of Joe Eszterhas—*Showgirls*, *Basic Instinct*, *Sliver*, and even *Jagged Edge*—are purely male fantasies, at the expense of the women," says one writer. "All the titillating female-in-sexual-jeopardy films that are on television every night," adds a producer. Some of these films have been successful, but many have flopped. In 1995, four of the biggest "sexual sizzlers" failed—*The Scarlet Letter*, *Jade*, *Showgirls*, and *Kids*. All were written by men.

SEX AND POWER

Sexuality is connected with power in unequal relationships. In many film depictions, the male has it, and the woman is under his control. Few films recognize that prostitution, promiscuity, obsession, and dysfunctional relationships are issues connected with the female's lack of power and lack of choices. Men have their own issues around these subjects. But the way these issues work themselves out for the female is different than how they play out for the male.

"To want to be cherished, honored, respected can be very threatening to some men," says actress Sharon Stone. "When you own your sexuality . . . it forces them to be responsible for their own."[5]

The issue of responsibility is one aspect of sexuality. The potential danger to the woman from certain sexual relationships is another. "It's just too frightening and dangerous for women to have sex," says Lizzie Borden. "Women have to be cautious about the free-for-all sex they had in the 1970s. Although it's an issue for men and women, it affects women differently."

Women comprise the fastest growing number of AIDS cases. The transmission rate from HIV-positive men to their female sexual partners is twenty times higher than the transmission rate from HIV-positive women to their male sexual partners. Yet very few films show sex realistically. Male filmmakers either don't know this, don't care, decide to ignore reality, or decide that sexual behavior on-screen has no relationship to life. This lack of realism in films mirrors a reality that is more dangerous for women than for men.[6]

Many of the female filmmakers I spoke to were concerned about safe sex. "The big problem is that movies so often deal with fantasy, so there's no mention of condoms or safe sex," says Borden. "So the fantasy is we don't have to worry about AIDS. There is this dispensing of reality." Borden sees some hope in the new films. "In the more hip Generation X movies, you see the condoms. Those shows are based on what real people in real situations would do."

Since male filmmakers have more power over these images of female sexuality than women filmmakers, their exercise of that power can be dangerous to females who view these films as how things should be, as behavior to emulate. Female viewers buy into the Hollywood myth of female sexuality, not recognizing that following this behavior has different consequences than when the male emulates film behavior. Women are not holding up their films as sexual manuals, but they do ask for realism and a recognition of the context of female sexuality.

NEGATIVE IMAGES OF SEXUALITY

In their quest to show many different aspects of female sexuality and power, some women filmmakers are exploring negative images, by reversing the male and female images and asking, What would women do if they had the power?

Filmmaker Monika Treut reversed the power play in *Erotique*, exploring manipulation and murder and what happens when women get the upper hand sexually. "I wanted to flesh out a powerful woman in a patriarchal society who imitates male power. She needed to be manipulative and have all kinds of tricks. Men and women are surprised when they encounter a female who is absolutely in control of her sexuality and is projecting an image of a powerful female. It's still an exception. This is an image of a woman who knows what she wants, goes after it, and has a sense of how other people respond to her sexuality."

Treut wants to explore the full sexuality of women, even if there's a cost involved. "We might have to alienate people first to try out as many possibilities at the moment as we can get. I wrote a book about the female images in the work of Marquis de Sade, the eighteenth-century novelist, and also the female images in the work of Leopold von Sacher-Masoch, the Austrian writer. The word *masochism* comes from his name. These are two examples of completely different images of women—powerful women, women who are aggressive, women who have an outspoken sexual interest, which they pursue. There are images in Greek mythology that are strong, powerful images that have been forgotten for some time—the Sirens and Medusa. Athena, the warrior goddess."

Jan Chapman and Jane Campion explored the perversity and complexity of sexuality in *The Piano.* "It's a matter of creating a character and talking about what she might do," says Chapman. "Both Jane and I knew women who exhibited this kind of womanly behavior which is contrived and capricious and perverse. In one scene Ada takes Stewart's hand knowing that Baines is watching and gains enjoyment from his discomfort."

If a filmmaker is only trying to create a character who's on a pedestal, a perfect human being, she can't explore these aspects of her sexuality. It's creating an ideal, rather than bringing the character to life. A number of female filmmakers, in their desire to explore a fuller sexual range, are exploring the dark side of sexuality.

Lizzie Borden explored phone sex in *Erotique,* another image of shifting power in the twentieth century. "I wanted to do something that reflected America when I chose the subject for *Erotique.* There are incredible phone skills this culture is developing. There's a way of flirting over the phone. Phone sex takes that to its logical conclusion. Everything's fast. We don't have the time to get there, so we'll do it over the phone. In a phone sex place, men call just to have their orgasm with somebody. It's a three-dollar orgasm. That's not so bad. Of course, the trick is to keep the man on the phone for forty-five minutes."

Not all telephone flirtations are merely sexual. While interviewing women filmmakers for this book, three of them told me they had once fallen in love with a man over the phone—just by the sound of his voice. One woman pitched the idea to a male executive. His response? "But how could you fall in love with him? You never saw him." Little did he know about female love. One of the women later met the man. She discovered he was a little man—with a wonderful voice. And they got married.

22

I'LL TAKE ROMANCE

HOLLYWOOD KNOWS that love and sex sell. But many of its greatest films are not about sex, but about romance. The slow, developing relationship. About love. Falling in love. Being in love. Falling out of love. Falling in love again.

A number of these film romances have been written by women or by male-female teams, with many adapted from books or plays: *Carousel* (screenplay by Phoebe and Henry Ephron, 1956), *The Long Hot Summer* (the 1958 film version by Irving Ravetch and Harriet Frank, Jr., who also wrote *Murphy's Romance,* 1985), the film versions of *The Barretts of Wimpole Street* (1934) and *Goodbye Mr. Chips* (1939) (both by Claudine West), *Anna and the King of Siam* (Sally Benson, 1946), *The Heiress* (Ruth and Augustus Goetz, 1949), *It's a Wonderful Life* and *Seven Brides for Seven Brothers* (both by Frances Goodrich and Albert Hackett, 1946, 1954), *Adam's Rib* (Ruth Gordon and Garson Kanin, 1949), *David and Lisa* (Eleanor Perry, 1963), *Prince of Tides* (Pat Conroy and Becky Johnston, 1992), *Magnificent Obsession* (Sara Y. Mason and Victor Heerman, 1935 and 1954), *Crossing Delancey* (Susan Sandler, 1987), and *Look Who's Talking* (Amy Heckerling, 1990).

What are the elements of the romance? What are women's romantic longings, and how are those put into film? Romance needs chemistry and relationship and love. A filmmaker can get by creating sex scenes without it, but it won't work in romantic comedies.

Writer Treva Silverman wrote for *The Mary Tyler Moore Show* for a number of years and was one of the uncredited writers who did rewrites for *Romancing the Stone* (written by the late Diane Thomas). Treva was asked to help solve a very specific problem: "The heroine, Joan Wilder, was not sympathetic in the first scene. And that's essential for romantic comedy. You have to say to yourself, 'Oh, I want her to get exactly what she wants and I want him to get exactly what he wants,' so that you're really on their sides. So that the second they meet each other, you say, 'Oh, I hope it works out!' "

What did Silverman do to make Joan sympathetic? "I decided that Joan should have a cat in her opening scene. I thought that if she starts talking to her cat and being mushy-sweet and nice, then it's an instant, 'Oh, she loves the cat. She's got to be pretty good.' The cat softened her and made her appealing. Charlie Chaplin once said, 'In the opening shot, if a man kicks a dog, he's the villain. If he pets the dog, he's the hero.' "

A great romance depends on the same elements that make a strong female character. "In a romance," says Silverman, "you need a spirited and independent woman. That kind of woman is usually perceived as sexual, because from a man's point of view—totally on an unconscious level—if a woman is spirited and independent and knows her own mind and has a kind of feistiness, there is an assumption that she's going to be an active, curious, inventive sexual partner."

Writer-director Nora Ephron (*When Harry Met Sally, Sleepless in Seattle*) agrees. "All the great romantic comedies are based on equality. I don't think these movies work unless the women are strong. Romantic comedies are based on conflict, and you can't have a conflict between a weak person and a strong person. The women have to have will."

A great romance depends on the same elements that make a good story. "So many romantic comedies involve some antagonism," says

Silverman. "Particularly early antagonism. The implication that there's going to be sparks. Conflict is important because it distances them and reminds people that he's a man, she's a woman, they're different. It's sexual because it keeps underlining his maleness and her femaleness. They're different, and boy will it be dynamite when they get together."

These conflicts might be about class, values, different backgrounds, a misunderstanding or misinterpretation, or just bad timing. She's getting ready to marry the wrong man—and then they meet.

To make the romance work, the female has to be as smart, witty, and clever as the man.

"A lot of this conflict is expressed verbally," says Silverman. "They're verbal and quick and clever. A passive woman who says, 'My, my, isn't that fascinating?' isn't going to hold our interest. Tracy and Hepburn are romantic characters. Their verbal sparring is a hint of things to come, showing how attuned they are to each other. It's a kind of foreplay, a kind of dance. They finish each other's sentences. She knows how to answer him. He knows how to answer her. On an unconscious level it tells us what their sexual relationship is going to be. There's a hint of thrust and parry or, if you prefer, thrust and moan."

The romance doesn't move quickly to sex. Before they get to bed, there's the slow development.

"You don't want the sex to happen too fast," continues Silverman. "Romantic comedy is romance. It echoes people's fantasies on a lovely level of what the perfect romance would be if only they could attain it. Everybody's always aching for that first touch, the first intimacy, the first going to bed together. In real life the first touches do show if there's going to be chemistry. I know people who have said, 'The minute he held my hand, it was one of the most exciting moments I've ever had in my life.' It's either there or it isn't. He's not much to look at, but he's a great hand-holder. It can even be the way someone puts his hand on your shoulder, the electricity, or the way his voice sounds."

The romance has recently been explored on television, through the Harlequin Romances produced by Alliance Films. When the company had to choose which books of the thousands to use, they had to think about a 1990s view of romance and take the women's perspective into account. Although the president of Alliance is a man and the producers of Harlequin Romances were men, there were three woman executives at Alliance who were also making choices.

"We had access to sixteen thousand titles," says Susan Minas, one of the three. "When we chose which titles to use, we decided we wanted women who are proactive and who drive the stories."

Almost immediately in the development of the stories, a difference emerged between what men found romantic and sexy and how women saw romance. Alliance executive Noreen Halpern comments, "When the men were rewriting, they were creating a woman that appealed to them—a woman who was totally on top of everything, totally aggressive sexually. Male erotica has a lot to do with many partners, as many as you can have." The women noticed another difference. "The men wanted to get them naked. 'If it's naked, it's hot.' We think it's more exciting to see someone touch like in the 1940s. Or like in *The Lover*. Or as in *The Sea of Love*—the huge tension and buildup. It isn't just about people naked."

Another difference was in the character of the female. "The men felt the woman had to be totally gorgeous, sexy and stunning," says Minas. "Of course, the woman should be attractive or at least become more attractive as she becomes more of a person through the love story, but for women to really like a woman on-screen and to really relate to her, she doesn't have to be a sexy babe. The men had casting ideas of *Baywatch*-type women. We felt we needed someone likable, somebody we could relate to. It had to be about emotion—about what's happening in the air between two people as opposed to wham, bam, thank you ma'am."

This casting choice did not just relate to the woman. Alliance executive Christine Shipton clarifies: "It's also not about having some beautiful model-looking guy. It's about having a guy who's a good enough actor, who can make you believe he has tremendous yearning, caring, desire, and strength. When a man looks at a woman, he needs to be soft as opposed to lecherous."

"But not too soft," Minas adds. "Harlequin tried the gentleman who's all the way gentle. But the readers wrote in and said, 'Please give us the alpha man—warm and tender and vulnerable because he loves her so much, but with a strength about him.' "

The issues around women also influence the kind of romance that was chosen.

"Many of the stories are about loneliness—not that the women are losers, it's just that one part of their life has not been fulfilled," says Shipton. "It's a yearning. Sometimes they've decided, I have my life, I like my life, I'm not looking for anything else . . . and then—she meets him."

"Sometimes the two are thrown together. Sometimes there's a sense of rescue, as long as they remain equal," says Halpern, emphasizing that the rescue must be mutual. "The man is rescued also. The woman has never known a great sexual adventure or perfect love. The man has never been in love. She'll teach him the real value of life—which is love. What's important is that he loves the real her. He discovers something that he's never really known before, which is that a woman who's intelligent and exciting and strong and powerful can be a much more interesting partner."

A great romance shows character transformation, growth, and change. "I see *Romancing the Stone* as a wonderful example of a Harlequin-type romance in terms of the woman discovering who she is," says Shipton. "It's a love story in the middle of a huge adventure—and the man is definitely tamed and changed throughout the story."

I'LL TAKE REALITY

The romance often implies a fantasy. Some women filmmakers, though, explore the reality, the truth about love.

Nora Ephron began as a journalist, "so I'm always going to be interested in what you would call the truth. The truth is always more interesting than something black and white. It has to do with complexity. What's interesting is in the details. I see little mirrors on experiences and feelings that I've had, and I try to use that in a film."

Ephron has put this view into many of her romantic comedies. "I'm interested in whatever you would call the gap between fantasy and reality. I'm not so much interested in romance, but in men and women and the difference between them. That's what *When Harry Met Sally* is about. It's about how men and women look at the same thing in completely different ways. Scene after scene. *Sleepless in Seattle* is about the different way this one man and this one woman look at romance. It's not that I don't think men are romantic. I think they just look at romance in different ways.

"In both these films, almost every single scene is about the difference between men and women. Can men and women be friends? What their first dates are like. In *Sleepless,* the obvious difference is that men watch *The Dirty Dozen* and women watch *An Affair to Remember.* But there's also the running joke in that movie about how aggressive women are romantically."

In overly romantic movies, the lovers just "realize" they're in love. In realistic movies, they work it out. "Isn't it lovely how practically nobody ever has to go into therapy in the movies to make their love life work?" says Treva Silverman.

Silverman thinks *Annie Hall* is "one of the best romances ever because it's so much closer to what really does take place in relationships. They were in therapy. They both understood who each other was. He adored being funny in front of Annie because she appreciated it and thought it was great. That's why the scene with the lobster is so memorable. The person you're with, you understand each other's everything—language and humor. When they don't get it, that isn't a sexual tension. That's a who-needs-it? tension."

Some of the truth of romance in the twentieth century might be about struggle, divorce, and older characters. "I'd like to see more exploration of the romance of the second marriage," says Silverman. "Unfortunately, the Hollywood reality says that to sell anything these days, people have to be in their twenties and thirties. Male executives don't like anything where women are in their forties."

But with the large population of baby boomers in their forties and fifties who are still having sex (according to the latest reports) and still going to movies, there may be some changing images as women make more of these films. One of the changes that women will bring is a stop to the older man–younger woman casting that is so prevalent.

Women have noticed this casting problem as far back as the 1930s, when Bette Davis commented that men "see themselves as permanently appealing and think it [not] at all strange that they are making love to actresses who could well be their granddaughters."[7] It has not changed. "I'm so sick and tired of seeing the fantasy that's portrayed by the whole Hollywood structure," says producer Candida Royalle. "It's always the man who is twenty years older than the woman, and this is seen as perfectly normal."

In most cases it's a male fantasy. "When I was twenty-three I went out with twenty-three-year-old guys," says Royalle. "We never went out with men twenty years older than us—they would have been considered old fogies. But look at all the Hollywood films that show Michael Douglas, Robert de Niro, Al Pacino, Jack Nicholson—all men over fifty, with young women in their twenties or early thirties. Let the guys sleep with someone their own age."

Royallė is adamant about putting a stop to this. "We have to stop perpetuating this very painful ageism that's so prevalent in Hollywood movies. It's just horrible. It's not only unrealistic but it's brutal and damaging to women. It offends me tremendously. It's so wrong. And it's got to stop."

Look around for a good image of sexual older women. There are very few. "*Cocoon* was a wonderful film that showed positive role models of women over fifty," says Elizabeth Engstrom. "I know some wonderfully classy older women and widows who take good care of themselves, have a positive image of themselves, and have a sex life, even if it is a solitary one. I'd like to see more portrayals of independent women living good lives. We don't need to be partnered in order to be whole. Contemporary films make sex so significant, when in a healthy, whole person, sex is just another part of the magic of life. I'd like to see more love scenes among older people. That would be very positive."

As women create more films, they are questioning some other basics of Hollywood. That means questioning the beauty myth.

THE BEAUTY MYTH

Since men tend to be more visual than women, their view of women has demanded glamorous, strikingly beautiful, stunningly perfect stars. This view begins at the script stage and includes casting, how the woman is lit and photographed, directed, and costumed.

In my experience of consulting on almost two thousand scripts, I can remember only a very few where the woman was not described by her physical appearance. This is true about minor as well as major characters, by men *and* women writers. The range of general descriptions usually includes the word *attractive,* or *pretty,* or *beautiful,* and such adverbs as *very, quite,* and *striking,* to presumably help dimensionalize the woman. If the woman's looks do not range between "very attractive" and "strikingly beautiful," the writer usually clarifies that she's *homely* or *plain, overweight,* or *unattractive.*

These descriptions limit the female characters to nubile women between seventeen and thirty-nine. It leaves no room for a female Tommy Lee Jones, Harvey Keitel, de Niro, Pacino, or Anthony Hopkins.

Glamour. Beauty. It seems that this is what film is about. Casting director Jane Jenkins explains that "directors want the blond, glamorous babe. The producers say the leading lady has to be pretty."

Jenkins finds this viewpoint limiting. "There are many actresses who would be considered very pretty in the real world, but for film they have to be Hollywood beautiful. Not only does that leave out some of the great actresses, such as Kathy Bates, but even an actress like Sandra Bullock, who is adorable but not Hollywood beautiful, had to have exactly the right film to break through. However, there's a lot more latitude for size, shape, and variety of women in television."

Is this true for men? Although the predominant description for male protagonists is "ruggedly handsome," fewer male characters are defined by their appearance, and most definitions of supporting or minor male characters say little about their looks. Men are often defined by qualities such as intelligence, self-confidence, integrity, or attitude. "Men don't have to be drop-dead gorgeous," says casting director Janet Hirshenson, who is partnered with Jenkins. "It's the force of their personality that captures the audience. There's a wider range."

Through the illusion of film, the industry has sent a message that this view of women is the reality. Men go out looking for the perfectly beautiful babe. Women try to adapt to the image. Cinematographer Brianne Murphy knows the truth. "My job is to make them look as good as I can. I make people look more beautiful than they really are."

The beauty myth demands support from all the various professionals who create the magic of film, from writer to director to producer to cinematographer and including costume, makeup, and lighting. The illusion that Hollywood presents is that this is how women are or can be. Costumer Marilyn Vance-Straker knows better. "Most people do have figure problems, whether because they're high-waisted, or have very large breasts, or are thick in the hips; so we use fabric and design to diminish those qualities, and to emphasize their extraordinary qualities, whether that be great legs, or a slim figure, or a tiny waist."

The camera does not tell the truth. As a result, it holds up an impossible ideal for women and an unrealistic expectation for men.

Murphy says, "What a shock it is to be working with someone

you've only seen in makeup, then one morning you happen to catch them going into the makeup trailer and you say, 'Who's that?' And someone replies, 'That's the beautiful leading actress.' What a shock when someone looks that different."

"If we all walked around with our own hair stylist, makeup person, costumer, cameraman, and lighting designer, we would all be fabulous, unbelievably gorgeous," adds Vance-Straker.

Some women are rethinking this beauty myth. "I don't believe anyone should be glamorous if they're playing a part that's not supposed to be glamorous," says Vance-Straker. "They should look their best, they should be comfortable, but they need to fit that character. Makeup, hair, and costume should be helping them to find their character."

"I just don't agree with the idea of beauty as it's presented," says Murphy. "My favorite actors have been people like Julie Harris and currently Kathy Bates who don't fit into that beauty mold, because I think character and the performance transcends that. I think we're seeing that more and more. I think it will be healthier for everybody. Men aren't going to find that kind of woman in real life and women can't be that kind of woman."

This new viewpoint may even change which actresses we see on the screen. Now, not only are there few women over fifty or sixty, but when they are on the screen, they don't look their age—for a reason. Many actors and actresses have had face-lifts; plastic surgery around their eyes and chin, a little lift here, a little tuck there. Perhaps it's been done for self-preservation, so they can keep their jobs, or because those playing out the beauty myth have also bought into it. But it has limited our view of what is beautiful—and what is sexual.

IS THERE HOPE?

Many women filmmakers are excited and optimistic about the future. Monika Treut sees change. "A little bit is happening. We talk about

Hollywood movies trying to open up to new portrayals of women and men. And there are alternatives for marketing movies through video and the film festivals, which gives me hope for different kinds of films."

Exploring sexuality means exploring truth without exploitation, without removing character and nuance and emotion and humanity.

It's about exploring healthy images. Elizabeth Engstrom adds, "I don't think there's enough of showing single women who have good lives. I don't think we see enough of women who know how to express their sexuality in a normal, healthy way. Without being sleazy, dangerous, without being ugly, or laughable, or cartoonish. Let's explore what's natural and beautiful in women, partnerships, couples, and how they change over time. We all go through cycles and seasons. Sometimes we're like rabbits, wanting sex all the time, and other times we need to be left alone. A good partner understands that, and it's rarely portrayed with sensitivity."

New Zealand scriptwriter and script consultant Helene Wong believes there is the start of a new trend. "Some of our films, such as *The Piano,* are beginning to break through the traditionally accepted ways of sexual imagemaking on the screen. And it's most likely to be the women filmmakers who'll do this; kissing and making love and nudity could look quite different when done from a woman's point of view. When we have more women involved in scriptwriting and directing, we will have no less than a broader interpretation of the human race."

23

CASE STUDY

Beth Sullivan

DR. QUINN, Medicine Woman first aired on January 1, 1993. Beth Sullivan was the first woman to successfully create and sole executive-produce a dramatic series.

The series begins in 1867, following the main character, Michaela Quinn, chronologically, year by year. During the course of the series, she falls in love and marries. Although the series explores many issues, Beth discusses how it deals with issues related to romance, love, and sex.

"We were somewhat bound by the Victorian era and Michaela's likely personal history as an upper-class female in that era. She would not have had premarital sex, thus her sexual awakening in the course of the show at such a late age [mid-thirties] struck some as hopelessly old-fashioned. However, most people went with the historical authenticity, which was a cornerstone of the show, and enjoyed the opportunity, along with us, of exploring the complex psychological issues related to women and sex that are as alive and well today as they were in the 1800s. It has given us the basis to examine women's fears of vulnerability and dependency and, ultimately, intimacy, as they relate to sexual expression and equality.

"It's not as though these issues didn't exist then. It's just that they were the purview of the nascent women's rights movement. The post–Civil War years were a very volatile time for feminists. Having relegated women's rights issues to the abolition movement and then been denied their expected enfranchisement, they turned their attention to their own concerns with a vengeance. Elizabeth Cady Stanton and Susan B. Anthony and their cohorts were very active. They fought on many fronts for women's rights, including the vote. And they struggled within their own personal lives for greater equity in career choices, child rearing, and sexual matters. They fought for equality within their relationships, within their families, and within society.

"On the other hand, Michaela and Sully's relationship has always been very progressive in terms of everything except sex. As a woman embarking on what was then virtually a men-only career, that of medicine, she's had to overcome a wealth of prejudice and self-doubt. She had to endure the role of outcast, and in this she and Sully found a common thread beyond their physical attraction to one another. Sully himself chose a difficult road in his opposition to the rampant exploitation of the West, especially of his Cheyenne Indian friends. Though Michaela is much more educated and sophisticated than he, they found a basis for mutual respect and acceptance of one another's needs.

"As Michaela and Sully's relationship has developed, we've managed to portray their sexual passion for one another very intensely. We're aware that, as an eight o'clock family drama, many parents rely on the show not to offend, so we're careful about how the characters' sexual relationship is portrayed. We make sure not to indulge in the unnecessary or to exploit the obvious. Without exposing flesh or using illicit language, we've used symbolic imagery to communicate the intensity of attraction between the characters.

"In the pilot, Michaela was brought into the Indian camp and thrown into a teepee with Sully and they have to sleep there that night. There's an instant attraction. They both lie down to sleep, all bundled up in robes and separate from each other across the fire; there's that moment when she opens her eyes and looks at him while he's supposedly sleeping, and then puts her head down. And then the same thing happens with him. He opens his eyes and looks. It's across the fire and through the flames—there's heat, flames, a symbolic image of their intensity.

"When Michaela and Sully first got to know each other, they went on a trek to trace the source of some poison that was getting into the water supply. They ended up out alone together when they weren't very familiar with each other at all. She broke her arm in a fall and was fairly helpless and disheveled. He brushed her hair. And he buttoned her blouse for her. These moments were very sensual. There was a lot of tension and a lot of intrigue that was genuine and not coy, plus it was going somewhere for the long term. We didn't play it for exploitation, but for the care and gentleness and the relationship.

"When Michaela and Sully became engaged, he had problems with migraine headaches spawned by various changes in his life and in the lives of his friends, the Cheyenne Indians. He did a sweat and defied her medical advice. She went and stayed with him through this experience. The images we used were very sensual—the steam coming off the rocks . . . they were both sweating . . . and he proposed to her in a very erotic, steamy sort of way—literally and figuratively.

"Other women's issues related to romance, love, and sex have been explored through our supporting female characters in the show. Through Dorothy, we've dealt with concerns of aging and wife battering. Through Grace, we've challenged racial prejudice and misconceptions surrounding infertility. Through Myra, we've looked at sexual exploitation of women and the core issue of self-esteem. Through Colleen, we've examined both the joyful and the painful aspects of coming of age. And in the case of all these women, we've explored their particular struggles in striving for independence while trying to balance personal relationships in their lives. Though very traditional in many ways, all of them have sought to express themselves through occupations.

"Whenever the word *sex* comes up nowadays, it seems to be a point of controversy, a so-called moral battleground. Unfortunately, the concept of morality has been co-opted in recent times by conservative forces in an effort to suppress, among other things, sexual and reproductive freedom. It's time we reinstated the word *moral* to its rightful, nonpartisan stature.

"Human beings have been grappling with morals, ethics, and values for as long as we've been able to think in a sophisticated manner. Thousands of years of questioning and striving after what is the right way to live, and what are the basic premises from which to judge and make choices, have been buried by the current simplistic laissez-faire philosophy that asserts 'You're okay, I'm okay,' or 'There's two sides to every question.' Having a right to one's opinion is being dangerously confused with the notion that all opinions are somehow right. Having a right to one's point of view is quite different than asserting that opposing points of view are equally legitimate.

"With this in mind, *Dr. Quinn, Medicine Woman* actively seeks to deal with moral issues. Those that are timeless, immutable. From its inception, I've tried to guide the show to examine the broader aspects of life, including love, in terms of relationships and family and community. Two of the sustaining themes have always been to demonstrate how an individual can make a difference and how a community can be effective despite economic, cultural, and political differences.

"In a world in which people are having an increasingly difficult time understanding their own significance, we try to give a sense of how everyone can make a difference for having lived.

"To this end, Michaela and Sully have always been individuals attempting to live by the Golden Rule. To some that sounds obvious, perhaps simplistic, even corny, but I'm convinced that this most basic moral precept is in mortal danger and can't be emphasized enough. In a world where competition has reached a peak, we want to show characters consciously trying to live honorable lives, without treading on anyone else for their own needs. This is not to say they always achieve this goal. Both Michaela and Sully are imperfect; they may be blinded at times, but their intent is always present. In the course of any given show, if one of their flaws has interfered with doing what is right, they're at least made aware of it. They may not have conquered it. Problems aren't sewed up neatly, but progress is made.

"We've had several shows that focus on the flaws. As a doctor, Michaela's commitment is to heal, no matter what, no matter whom, no matter how much she disagrees with the person's actions or beliefs. She once had to treat one of the most odious men in town. During the course of that show, she comes to a place where she must reach into her humanity and pull for him as a person. She must find a way to sit down and communicate to him on a different level other than just technical skill. It strengthened her capacity to care and love in a different way than just through her medicine.

"Through the show, I'm getting to deal with many of the issues that I think are important. It's especially interesting because many of my experiences and Jane Seymour's experiences are parallel. She's forty-four and I'm forty-six. We both married since the show started. She just had twins in November, and I had twins in March.

"So we've played those experiences in the show, including pregnancy issues and how that relates to love and relationship issues. We've explored the fear of being too old to have children, as well as concerns about balancing career and family. Michaela learns there's no such thing as a superwoman. We've tried to communicate healthy prenatal issues subtlely.

"We've used women directors and writers on our shows, such as Gwen Arner and Sara Davidson. Gwen brings a certain sensitivity to it with her ability to portray the relationships between the women, and Sarah has created many of the sensual images that I described.

"We have not played it safe. My objective is to challenge not just the emotions, but the mind. In fact, I coined a motto for the writing staff to follow: 'In through the heart and out through the brain.' That's the guiding force in terms of what premises drive our stories."

PART SIX

A SOCIAL AND GLOBAL PERSPECTIVE

SOME SOCIAL BREAKTHROUGHS FOR WOMEN

1974: *A Case of Rape,* starring Elizabeth Montgomery, confronts the issue of rape from a woman's point of view.

1981: *The Willmar Eight,* directed by Lee Grant, changes discrimination laws within the banking industry. Her film *When Women Kill* helps change laws about spousal-abuse defense allowed in the courts.

1982–1987: *Cagney & Lacey,* created by Barbara Corday and Barbara Avedon, airs an episode where Mary Beth gets breast cancer, which helps change legislation to benefit women. The show deals with many issues that affect women, such as sexism, rape, abuse, pornography, etc.

1984: *Something About Amelia* wins an Emmy Award. It is the first television movie to deal with incest.

1984: *License to Kill,* produced by Dorothea Petrie, is the first television movie to confront the issue of drunk driving.

1984: *The Burning Bed,* starring Farrah Fawcett-Majors, deals with domestic abuse.

1985: Emmy Award–winner *Love Is Never Silent,* a story about deaf parents, executive-produced by Marian Rees, is the first film to use deaf actors in all the principal roles.

1991: Donna Mills produces *Runaway Father,* which helps change legislation to nail deadbeat dads.

1995: *Serving in Silence* airs. One of the first television films about discrimination against gays in the military, it's produced by Barbra Streisand, Glenn Close, and Cis Corman and written by Alison Cross.

24

WHAT IS OUR RESPONSIBILITY?

> If one is lucky, a solitary fantasy can
> totally transform one million realities.[1]
> —*Maya Angelou*

THE CAMERA IS A LENS that turns its eye on some little corner of the world. It not only records what it sees, but interprets what it sees. It pulls in the light, the images, the stories, leaving some things out, taking others in, changing the view, always selecting one thing, not another.

What the camera sees is determined by the filmmaker's view of the world. What is important? What is a good story? Who should it be about? What is my responsibility as a filmmaker?

The answers to these questions are determined by the experiences, background, creativity, culture, and gender of the filmmaker. "If we think of the evolution of films as a kind of mirror which reflects changing society, we must concede that the mirror has always been limited in its reflection, and possibly distorted," says Christine Mohanna in her article *A One-Sided Story: Women in the Movies.* "Our society conditions men and women. . . . It could be that they both see male and female roles through the same distorted lens."[2]

Even when the subject matter might be similar between a woman and a man, the approach is often different, because of the point of view. "As moviemakers, what we do for a living is mirror the culture," says producer Dawn Steel. "But the culture that we mirror depends on what we're looking at."

The camera records what it sees, but "movies and television shows are also huge shapers of culture and people's lives," says Mustang Pictures executive Melanie Ray. "We are such a link, a personal link with people all over the planet. We owe it to the work we have chosen to do to be well-informed, well-read, and balanced people who look at what we do as both a job and as what we do as human beings."

The camera not only reflects society, it shapes society. In so doing, it can change us and change our world. What existed before, now exists with a new consciousness. What we didn't know, now we know. Our perceptions change. New attitudes are formed. What we never cared about before, now we see differently. This leads to new judgments, new decisions, new opinions, new actions.

Since film has been dominated by the male point of view, a great deal of women's experiences have been left out. Some of these are stories about love, relationships, children, mothering, overcoming oppression, victimization. Others have been little-known stories about women's heroism and victories. Some of those experiences have been glaring social wrongs, which no one noticed until somebody turned the camera in that direction.

Certainly there have been thousands of sensitive films written, directed, and produced by men who have cared deeply about our society. Many have dealt with problems that affect all of us—pollution as a result of corporate irresponsibility, war, violence, the destruction of the rain forests, the lack of business ethics.

But many social problems affect women disproportionately to men because they affect the powerless, the disenfranchised, and the victims to a greater extent than the dominant culture.

According to government studies, two-thirds of the world's illiterates are women. There have been several films about illiteracy—all about men. *Stanley and Iris*, written by Harriet Frank, Jr., and Irving

Ravetch and directed by Martin Ritt, focused on the story of an illiterate man (played by Robert de Niro) and the woman who taught him to read (Jane Fonda). *Bridge to Silence,* written by Cynthia Cherbak and directed by Karen Arthur, told the story about a dyslexic man who had problems reading. For women, illiteracy does far more than keep them from getting a job. It's a way of keeping them oppressed, unable to make informed decisions, unable to exert any control over their lives. The woman's story of illiteracy has not yet been told.

In almost all sexual harassment incidents, women are the victims. *Disclosure* dealt with this subject, but the protagonist was a man. He fought back successfully and triumphed, although for a woman in that same scenario, she might have lost her job, her reputation, and suffered the stigma for years.

More women than men are stalked. Perhaps the best-known film about this subject is *Fatal Attraction*—about a man stalked by a woman.

TALK ABOUT RESPONSIBILITY

Many women filmmakers feel a responsibility to look carefully at the message they're sending, the stories they're telling. "The images that we make go out into the zeitgeist of life," says Dawn Steel. "It can't help but affect you when the images are negative. How can a woman feel good about herself walking out of a movie like *Showgirls*? How can you feel good about yourself when you see abusive images of women, or stupid images of women? But when you get bombarded by positive images, that affects you as well. My responsibility, as pretentious as this sounds, is to raise the consciousness of women about themselves. And self-image comes from images. Images of yourself."

If all entertainment sends some sort of message, this responsibility can weigh heavily on sensitive filmmakers who know the power of their media. Is their responsibility to solve the problems of the world through media? Most would answer no. Is their responsibility to be responsible? Yes.

For Oprah Winfrey, "Entertainment is the last value . . . I'm not just here to entertain. The intent is always, Is somebody going to be uplifted, enlightened, encouraged, or educated in some way? For me, the show is a mission, it really is."[3]

Few women deny that television and film have a powerful impact on this society. But how far does it go? "I have come to believe that there is an ability for media to change society," says Trina McQueen, president of the Discovery Channel in Toronto, Canada. "But that ability is not universal and not total and not predictable. We have a social responsibility for what we put on television, absolutely. I really do believe that what we put on television can, to a certain extent, affect the behavior of the people who watch it. It has an impact."

Although women may not know the answer about the overall social impact, many feel the impact on their own lives. "There are so many points of view regarding the actual impact of movies on viewers' psyches and consciousness. I don't know if anybody really has the answer," says Janet Yang. "Because I'm a sensitive person, if I sit in a movie that has very powerful messages one way or the other, I tend to absorb them. Other people can sit through, let's say, a very violent movie and not feel affected."

Many women have trained themselves to be sensitive, because they've had to. They've had to learn to see children's problems before they say it, to read the mood of the husband when he can't articulate it, to understand instinctively when something is wrong with a friend. Yang believes that this sensitivity is, perhaps, "inherited, or genetic. I think our pores are just more open than men's. It's a curse in one way and a blessing in another." Having this sensitivity leads to the questions: Who or what are filmmakers responsible to? How do they exercise that responsibility?

For some, their first responsibility is an artistic one—to simply be true to themselves.

"I think my responsibility is to write as authentically as possible, and write what the character deserves," says Hilary Henkin. "Am I true to the voice of the character I am writing? It's a matter of working with integrity."

"The only thing you can ask any artist is: Be true to your own voice," says Judith Claire, who wrote *Chanel Solitaire* and, as a career counselor, has helped other writers deal with these issues. "You can't dictate what's right or wrong to write about, because that sets boundaries, which are counter to the creative process. You have to let your mind and spirit roam free. That's how you make discoveries and surprise yourself. For a writer, it's telling stories that are as individual as you are, with characters that are as true as you can make them. You're striving to create with as much skill, attention, and detail as possible. It's hard work, but you do it because you want your script to reverberate with integrity, insight, and wonder. Whatever the genre, you want to touch the audience, stir their imaginations, encourage them and expand their lives. To do that, you have to be authentic."

"What is the truth of the character?" asks Australian producer Sandra Levy. "If I find something that is true and if I believe that I'm doing it as well as I can, then I'm filling that part of responsibility. I would not be comfortable with making sexist, racist material, or exploitive material. I hope that the material that I make that travels the world has more going for it than just the lowest values of human interaction. Perhaps women are looking for this because few of us come into this business because we want to make money. We feel we have things to say. We have observations to make. We have creative relationships to explore. So what we want to do is express a view of characterization and a view of drama which is the truth."

For writer Diane English, creator of *Murphy Brown*, there's a responsibility to present a balanced point of view. "Murphy Brown is a character with a distinctly liberal point of view. But that does not mean we have not been responsible. We have several continuing characters . . . who have the opposite point of view. Jerry Gold is a character Murphy might marry—yet he does not support gun control, and he calls Murphy on every aspect of her liberal agenda. We give him equal time, and find their arguments make good debates. The airways are public airways, and there are more than just liberals watching *Murphy Brown.* I don't believe the audience should only see one side of the debate." English was interested in exploring political and social satire because "it questions the people calling the shots. It gets the audience involved because it's about important public events that are bigger than we are, more dramatic."[4]

Issues make good drama. But being responsible to one's society, one's vision, one's gender can weigh heavily on some filmmakers.

"The question of responsibility is a balance that I struggle with all the time in my work," says writer Anna Hamilton Phelan, who wrote the scripts for *Mask* and *Gorillas in the Mist.* "I have an enormous sense of responsibility to my gender. And about race. As I get older, I realize it's a part of my being. It's not going to go away. So I just go with it and do the best I can."

It's particularly difficult because these topics are not easily sold. Putting the positive into one's work is not always seen as dramatic, high concept, or commercial.

"Sometimes it's like battling through molasses to get a good film done," continues Phelan. "Sometimes I want to just walk away from the whole thing. But the only way to battle media is with media, to keep feeding it with more positive things because it's out there. It is so much a part of everyone's lives now. You cannot deny it."

As a writer, Phelan's sense of responsibility includes providing an important balance through the characters that she creates. "Sigourney Weaver once said to me, 'Anna, if you and other writers stop writing about female characters, then our daughters and our granddaughters will have no female images on the screen to identify with at all.' That's an enormous obligation and responsibility."

The producer's sense of responsibility can be even greater. "I feel many levels of responsibility," says Janet Yang. "First to myself, and what I put my name on. I feel a responsibility to my company and to the company that finances us. I feel responsibility to women. I feel a responsibility to Asian Americans. I feel a responsibility to the public at large. Somehow within yourself, you recognize where those balances of responsibilities lie. It's something that requires, I think, some real consideration."

There is also moral responsibility. British director Sallie Aprahamian asks, "Where does our moral responsibility come in? Every subject has an issue and moral to it. In telling a story, we have a whole series of options before us which relate to society's responsibility, individual responsibility, the prejudices that might exist over a character's behavior. For instance, the majority of love scenes show people falling into bed, without any debate about contraception or love or consequences or responsibilities. Writers and producers might not want to deal with it. They might say that raising these issues gets in the way of the scene, but the reality is that every show presents a message."

No matter how much responsibility these women might feel, the stories they want to tell are not well accepted by the male decision makers. "People who actually talk about issues, who openly say they're going to deal with issues, are not looked on fondly by most producers," says Aprahamian. "The new shows created by British TV do not perceive themselves as about issues. They're comfortable period pieces, a bit of music, a nice central character that we all like—he's a really good guy—set in a beautiful countryside."

But every film, whether directly about social issues or not, does communicate ideas and issues. It's the nature of the medium. It can't help it. If it's an underdog triumph film (like *Rocky* or *Places in the Heart*), it says "you can do it." If it's a story about war and combat, the message might be about glory and honor (*Glory*), getting along (*Hogan's Heroes*), heroics (*The Guns of Navarone*), or even the stupidity of war (*Gallipoli*). From television we receive messages—which may or may not be true—about the lives of the rich and famous, the working class, the professional woman, the beautiful and young.

For many decision makers, it's not the message that's important, it's the question: Does it entertain?

SOCIAL MESSAGE OR ENTERTAINMENT?

Film and television viewers demand to be entertained, and smart programmers recognize this if they want to keep their jobs. Not only is the demand for entertainment part of every movie, dramatic series, and situation comedy, but the demand is part of educational television, documentaries, and interactive media. If we don't enjoy it, we won't watch it.

Is entertainment incompatible with the desire to be responsible? It would seem not. Women filmmakers recognize that these two elements can and must go together. Most mainstream women filmmakers shy away from any desire to do message drama. That is not their intention. In fact, most understand the dangers of dealing with issue-oriented material.

Sallie Aprahamian explains that social issue films must be dealt with carefully. "It always must be story- and character-led, not led by the issues. If you don't have a vibrant character, it doesn't matter whether the issue comes into your show or not. It comes back to the quality of the story again and again, then to your moral point of view and how you tell it."

Diane English knows that one can lose audiences when dealing with issues. It depends on the execution of how issues and entertainment are put together. English also believes that "in a strictly storytelling sense, debates dealing with moral issues create better television. Having a strong point of view is often more entertaining than not having one. It's all in the execution. We work hard to make sure our shows are funny. . . . We need to be very, very funny because there is a point of view, challenging material, and topics which require people to think. If the show wasn't entertaining on some level, people wouldn't allow us to do what we do."[5]

Sunta Izzicupo, vice president of television movies at CBS, sees a similar distinction that must be made between entertainment and social issues. "The best movies of the week start by telling a good story, with honest, nonexploitive characters, with a compelling script.

If it also has socially redeeming qualities, that's all the better. But I think that when you set out to do a socially redeeming, 'important' movie, you often fail because it's bloodless. The story has to bring people in first, and then you can hit them with a message or sway their beliefs, or antagonize them into action—whatever you want to do."

When it all comes together, it's one of the real perks of the job, according to producer and former network executive Barbara Corday. "A lot of people who work in the TV-movie business have the incredible luxury of once in a while doing one of those great socially perceptive and important films. In theory, it's hard. It's very hard because you can't let the message become the show. You have to entertain first, and whatever message there is has to be done in an entertaining, acceptable way."

But the payoff of creating a show with issues and entertainment can be bigger, because it reaches people on more levels. Myth consultant Pamela Jaye Smith sees that these fit naturally together. "Entertainment is the easiest form of teaching. It opens doors. Because film hits so many senses at once—the visual, the aural, and implies the sense of touch—film and television have a powerful impact on the brain. Unfortunately, not everyone working in media understands this power, so you have many people playing with a loaded gun, not even knowing what a gun is."

Even when a film is purely entertaining, what is being entertained needs to be considered. Zanne Devine, vice president of production at Universal Studios, says, "A writer once said to me, 'Making entertaining movies is not bad. It's all about what you chose to entertain in people.' I am not interested in entertaining people's violent feelings toward women, or the violent images that go along with those feelings. I don't like it in my life and I don't want to bring it into the world. I'm interested in contributing all kinds of things. Not this, however you define it, whether it's violence, rape, derogatory comments, sexual metaphors. I don't want to advocate making a particular movie because I don't want blood on my hands."

French director Agnes Varda sees that the film artist is almost honor-bound to respond to the problem. "It might seem ridiculous to just make a film when you see what's happening. The world is such a mess. Two-thirds of the world's population doesn't have running water. Millions of women still have clitorectomies and wear veils and have to obey the father. Women are underpaid. Racism is back. It makes you ashamed to be a human being. But since we are on the edge of entertainment, whatever meaning we wish to give it, we can still approach art as a medium to touch and move people, to teach something about life. And we have to be entertaining. We have to give them something which can show good humor, good emotion, that communicates something. We can still reach different people on the level of sensitivity through a universal feeling."

BUT WILL IT MAKE MONEY?

It's not enough to just be entertaining, or even socially engaging. There's another balance that is demanded of filmmakers. Their films must be commercially successful—they must make money.

"There's a tension between the social message and film and television as a commercial enterprise," says producer-executive Sara Duvall. "We work in a unique field that *demands* that we be successful on a commercial level. Nobody is in the business to lose money, to make a film that no one wants to see, to exercise their art without recognizing that film is a collective experience—people don't make films just for themselves."

But are responsibility and commercialism incompatible? Although many believe they are, there is plenty of evidence to the contrary.

Executive Geraldine Laybourne, former president of Nickelodeon, sees that they are actually mutually inclusive. "I have a very strong sense of responsibility and it's first and foremost to our audience and secondly to our shareholders. Basically we believe that what is good for kids is good for business, and it certainly has proven out that way—Nickelodeon has grown at twenty-eight percent for the last five or six years and continues on that track."

The best films have been all four: true to an artistic vision, socially responsible, entertaining, and commercial. In the process, they have helped shape society. Some of the most profound changes have come about through Movies of the Week. Many of the most influential MOWs have either been produced or directed or written by women or have changed women's lives by tackling controversial subject matter that particularly affects their lives.

MAKING CHANGES

Since the Movie of the Week began in 1964, MOWs have become a form particularly able to deal with social issues. NBC produced *A Case of Rape* in 1974, one of the first films that dealt honestly with rape and its aftermath. The issue of domestic abuse was opened up through *The Burning Bed* in 1984. *The Rideout Case* (or *Rape and Marriage*) raised the issue that marriage didn't mean that a man could do whatever he wanted with his wife. *Friendly Fire* dealt with a woman who lost her son to friendly fire in the Vietnam War. *A Fallen Angel* and *Do You Know the Muffin Man* raised issues about child molestation.

The power of many of these films was greatly attributed to the award-winning performances of their actresses. In a number of instances, these were their breakout roles. Elizabeth Montgomery, who made her reputation in *Bewitched*, appeared in *A Case of Rape*. Farrah Fawcett-Majors moved from *Charlie's Angels* to *The Burning Bed*, and comedienne Carol Burnett starred in *Friendly Fire*.

Australian-Asian filmmaker Pauline Chan sees that women are often more able to address these problems because they're the outsiders. "Because men are the people who are running the show, they want to think that everything is working perfectly. They're supposed to be doing a good job, so they don't want to know about a problem. They would prefer to think they are little problems that don't need addressing. But the women don't feel that sense of responsibility because they're not running the show. They can be the objective bystanders. In a sense, the outsider has a better possibility of making change because she can observe in a more objective way. She's not in the thick of it. And she can just sit there and after a while she looks and she says, 'You know, I think things could be done better.' "

Women turn the lens on their domestic world and see problems that have not been addressed or even talked about. *Something About Amelia* (1984) was one of the most important MOWs, turning its eye on the issue of incest. "Sixty million people watched this film on one night," says its director, Randa Haines. "I remember being amazed by that—the power of that medium to reach that many people. Very wisely ABC put hotline numbers into each area for people to call. There were thousands of phone calls and thousands of letters from people saying, 'I'm in that situation,' 'I'm a father in that situation,' 'I'm a child in that situation.' Children called after school the next day, as did hundreds of women who were fifty years old who'd never told anybody what had happened to them. It really opened up a floodgate of emotional and social response. Schools and psychologists and social agencies began to talk about it.

"People felt less alone. They began to share what had happened. They realized they could find help. It was the beginning of an awareness that is very much present today."

Raising consciousness, creating awareness, and even changing laws have all been the result of these films. Actress Donna Mills produced *Runaway Father*, "a groundbreaking film about deadbeat dads. It's about a woman who has small children; the guy leaves and doesn't pay child support. She goes after him and gets him. It used to be that fathers who wouldn't pay their child support would go to Florida. But this film helped create new legislation to get deadbeat dads. Now they've made it a law that the IRS can go after them."

Says Mills, "I also did *My Name Is Kate*, about alcoholism, and *Dangerous Intentions*, about domestic violence. After *Dangerous Intentions* we ran an 800 number and received thousands of phone calls from victims of domestic abuse."

Donna Mills, like many producers, puts her role as producer in perspective. "I don't think a TV movie ever is singly responsible for social change, but it helps."

Although it may not be singly responsible, studies show that movies actually have more impact than message programming. According to Dr. Richard T. Hezel, information programs on social problems that are designed to impact behavior often have low ratings, and the impact is minor. But "made-for-TV movies, on the other hand . . . may frequently achieve larger gross behavior impact than information programs, in part because of their larger audiences, their forceful dramatic presentation of the social problems, and perhaps because of audience tolerance for incidental information that is presented indirectly within an entertainment format."[6]

Producer-director-actress Lee Grant has used both the documentary and the MOW format to explore issues of oppression, discrimination, and social irresponsibility.

"I began as an actress who was blacklisted during the 1950s. I'm so grateful to that experience, because my social consciousness came from this event. I had been traumatized. I have a strong Cassandra sense of the future—as if I can see the handwriting on the wall. I often feel, If this is not given a voice, we're in real trouble. Documentaries were a great outlet for me."

Her first documentary was called *The Willmar Eight.* "This was about eight women who went on strike against a bank in Willmar, Minnesota, because the president of the bank discriminated against women, not allowing them to be promoted beyond cashier."

After making a number of documentaries about subjects ranging from battering to sex change to the family court system, Grant began parlaying them into Movies of the Week for television. "We were involved way before *Inside Edition* with making films out of news.

"I made *Down and Out in America,* which said everything that I ever wanted to say about what the Reagan years did to this country. We used a crisis situation from *Down and Out* to make *No Place Like Home,* about a working-class family who thought they were safe. We set it in Pittsburgh, where all those iron factories and steel mills closed down. They ended up going right through the safety net onto the street. And it's the story about how a woman, played by Christine Lahti, kept her family together and kept going.

"*Women on Trial* was an exposé of the family court system in Houston, Texas. *Nobody's Child* was about a normal child who was put into a mental institution because her family couldn't handle her."

All of these films had an impact on society. "The biggest buyers of *The Willmar Eight* were those in the banking industry. The event in that small town had a large affect on how banks began to treat women in management. Although my film didn't help the Willmar Eight, it did help women in banking. It helped that little voice get bigger.

"*When Women Kill* was about all kinds of women who kill—many were battered women who killed their husbands. When I did that film, spousal abuse wasn't something you could bring up in court, so a lot of these women were doing fifteen years to life in prison for a situation that was just totally out of hand. Now the battered woman syndrome is acceptable in courts.

"As result of *When Women Kill,* we got Mario Cuomo, who was then governor of New York, to release one of the women who were in jail. She was reported to have killed her stepfather, but nobody had any evidence. After doing *Women on Trial,* the judge who had taken children away from women who brought up spousal abuse in court wasn't elected again."

Grant recognizes her motivation behind all her films. "I think I have a saving-him/saving-her kind of button. If situations can be brought out, maybe people can be saved. It's my only outlet. It's the only way I know to do something that has a real impact. If there's a voice for the problem, at least something can happen."

In my interviews with women, I was surprised at the number who felt passionately committed to making their films count for more than just entertainment. Some used religious and spiritual references to articulate this passion, identifying it as a "calling," or "missionary zeal," or a "passionate commitment." They spoke with energy, intensity, and passion. However, none of these women were focusing on the message as message. This was not about proselytizing or converting. Most were focusing on their desire to tell a truth that had not been told before but that they considered vitally important. They felt someone, or women in general, or an ethnic group, had been wronged. Or felt there was some situation that simply had to be addressed and film was the best way to do this.

Some women were adamant about not using the words *responsibility* or *message,* and even kept emphasizing *entertainment.* Yet when I looked at their work or listened to them talk about the films they were most proud of, their sense of responsibility was clear.

The overall message was one of balancing responsibility, artistry, and truth.

GAUGING THE RESPONSE

On many of these socially conscious films, response is gauged in a number of ways. Most have an 800 number placed at the end of the film, as did *Something About Amelia* and *Dangerous Intentions,* and hundreds or thousands of people may call for help, advice, or to share their stories. In many cases, social service agencies receive responses for several days, or up to a month, often doubling or tripling the number of calls they normally receive. Producers and networks talk to sociologists and psychologists who tell them that consciousness has been raised about the issue or that the movie helped their clients.

With other films, response is more difficult to assess. "A controversial film like *Serving in Silence* [produced by Barbra Streisand's company, Barwood Films, and written by Alison Cross about a lesbian colonel in the army] will receive both positive and negative responses," says NBC vice president Roz Weiman. "The positive responses ranged from people saying, 'It's a pleasure to see such an articulate, well-acted film,' to those much more specifically addressing the issue. People were delighted that they were able to see a very positive portrayal of a person who is a lesbian as well as a military person because it comforted them, gave them a sense of strength because they were lesbians themselves or had lesbian family members. We did get some very touching notes from mothers of lesbians, family members who identified and were touched by the portrayal of the family reaction."[7]

These issues are not just being addressed with the Movie of the Week form, but have been addressed in series as well. Barbara Corday was one of the cocreators of *Cagney & Lacey*, which aired from 1982 to 1988 and was one of the first television series created by women, about women. "Traditionally there have been a great many comedy shows that have starred women—from *I Love Lucy* to *Ann Sothern* to *Roseanne* to *Murphy Brown*—but few women have had their own one-hour drama shows. When I first worked at ABC in 1979, it was a fairly accepted slogan that women couldn't carry a one-hour show."

Once the show went on the air, it became a critically acclaimed series, winning a number of Emmy Awards. The show was one of the first times that social issues were dealt with in the context of a series. "Within the show, we dealt with problems of rape, alcoholism, racism, sexism. A series has the ability to constantly pick at people, saying, Remember this, remember this, remember this."

What was the response? "The mail was extraordinary. We got beautifully typed letters as well as letters written on the back of a shirt cardboard, which showed us that we were reaching a cross section of the population. People particularly responded to the character of Mary Beth Lacey, who was a housewife, a working-class mom—she had kids, had a husband. They were trying to make ends meet. We had mail from women who felt that for the first time on television, people in their situation were being seen and being portrayed not just sympathetically but in an empathetic, realistic way. We were mirroring what was really going on out there. We were talking about day care problems and child care problems and husband-wife problems and who makes more money and who still wears the pants and how does that affect sex—all these things that nobody had ever talked about on television before. We dealt with issues about date rape before anybody else. We did alcoholism. We did pornography, breast cancer, sexism in the workplace—every social issue of the day that you could possibly have done.

"We didn't just deal with women's issues. We did one episode where Mary Beth was taken hostage. Police departments all over the country used that episode to train policemen about how to act in a hostage situation."

Corday is even more pleased with the impact the show made on modeling relationships. "The things I loved most about this show were the unspoken images, such as Mary Beth walking in from work and Harvey's making dinner and she gives him a kiss, he gives her a kiss, and they start to talk and she doesn't say, 'Oh, honey, you made dinner, thank you so much.' Dinner is for everybody. It's not one person's job to make dinner. Those are the kinds of things we were able to do in ways that were very subtle, but people got it."

In spite of their success, shows about social issues have not been encouraged. Why? If media is so powerful, if socially conscious films have been artistically and commercially successful, why do women feel there is still such an unwillingness to green-light projects on social problems they consider important?

"I don't think it's a conspiracy," says producer Janet Yang. "I just think men don't notice. They don't know better. It's a lack of exposure, a lack of education. It's also the economic pressures and not knowing what is possible. Not having the awareness and the voices to bring something new to the screen."

And there's another reason. Films about social problems are often not encouraged because a large share of the market for both television and film is international. "We're always told that our movies are too 'soft' for a foreign audience," says Sunta Izzicupo. "They're about our own domestic social issues. And other countries are often not interested in those topics. We're usually told that the foreign market wants male action and women-in-jeopardy movies."

"Other countries are going to deal with social issues in terms of their own domestic situation," says Simon Hart, president and CEO of Ellipse Program USA. "Other cultures don't really care about the Texas cheerleading mom. They don't know who Amy Fisher is. Those are things that are not international social issues but more common to the United States."

Whether domestic or foreign, every image touches those who see it. No more is the influence of a film just within its borders. Now the international market is the largest buyer of American films, with up to 60 percent of the profits from a movie coming from the foreign markets. That brings up new issues about responsibility.

25

GLOBAL INTERRELATIONSHIPS

WE LIVE IN the global village. The images that we convey now affect the remotest areas of the world. There are few places on earth that are not affected by television or film.

Producer Gale Anne Hurd recounts going to a very remote island in Micronesia that had only one generator to power up a television or VCR. There she discovered that everyone had seen *Terminator 2*: "It was terrifying. I didn't want to invade their culture with something that would impact them the way it did. Here were these peaceful people living in paradise and they had all become fans of Arnold Schwarzenegger and urban, action-oriented entertainment. At that moment, I realized that whatever you may think your responsibility is, it's overwhelming. It changed my perspective on the influence that I have as a producer."

Baywatch is now seen in the Middle East, *True Lies* in China. In Japan the husbands rent American home videos for their stay-at-home wives. What happens to cultures affected by Sylvester Stallone's image of violence? By *Baywatch*'s image of women? By *Showgirls*'s image of sexuality? What happens when every culture is distorted by images of American life?

The effect of television on other cultures is enormous, and sometimes unexpected.

Anna Hamilton Phelan tells the story of a Writers Guild arbitration that got resolved in an unusual way. "Some writers from the Writers Guild of America were not getting foreign revenues owed them for episodes they had written of *I Love Lucy* which were now being shown in India. The producer told them that there were no revenues coming from that country, that no one in India watched *I Love Lucy*. Shortly after that, someone from the Writers Guild happened to be in a little village in India and noticed that many of the children were named Lucy, Ricky, Ethel, and Fred. That was the beginning of a lawsuit, so these writers could get what was due them."

These effects from television are innocuous and seemingly quite harmless. Others are less so.

A number of executives speak about their concern that television is destroying culture. One executive, who asks not to be named, says, "So many cultures are being destroyed because of the influence of *Baywatch* or *Dallas* or the constant images of beautiful young women. Suddenly their black or brown skin isn't beautiful anymore. Television is telling them you have to be blond, blue-eyed, and white. We're destroying the value systems of these countries by exporting these images of sex and by exporting the violence of a *Pulp Fiction* or *Die Hard* or the latest Jean-Claude Van Damme or Arnold Schwarzenegger or Chuck Norris film."

Janet Yang has seen the power of international media firsthand—for good or bad—by taking American movies to China and seeing how the Chinese were affected by some of our best films, such as *To Kill a Mockingbird*. "It told me that the power of media to affect lives is very strong. I don't think anybody is immune to it. I don't think there's a country in the world that is not attracted to the medium. And the technology, the fact that it's larger than life, helps our stars become icons, symbols, legends, increasing that power. They transcend cultures. It's no accident that movies are one of our biggest exports. America has developed some very, very strong skills in storytelling, in directing, in performance, and in marketing. We have created a phenomenon. A worldwide phenomenon. No matter where you travel, anywhere in the world, people recognize Tom Cruise, Harrison Ford, Bruce Willis."

"There's so much money coming from foreign," says Anna Hamilton Phelan, "that the buyer cares less about script, and less and less values writers and producers and even directors, and more and more values stars. Since the early 1990s studios began preselling their films before they were made. They just had to say, 'We got Arnold Schwarzenegger,' and nobody cared about anything else. They didn't care about how good the movie would be, they just knew that if they had Arnold, they could make a profit."

Tom and Arnold, Bruce and Harrison drive the foreign market, leaving little room for the woman's point of view or for the outsider who wants to raise global consciousness. But that doesn't stop this desire to influence. "As conscious and awake people, we can recognize we have a field of influence," says myth consultant Pamela Jaye Smith. "The more awake and aware you are, the wider your field of awareness and influence is. So that it's not just 'me,' the individual, my family, my company, my culture, my stockholders. It gets bigger and bigger and bigger. You hope you have people creating these films who are simply, by definition, more aware. If the filmmakers are aware of their influence and act responsibly, you can take these images and bring them into people's homes and all of a sudden what you've done is you've opened their eyes. That's one of the reasons why filmmaking is so immediate, so powerful. It's like taking a light and shining it into the dark."

But it wasn't meant to be easy. "It's an obligation that puts a great deal of pressure on the filmmaker," continues Smith, "but if we allow our sensitivity to happen, if we allow ourselves to have feelings for the larger world, to connect through a global perspective with women, with people around the world, then we can make a difference."

INFLUENCING CONSCIOUSLY

Some women filmmakers, trying to hold a light to the darkness, approach the problem with educational films. Chinese director Irene Tung recognized the power of the media as early as the Second World War.

"My brother was part of the group that opened up the Burma Road toward the end of World War II, and he came back with a story about movies shown in Burma. I asked, 'How can they see a movie? They don't have a movie house. They don't have electricity.' He said, 'They have a generator.' Then I sat and I thought, That would be a wonderful tool for the Chinese peasants to use for education. So I was one of the first to start the audio/visual education in China. I went to New York to learn filmmaking—and came back and made films. Some were about the scenery and the beauty of China, but I also made educational films. I made one showing soldiers how to clean their dormitory. One teaching these villagers how to play basketball. Another about how to care for the trees. How to cut them. How to transport them. Particularly in the ice, in winter. I made a feature film about the people in Mongolia. I filmed some of the Korean War, where I was nearly killed."

Tung has seen the developing impact of media in China. "Close to 85 percent of all the Chinese now have television. Movie theaters are now in even small cities and small country towns. In mountain areas they bring projectors to show movies. In villages, movies are shown at weddings; the hostess of the wedding can choose what kind of film from a list. The women and older men stay home and watch TV, the men go to the movies—which are now open twenty-four hours. On Saturday and Sunday they can see five movies in the same theater complex on the same ticket."

Does it matter what is being watched around the world? Barbara Pyle, vice president of environmental policy at Turner Broadcasting Systems, is convinced that it does. "It's an absolute fact that people emulate behavior that they see on television."

Pyle has been studying ways television is used to address social and environmental problems. "The media can affect society positively. I've been documenting this particular phenomenon since 1984. It was pioneered by Miguel Sabido in Mexico. In a soap opera produced in Peru, called *Simply Maria,* one of the characters was a maid. In this story, she bought a Singer sewing machine, went to night classes, learned how to sew, and was able to quit her job. She opened her own sewing shop and was very successful. The maids were watching this soap opera, and when she went to school, they went to school. When Maria bought a sewing machine, they did. It was so successful that you could not buy a Singer sewing machine in Peru for months, because they were so backordered. Once Sabido saw what this program could do by accident, he asked himself, What if we did this on purpose? What if we produced soap operas and incorporated into them the value of having a small family, the value of being able to control your own fertility, the value of getting a decent education? What if we use them to show that you can be macho without being violent?

"They've done several of these *telenovelas* in Mexico. They deal with issues such as the empowerment of women, population, education, and much more—issues that everyone should care about—woven into these shows in a very clever way. Local production companies and television stations have started to do this kind of programming in the Philippines, India, and in many other countries."

Pyle continues, "I am heartened to see that the soap operas for social change are really taking hold. There was a recent meeting in Los Angeles hosted by Population Communications International in which soap opera producers and directors from the United States attended to learn the details about how these soaps actually work and possibly to adopt some of these methods for North American soap operas. It's things like this that really give me hope."

Cecile Guidote Alvarez is an international filmmaker whose work has been featured by Barbara Pyle in *People Count,* a series about the issues debated at United Nations summits and conferences. Alvarez has been a television producer in the Philippines since 1962. "Unfortunately, too many of the executives have this so-called happy formula that the masses want only sex and violence—it's the general commercial fare. We in the Earthsavers Movement and my colleagues in the Philippine Center of the International Theatre Institute are trying to present an alternative diet for the minds of our people. We've been doing docudramas about the death of students from hazing, trying to wake them out of this stupor of drugs. We do stories on the plight of overseas Filipinos. We deal with crime and corruption and reflect on the burning issues of the day because we have faith that media arts is a catalyst for social change."

Alvarez sees television as vital to resolving basic identity issues of the Philippines. "The identity crisis of the country is not going to be resolved unless we forge our own identity. The face of the country will never be full unless we've really included all of this rich variety of ethnic strains. And we can't be mesmerized only by Madonna and McDonald's culture."

Filmmaker Maria de Carmen Lara from Mexico has made documentaries on prostitution, abortion, AIDS, and the dangerous situations faced by garment workers. "Most of my work in these last two years has been about women's sexuality and gender. It's very important now to talk about gender in Mexico. Many of the problems are affecting women more than men, and women are the victims of male dominance."

Her 1979 film on abortion changed laws. Her film about AIDS addressed the problem of AIDS in Mexico. "The husbands go to the United States to work in the fields. They go to the city. They don't use condoms, they have sex with women in the United States, or share a plastic doll, return with AIDS. But they never tell their wives that they are infected. In the United States the AIDS programs don't deal with Latin Americans, so these workers aren't educated about it." By making documentaries about these subjects, de Lara has been able to begin a discussion, educate the women, and raise consciousness about an issue that has a profound effect on Mexican society. "It's difficult to know the real impact," says Carmen de Lara, "but many of the men are now asking to be tested."[8]

Within their own countries, women are creating programming that is impacting the culture. Other women are working internationally on coproductions, believing this is the wave of the future, and believing that American culture must not be the only culture that dominates the media.

THINK GLOBALLY

Since working globally is the wave of the future, some women are putting in the time and effort to set up the parameters. Marla Ginsburg is an American in Paris, working as a producer and executive in charge of international coproduction for Gaumont Television, the same parent company where Alice Guy Blaché began in 1895. Ginsburg sees that there is much to be learned from each other. "I don't think it's a question of Americans coming over to Europe and teaching people how to do things. I think we in the United States have a different technique, and some of the things we do are better and some are not."

Working on coproductions is difficult, partly because we're not all moving to the same rhythm. "Basically it's as if someone said, 'We're going to dance now,' and no one identified what music we'd be dancing to. So one goes out to do the fox-trot, the other one's doing the tango, another is doing salsa—everybody's moving to a different rhythm. The key to coproduction is to understand that it's all dance. Just because one country's doing the waltz and another is doing the tango doesn't make it better. It's different. You have to be utterly willing to embrace those differences or it's over before you've started."

If countries are not learning from each other, they will be missing out on talent that can come from anywhere in the world. Australians such as Gillian Armstrong are now A-list directors in the United States. Other directors, such as Katja von Garnier from Germany, Pauline Chan from Australia, or Gaylene Preston from New Zealand, are being courted by American production companies and studios.

Some of the great actresses come from other countries, including Sophia Loren from Italy, Greta Scacchi from Australia, Isabelle Huppert from France, Sonia Braga from Brazil, Emma Thompson and Jane Seymour from Great Britain, to name a few.

Margaret Loesch from Fox Children's Network has been open to the creative possibilities of international talent. "Two of the biggest hits I've ever been associated with were born out of other countries: *The Smurfs* came from Belgium and *Power Rangers* was from Japan."

Loesch is aware of what we can offer other countries and of what other countries can offer us. What does she want to see? "We know American product is very popular worldwide, but there does have to be balance to be successful, and also to be responsible. I'd like to see more local product in our programming overseas. To be both successful and responsible we have to nurture the local level, the local artist, the local writer. There are great stories and great characters and great ideas from somewhere other than the United States, and I think we need to ferret them out."

Like Margaret Loesch, many women are looking to impact both media and culture in a positive way. They also realize that to do that will take preparation, talent, support from women and men, and knowledge of what it takes to make it in this business.

26

WHAT MUST WE DO?

WOMEN HAVE MADE great strides in the last ten years. At most studios and networks, women make up 35 to 50 percent of middle management and have broken through glass ceilings in many areas. Penny Marshall, Barbra Streisand, Penelope Spheeris, Gillian Armstrong, and Jodie Foster are now all considered A-list directors and have created films that have grossed more than $100 million. Female producers in television and film are winning Emmy Awards and Academy Awards. In 1994 the top-grossing film, *Forrest Gump,* was produced and developed by Wendy Finerman. The third top grossing film, *True Lies,* also included a female producer, Stephanie Austin.

There is no reason to think that these strides won't continue. In early 1996, Nikki Rocco became president of distribution at Universal Studios, the first woman to crack the glass ceiling in that area. By the end of the century we might see another female president of a studio, more women in higher management, more women directors, producers, and writers, and perhaps more women on boards of directors.

However, behind the scenes, there are still few women. The International Photographers Guild, which shoots most union features and television, is only 11 percent women, and the American Society of Cinematographers has only four females of their more than one hundred members. There are still only 5 percent female composers. Only 20 percent of all feature films produced in 1994 had female producers. Less than 10 percent of all feature films and television films have female directors, although women do better on television taped shows (such as sitcoms), directing slightly more than 20 percent of those shows. Only 12 to 15 percent of all feature films are written or cowritten by women. Few women serve on crews of feature films or television series.[9]

The changes are slow to come, but there is progress. The first all-female front line in the control room is now on the hit CBS show *The Nanny*, with women holding positions as director, technical director, associate director, and script supervisor; plus more than 50 percent of the producers are women, including the star of the show, Fran Drescher. Composer Shirley Walker is the first female to score the music for an entire prime-time television series, *Space: Above and Beyond*.

Other statistics look better. Many film schools are now 50 percent women. In Australia, some graduating classes are now 80 percent women. In movies and miniseries on networks and cable, 54 percent have female leading characters and 55 percent have female producers in their credits. About 27 percent of these made-for-TV films are written or cowritten by women.

In many countries around the world, including Germany, New Zealand, Australia, and Sweden, about 35 to 40 percent of producers are women. In England, nine of the thirty-eight recurring hit drama series were devised solely or partly by women. This overall rate of creating successful shows is higher than for men.

Women directors and writers don't do as well, although New Zealand has one of the best records, with 21 percent female directors and 35 percent female writers. India has some of the lowest numbers, with only 5 to 10 percent women in all these categories, although that is improving.

There is much to celebrate about the gains made in the last twenty years. There is also much work to be done.

CBS executive Sunta Izzicupo describes the situation that prevails in much of the industry. "Women do not have, for the most part, meteoric rises. Women have to prove themselves to men. And the women I know have had to have done every job along the way. You don't just show up as a vice president. Often the steps that men don't have to go through, we do twice. We skip nothing."

If women want their influence to continue, there is much that they can do. A number of the most successful women in this business have specific advice that can help women continue to make an impact.

BE PREPARED

It is essential that women continue to be very good at what they do. In the 1920s, women were left behind because they weren't wanted. This time it's essential that they not be left behind because they aren't prepared.

Women in Film founder Tichi Wilkerson Kassel sees preparation as essential. "Women must continue to educate themselves, to get more strength and power, and continue to pursue their dreams. Women still have to work harder, be smarter; they cannot become complacent. They must be more clear and more direct. Women are not as easily forgiven their trespasses. We have less leeway for errors."

Some of this preparation means knowing their craft well, whether it's directing, producing, writing, or any other field. It means having an understanding of how the business works. It means having the highest professional standards. It also means being prepared for the twenty-first century and for the challenges of being part of the media of the future—high-resolution television, interactive and computer games, new technology, cyberspace, the information highway.

Joyce Schwarz is a new-media consultant and has written on the new technology. She defines these fields: "We're talking about a field called emerging technologies; about a new economy based on information and technology; about the convergence of computers, the convergence of entertainment, the convergence of telecommunications and the wireless industry. Interactive is only a small part of the new media. By the year 2000, about 8 percent of homes will have interactive TV, but by that same year we'll have an industry on the Internet's World Wide Web worth over $1 billion. There are now twenty million people on the Web. It will be in about 30 percent of the homes by then."

Schwarz is aware of the stereotype of women being afraid of technology; that must be overcome. "Unfortunately, many woman are technologically still somewhat phobic. They seem to think that you have to be a technologist or engineer to understand this. I'm still one of the minority of women leaders in this field. It's a young-guys' network with really fierce competition. Women have to get into the field or they're going to be left outside. All aspects of our lives are going to be changed in the next ten years whether we like it or not. There was a glass ceiling in the other world. There will be a glass basement in this one unless women get skills to do this new media. If women don't get technologically savvy, I don't see how we're going to survive the changes in this industry in the next ten years. Through this, we can have a woman's underground. We can communicate with women leaders around the world. We can raise our consciousness. We can consciously try to make connections with women."

THINKING AHEAD

Being prepared for the future means having a goal.

"Men usually have a five-year plan," says actress Marlo Thomas. "They think about where they're going, what they want to do, how much money they want to save, what they want to accomplish. Very few women do that. Perhaps it's because women are not so sure their lives are that controllable. They have children to tend to and husbands to deal with, so they might wonder if they can be in control of their five-year plan when there are so many other people that are the rudder of their boat. This makes it harder for them to have a definite direction."

Thomas has advice about how to start making these plans. "Part of that plan is not to be afraid to dream and fantasize—to think about the personal dream you had when you were twelve. What you thought about. What you dared to think about. We have to dare to dream again and to dare to be an adventurer. We have to have some kind of idea as to where we want to get to so we can get there."

To get there, begin with reflection.

THINKING ABOUT IT

The film business is an active, practical business. It attracts people used to doing, rather than reflecting. It is not a business where people spend time sitting back and philosophizing and theorizing about it. Filmmakers are known for getting in there and making it happen.

Yet in order to move forward, in order to create change, women need to reflect. That means finding time, finding a balance between excessive activity and time for themselves.

Canadian National Film Board executive Marilyn Belec from Nova Scotia has been able to encourage and help fund women filmmakers, direct an employment equity program, create a mentoring program for women, and help found Women in Film Nova Scotia, by leaving herself thinking space. "One of the things I'm good at is thinking, coming up with ideas. They pour out of me all day long. If I could give my other jobs away and concentrate on ideas, that would be a much better use of my time."

She sees the necessity of centering, of feeding her own spiritual needs in order to do her work well.

"There isn't enough spiritual room in my life. I have no time to be by myself, without having an obligation to somebody. I think about my work. I wake up and I'm thinking about what I have to do, morning to night."

Nova Scotia writer Lulu Keating agrees. "It's so important to center. We need a spiritual space, a holistic approach to how we define the quality of our time. There's so much spiritual growth that happens by mulling over issues, to meditate on an issue deeply enough so it's worth bothering. There's no point in our work otherwise."

Why is this a woman's issue? If women are re-creating part of the business, they cannot do it without reflecting, considering, thinking about what has gone before and what they hope to see instead. Their impact on the business demands this centering.

ACTION

The movement includes not just thinking about a five-year plan or what needs to be done, but putting it into action.

Barbara Barde, head of the Women's Television Network in Canada, sees a problem that women need to address. "A lot of women are not focused enough. They don't know what they want to do. You have to ask yourself, What do I want to do, and what skills do I need to do it? How am I going to achieve it? Come up with a game plan and don't vary.

"Recently, a study was done at the Ryerson Film School in Canada. They discovered that the incoming class is 60 percent female, 40 percent male. The graduating class is the reverse, 60 percent male, 40 percent female. I would like to find out why that happens. Part of the reason may be that there aren't female instructors, so they [the women students] don't see role models. But some of the women instructors say that the women often aren't as focused as the men. They don't know what they want to do upon graduation."

SUPPORT NETWORKS

Women don't make it alone. Every woman at the top—even at the middle—has had help along the way. Once women enter the business, it seems essential that they receive support from other women. Marlo Thomas suggests doing for each other what men have always done.

"What we can give each other now is a kind of cheering section and say, 'Go girl, go. I'm here. I'm listening. I'm interested.' We can mentor. We can trade notes. We can tell each other where the good guys are so we don't go where the bad guys are, where we're gonna get sabotaged, where somebody's going to take our film away from us. We have to help each other not give away our power."

Where do learn about how to support each other? Some women suggest taking lessons from the men.

"The men who are extremely successful in business always advise the same thing: Help people out," says Sara Duvall. "Bring people into the industry. The jobs that aren't appropriate for you, give them off to people you like and trust and would like to see do better. The men who are really successful understand that balanced perspective."

Fox executive Laura Ziskin believes we may have to change our attitudes about support. "We have to focus on women helping other women. Because we are a minority, we tend to think that there can only be one. If I want to go to a studio and they already have a woman producer, well, I assume they're not going to want me because they already have their woman. Men don't think they're not going to want them because they already have their man. Can there be only one woman head of a studio? Maybe there will be five women studio heads. Women must always promote each other. It is really important."

For Zanne Devine at Universal Pictures, support means being proactive. "I think that we have to be awake and be proactive in the direction of our lives as individuals and also the direction of our lives in terms of supporting other women. We need to ask ourselves, What are we going to do? It doesn't have to be about signing petitions and making rallies and whatever. It's about empowerment. It's about knowing the system and working within the system to make the system change. We can work within the parameters of our situation. If there are only three women actors who open movies, let's at least be aggressively searching for material for those three. We can make the point of asking ourselves, Have I ever, in the last twelve months of doing my job, fought for a female director to get a movie green-lit? If the answer is no, well, guilty as charged.

"We have to be in touch," continues Devine. "How do we wake ourselves up?" She also asks another question: "How do we wake others up and say, 'Wait a minute. It doesn't feel very good, to look around the table and see that the decision makers are all male.' Some people don't care about that. I do. I'm attracted to decision-making authority and I look and say, 'Hey, I'm not represented there. I don't like that. I want to do something about it.' "

Some of the waking up means looking for one's own sphere of influence, asking, What can I do? When television producer Marian Rees asked that question, it led to the hiring of female interns on many of her films. By 1995 more than five hundred women had worked with her on her productions.

Other women use their influence to speak out.

TAKING RESPONSIBILITY: SPEAKING OUT

Once women reach positions of power, it becomes important to speak out about what they see around them. Although some women don't want to make waves because it might jeopardize their own positions, a great many women see that it's important to let the woman's point of view be expressed. This might mean speaking up about subjects that people don't want to talk about. "We have to be comfortable saying,

'Here's my point of view,' " says Zanne Devine. "My point of view of a movie like *Showgirls* is that I don't want to make that kind of movie. I don't want to support them. I don't want to advocate them. I don't want to go to them. And if I was in the room, I would say that."

Of course, it all depends on how women speak up. Devine sees that one still has to use diplomatic skills in order to give one's word more impact. "When I speak up, I try very hard to speak as an individual in a nonaccusational way, and to speak from my experience and my agenda. I don't think any of my colleagues would be surprised to hear that there are certain parameters around movies I'll support and movies I won't. Of course, if the decision makers in the room—male or female—advocate doing a movie about a serial killer who enjoys killing women—well, if that's their thing, they're going to do it. But I do try to say my piece, as long as I've still got a seat around the table. As long as I still have the opportunity to fight for what I believe in. If me speaking up first causes one other person to nod in agreement, then at least you've got people thinking."

DON'T TAKE IT PERSONALLY

Speaking out can bring a reaction from others. For some women, being in the spotlight, saying something that might be misinterpreted, putting themselves out there in any way, is fearful because it often leads to a negative response. This negative response can be a rejection of their opinion, ideas, or script. Many executives see that sometimes women think too small because of being sensitive, not just to failure but to criticism. They downplay their influence. When they do get a negative response to what they've done, they take it personally.

Producer Dawn Steel sees this as a problem that women must overcome. "They take things too personally; way, way too personally. And they don't persevere in the same way that men do because they do take things personally. They don't come back up at bat. It's a hard lesson for women to learn. If someone says, 'I don't like your idea,' it's personal, but we have to get a much thicker skin than we're born with. We get too sensitive. Tom Hanks said in *A League of Their Own*, 'There's no crying in baseball.' I say, 'There's no crying in business!' Period. Exclamation point."

A number of women emphasize that success and failure in any endeavor can be moral judgments to women "and game calls to men." For the man, business can be seen more as a game. Failure might be called "losing my toys," whereas women personalize failure.[10]

My own saying has been, "Don't take it personally, even when it's meant to be."

To persevere, director Devorah Cutler emphasises, "Get a good team around you. And don't discount *anyone*, because you never know who it might be who'll help you realize your vision."

THE LAST MILE IS THE HARDEST

Evi Stangassinger is a former producer, now the highest ranking woman in production at the Munich Film School in Germany. She looked at the position of successful women and analyzed what it means for them to be truly successful. "Once you find your own way, you have the position and the ability to influence others. A lot of women say, 'I found the way for me. I was pretty successful.' They get money. They get a lot of holidays. But they're not happy anymore. They have no more strength. There's something—it's like a dumpling in the stomach. I analyzed that dumpling. What is the reason? Why are they not really happy? They have many explanations, but not the real explanation. We must say, 'This is not the end—our success. Now we must give it on, like a wave.' It takes still more power and strength to say, 'In what way can I help? What can I do?'

Stangassinger emphasizes that our work is not just for ourselves, but if influence is to continue, it must also be done for others. "It is like a marathon run. The first two-thirds is you; the last third, the stronger part, is to give it on. Otherwise, at the end you're not successful anymore. A person who wants to change things needs a lot of time for herself to think about things, and then she needs to give it on. We have to ask ourselves at least twice a week, Did we do it right? Did we really help? Are we still on the right way?"

Have we made a difference? Do we make a difference? The answer is clear. It is a difference that impacts the business on every level and ripples out around the world.

27

CASE STUDY

Agnieszka Holland

AGNIESZKA HOLLAND is one of the most global filmmakers. She has directed films in six countries, on subjects that cover such social and global issues as Communism and tyranny (*To Kill a Priest*), the Holocaust (*Europa, Europa*), the loneliness and friendship of children (*The Secret Garden*), and intimacy and tyranny (*Angry Harvest*). In 1994 she came to Los Angeles to direct her first American film for TV, *Red Wind.*

"I wanted to become a director because I had a creative personality and I wanted to express myself. I need the interaction with others and I found that moviemaking is the best way to use all the skills I have.

"In general I want to communicate with the people through something that has an artistic quality. I'm more of a storyteller than politically motivated.

"*To Kill a Priest,* one of my less known films, was the only militant movie I did. Based on a true-life incident that took place in Poland in the 1980s, it's about a priest working for the Movement in a brutally repressed society who was killed by the secret police. I was much more fascinated by the killer than the priest. I liked looking at the light and dark sides of the story. Also, my father was killed by political police when I was thirteen. The story of the priest was an extremely important event to the Polish people. I felt the weight of the social and political responsibility.

"After the movie was completed, the political situation in Communist countries changed, and in some ways it became a historical movie. But it was talked about a lot in Poland. I'm sort of a celebrity there. It had an enormous audience in the underground. When it was possible to show it in the theaters, no one was so much interested. That is a weakness of the militant movies—they have only one dimension. When the reality changes, they lose their power.

"Although films can impact society, that's not my agenda. I try to be open and to take filmmaking as a kind of job. I don't tell myself that I have a duty to myself or society. I believe if something is important enough for me, it will be important for some others.

"I don't think I have the ability to educate or change people's minds through my films. However, I think the filmmaker does have a responsibility. For instance, I think showing violent movies to kids is irresponsible. I also have a responsibility with adult films, since I think films can influence behavior of groups of people negatively, but I don't believe they can change people's minds in a good way. Of course, they can help people feel better for a while or understand better certain things, but I'm skeptical about the capacity of film to change somebody in a deep way—to make a good person from a bad one.

"People ask me what is the message of my movies and I say 'that life is complicated.' Something I don't like about American films is that they think the division between good and evil is simple and that you can exorcise the devil. That's why I don't like the concept of the thriller. You kill the exterior evil and they think man will be happy. But for me the problem is that the evil is part of our self.

"I'm bothered by the fact that often the movies that are the most popular are sometimes the most stupid. It's like a plague.

"From the storytelling point of view, American movies are very similar. Very few movies have different rhythms, or a different aesthetic or different way to tell the story, which means the people are used to only one kind of storytelling. It's like killing the individual language and the individual expression. Can you recognize where a movie originates from without a strong voice? If there's no voice, there is no personality. If no personality, there's no respect for the uniqueness of the individual.

"I'm familiar with the process of moviemaking in many countries because I've been a director in Poland, France, England, Germany, Czechoslovakia, and the United States. Although Poland is a traditional society, I've never had a problem with my authority as a woman director. I was accepted very easily there, and also in Prague. The Germans don't have a problem with me as a woman. They accept the authority. If I play the role of the director, then I have the authority. And I had a very nice experience here, in the United States.

"But in France I had some problems with the crew. Big problems. Several times. Some people were unable to accept that a woman had so strong authority, that they had to accept it and adhere to it.

"I never have a problem with actors. They are like children and I am like a mother. It's different with the crew because it is much more of a power game. On the set, I try to give the others the feeling that they can be better, more creative than before. It's a collaboration, an exchange. I'm a director because I enjoy the work, not because I enjoy authority. Some crew members are used to having a male director who is tyrannical and very authoritative and they are lost if I'm treating them as an equal.

"Of course, there are problems for more reasons than just because I'm a woman. I also had problems because of the political situation and my political opinions. And the fact that I'm Jewish. I had so many problems because of these different issues and I never realized I could have problems just for being a woman. Until recently, the problems of the world were more interesting to me than women's problems.

"I'm not feminist or sexist. I've always been more comfortable showing men characters than women because I can watch them from outside, have more distance, be more objective. Before I didn't have deep friendships with women. My best friendships were with men. Now it's changing.

"Now I try to make my women stronger and more complicated. A couple of years ago, I wasn't so interested in that kind of character. Women are interesting to me not because of the feminist perspective but because of their woman's point of view, of their particular experience. Their sex makes it richer.

"I don't know much about sociology. I've always liked to pick characters that reveal something about the human condition. But I'm now more interested in looking at strong women and the price they pay for that strength. They are forced to play many roles—being the mother, the wife, the professional. I'm also interested in a woman's sexual identity, in the kind of sexual roles women play.

"I'm interested in the theme of identity. Who you are. In which way are we free to choose and create our destiny and in what ways must we depend on one another? How much freedom do we really have?

"Our freedom means who we are really. Are we what another person wants us to be? Are we how other people see us? Or can we create something independent of this exterior prison? Some of our freedom is also defined by the politics and the economics of the society.

"The social and political standing of women is changing in a very dramatic way. The next century will be a century of women, because man has lost the capacity for leadership.

"Unemployment becomes a global problem. There won't be enough work or food. Men are unable to play their roles of hunter. They have to find another way to build their identity. They'll need to find fulfillment within the family or through being with children, which is more related to 'feminine' values. They'll need to become more nurturing, because it's the only way for them to survive.

"The real conflict in reality is not in class war or religious war but in the roles of the sexes. The subject of how women's and men's identities are going to change in the next century is one of the major themes to explore in the future of film."

NOTES

PART ONE

1. *The Wit and Wisdom of Women* (Philadelphia: Running Press, 1993), p. 43.

2. *The Memoirs of Alice Guy Blaché*, trans. Roberta and Simone Blaché, ed. Anthony Slide (Metuchen, NJ: Scarecrow Press, 1986) p. 15.

3. Ibid. p. 24.

4. From *Women Who Made the Movies,* a videotape by Gwendolyn Foster-Dixon and Wheeler Dixon, 1992, from Women Who Make Movies catalogue.

5. This information was clarified in an interview with Anthony Slide but can also be found in his book *Early Women Directors* (London: A. S. Barnes and Company; South Brunswick and New York: Thomas Yoseloff Ltd., 1977) pp. 9–10.

6. William Arnold, "Heroine of the Silent Screen," *Seattle Post-Intelligencer,* 27 November 1989.

7. Ibid.

8. Nancy Dowd, "The Woman Director Through the Years," from Special Report: The Woman Director, *Action,* p. 16.

9. Most of this quote is taken from our interview, with some additional information from "Approaching the Art of Arzner" by Francine Parker, from Special Report: The Woman Director, *Action,* p. 9.

10. This is a combination of an interview and the article "Discovering Ida Lupino" by Francine Parker, from Special Report: The Woman Director, *Action,* p. 19.

11. "Margaret Booth Still Working After 62 Years of Editing," *Hollywood Reporter,* April 3, 1978.

12. From *Movie Memories,* "No Stand-In for Mabel Normand" by Raymond Lee, 1955.

13. Ibid.

14. UCLA Film and Television Archive, Women Screenwriters in the Hollywood Studios film series, February 14–March 18, 1995; thank you to Jack Nalon and Writers Guild of America West.

15. Ibid.

16. William Bakewell, *Hollywood Be Thy Name* (Metuchen, NJ: Scarecrow Press, 1991), p. 27.

17. Ally Acker, *Reel Women: Pioneers of the Cinema, 1896 to the Present* (New York: Continuum, 1993), pp. 196–198.

18. Joseph McBride, *Hawks on Hawks* (Berkeley: University of California Press, 1982), p. 138.

19. Jeanine Basinger, *A Woman's View: How Hollywood Spoke to Women, 1930–1960* (New York: Alfred A. Knopf, 1993), p. 179.

20. From *Women Who Made the Movies,* a videotape by Gwendolyn Foster-Dixon and Wheeler Dixon, 1992, from Women Who Make Movies catalogue.

21. Quoted from the film *The Wonderful Horrible Life of Leni Riefenstahl* by Ray Mueller; Kino International is the U.S. distributor.

22. I interviewed Matilde in Mexico City in June 1995 along with a group of several other women writers. Most of these quotes are taken from the documentary *My Filmmaking, My Life: Matilde Landeta,* a film by Patricia Diaz, 1990, from Women Who Make Movies catalogue.

23. Ibid.

24. UCLA Film and Television Archive, Women Screenwriters in the Hollywood Studios film series, February 14–March 18, 1995; thank you to Jack Nalon and Writers Guild of America West.

25. Marsha McCreadie, *The Women Who Write the Movies* (New York: Birch Lane Press, 1994), p. 140.

26. Ibid. p. 72.

27. From "Let Us Now Praise Famous Women: Archive Program Celebrates Women Screenwriters" by Laura Kaiser, *Archive,* April/May 1995, p. 5.

28. From the PBS series *The American Cinema,* Fall 1995.

29. From *Premiere* magazine's Women in Hollywood special issue, 1993, p. 57.

PART TWO

1. *The Quotable Woman,* (Philadelphia: Running Press, 1991), p. 27.

2. Jeffrey Daniels. "Why Majors Only Break Even," *Hollywood Reporter,* 12 February 1996.

3. "Women Communicating: Studies of Women's Talk" edited by Barbara Bate

and Anita Taylor, "Implementing Feminist Principles in a Bureaucracy: Studio D, the National Film Board of Canada" by Anita Taylor p. 297.

4. "Becoming Jodie Foster," interview by Tom Allen, *MovieMaker* magazine, November/December 1995, p. 29.

5. Ron Miller, "Shattering TV's Glass Ceiling: Women Continue to Build Industry Power," *San Jose Mercury News,* April 30, 1995. The women directors statistic comes from the Directors Guild of America Affirmative Action Summary Comparison Report dated February 27, 1996. Women directors for television movies, miniseries, and feature films make up just under 10 percent, and women directors for taped shows such as situation comedies make up about 20 percent.

PART THREE

1. *The Wit and Wisdom of Women* (Philadelphia: Running Press, 1993), p. 163.

2. "Women in Hollywood," *WGAW Journal,* February 1990.

3. Meri Nana-Ama Danquah, "Crashing the Glass Ceiling," *Writers Guild Journal,* p. 13.

4. Ibid.

5. From the *Hollywood Reporter* Women in Entertainment issue, December 12, 1995, p. S-21.

6. Richard Corliss, Women of the Year article, *Time,* November 13, 1995, p. 61.

7. Lillian Russ, "The Huston Chronicle," *The New Yorker,* January 29, 1996, p. 25.

8. From Women in Film Crystal Awards speech, 1992.

9. Aristotle, *The Poetics,* trans. S. H. Butcher, intro. Francis Fergusson (New York: Hill and Wang, 1961), p. 81.

10. Alan Riding, "Liberté, Egalité, Fraternité? 2 out of 3 for These Directors," *New York Times,* 9 April 1995.

11. Richard Corliss, Women of the Year article, *Time,* November 13, 1995, p. 61.

PART FOUR

1. From *Woman of the House,* "Women in Film" episode, written by Linda Bloodworth-Thomason, aired Summer 1995.

2. Roseanne Barr, from the Turner Network documentary *Century of Women.*

3. "Becoming Jodie Foster," interview by Tom Allen, *MovieMaker* magazine, November/December 1995, p. 40.

4. Laurie Werner, "Schwarzenegger, Stallone, Streep," *Los Angeles Times Calendar,* 25 September 1994, p. 3.

5. Ibid.

6. According to a letter I received from Amany Aboul Fadl Farag, the source for the statistics is an academic study by Mona Said El Hadidi, presented to the faculty of mass communication, Cairo University. It was also published in *Al Usra,* No. 1, 11 May 1994, p. 15.

7. From *Soviet Women Filmmakers,* a videotape by Sally Potter, 1990; a Triple Vision production.

8. Chris Willman, "60 and Still Stealing Scenes," *Los Angeles Times,* 22 December 1994.

9. From information on Girl Games, and Melissa Fletcher Stoeltje, "Just for Girls," *Houston Chronicle,* August 3, 1995.

10. From outtakes of a video interview by Canadian producer Lili Fournier. Thank you, Lili.

PART FIVE

1. Phyllis J. Read and Bernard L. Whitlieb, *The Book of Women's Firsts* (New York: Random House, 1992), p. 227.

2. *The Wit and Wisdom of Women* (Philadelphia: Running Press, 1993), p. 69.

3. From an article that Laura sent me about sensuality, called "Intimate Succulence, Exquisite Intimacies: A Philosophical Dissertation about Cooking," trans. Yareli Arizmendi. Thank you to Caroline Rivera for contacting Laura and translating my question to her.

4. Daniel Goleman, "Sex Fantasy Research Called Blind to Women," *New York Times,* 14 June 1995.

5. From outtakes of a video interview conducted by Canadian producer Lili Fournier. Thank you, Lili.

6. Facts on women and HIV/AIDS from the Los Angeles City Commission on the Status of Women.

7. Sharon Bernstein, "But Is There Hope for the Future?" *Los Angeles Times Calendar,* 11 November 1990, p. 88.

PART SIX

1. *The Quotable Woman* (Philadelphia: Running Press, 1991), p. 186.

2. Christine Mohanna, "A One-Sided Story: Women in the Movies," *Woman in Film Journal,* 1972, p. 7.

3. *Emmy Magazine,* 10th Annual Hall of Fame issue, 1994, p. 46.

4. "Diane English" from *The Journal,* July 1991, p. 17.

5. Ibid. p. 18.

6. From "The Impact of Commercial Television Entertainment Programs on

Human Service Agency Requests and Reports" by Richard T. Hezel, Ph.D. For further information, refer to "The Impact of Social Issue Television Programming on Attitudes Toward Rape" by Barbara J. Wilson, Daniel Linz, Edward Donnerstein, Horst Stipp. Thank you to NBC for sharing this information.

7. *Serving in Silence* was produced by Barbra Streisand, Glenn Close, Craig Zadan, Neil Meron, and Cis Corman; written by Alison Cross; and directed by Jeff Bleckner.

8. This same problem was addressed by Lebanese director Janane Mallal in her film *Badrieh,* for the Lebanese Broadcasting Corporation International C-33 channel. The woman and her children with AIDS become outcasts in their own village. This documentary won a first prize in health reporting on CNN and helped reintegrate the woman into her village.

9. From the DGA Affirmative Action Summary Comparison Reports, 1990–1994.

10. Colleen O'Connor, "The Sweet Smell of Failure," *The Oregonian,* 1 December 1994. O'Connor also makes reference to two books on this subject, *The Male/Female Difference* by Carole Hyatt and *When Smart People Fail* by Linda Gottlieb.

SELECTED BIBLIOGRAPHY

Acker, Ally. *Reel Women: Pioneers of the Cinema, 1896 to the Present.* New York: The Continuum Publishing Company, 1993.

Baehr, Helen, and Gillian Dyer. *Boxed In: Women and Television.* London: Pandora Press, 1987.

Bakewell, William. *Hollywood Be Thy Name.* Metuchen, NJ: Scarecrow Press, 1991.

Basinger, Jeanine. *A Woman's View: How Hollywood Spoke to Women, 1930–1960.* New York: Alfred A. Knopf, Inc., 1993.

Blonski, Annette, Barbara Creed, and Freda Freiberg. *Don't Shoot, Darling! Women's Independent Filmmaking in Australia.* Australia: Greenhouse Publications Pty Ltd., 1987.

Bright, Susie. *Herotica: A Collection of Women's Erotic Fiction.* San Francisco: Down There Press, 1988.

Brownlow, Kevin. *The Parade's Gone By . . .* New York: Ballantine Books, 1969.

Cook, Pam, and Philip Dodd. *Women and Film: A Sight and Sound Reader.* Philadelphia: Temple University Press, 1993.

Cox, Eva, and Sharon Laura. *What Do I Wear for a Hurricane? Women in Australian Film, Television, Video, and Radio Industries.* Commissioned by the Australian Film Commission and the National Working Party on the Portrayal of Women in the Media, November 1992.

Francke, Lizzie. *Script Girls: Women Screenwriters in Hollywood.* London: British Film Institute, 1994.

Garçon, François. *Gaumont: A Century of French Cinema.* New York: Harry N. Abrams, 1994.

Gilligan, Carol. *In a Different Voice: Psychological Theory and Women's Development.* Cambridge: Harvard University Press, 1982, 1993.

Haskell, Molly. *From Reverence to Rape: The Treatment of Women in the Movies.* New York: Penguin Books, 1973, 1974.

Kuhn, Annette, with Susannah Radstone. *The Women's Companion to International Film.* Berkeley and Los Angeles: University of California Press, 1990.

Maio, Kathi. *Feminist in the Dark: Reviewing the Movies.* Freedom, Calif.: The Crossing Press, 1988.

Mayne, Judith. *Directed by Dorothy Arzner.* Bloomington and Indianapolis: Indiana University Press, 1994.

McCreadie, Marsha. *The Women Who Write the Movies: From Frances Marion to Nora Ephron.* New York: Birch Lane Press, 1994.

McGilligan, Pat. *Backstory 2: Interviews with Screenwriters of the 1940s and 1950s.* Berkeley and Los Angeles: University of California Press, 1991.

Ollenburger, Jane C., and Helen A. Moore. *A Sociology of Women: The Intersection of Patriarchy, Capitalism and Colonization.* New Jersey: Prentice Hall, 1992.

Press, Andrea L. *Women Watching Television: Gender, Class, and Generation in the American Television Experience.* Philadelphia: University of Pennsylvania Press, 1991.

Quart, Barbara Koenig. *Women Directors: The Emergence of a New Cinema.* Westport, Conn.: Praeger Publishers, 1988.

Read, Phyllis J., and Bernard L. Whitlieb. *The Book of Women's Firsts.* New York: Random House, 1992.

Riefenstahl, Leni. *Leni Riefenstahl: A Memoir.* New York: First Picador USA edition, 1995.

Slide, Anthony. *Early Women Directors: Their Role in the Development of the Silent Cinema.* New York: A. S. Barnes, 1977.

Slide, Anthony. *The Memoirs of Alice Guy Blaché.* Metuchen, NJ: Scarecrow Press, 1986.

Smith, Sharon. *Women Who Make Movies.* New York: Hopkinson and Blake, 1975.

Toronto Women in Film and Television. *Changing Focus: The Future for Women in the Canadian Film and Television Industry.* Toronto: University of Toronto Press, 1991.

INDEX

0-595-26838-2

CPSIA information can be obtained at www.ICGtesting.com
Printed in the USA
LVOW050955280812

296299LV00005B/13/A

9 780595 268382